IF THE KAISER COMES

IF THE KAISER COMES

DEFENCE AGAINST A GERMAN INVASION OF BRITAIN IN THE FIRST WORLD WAR

MIKE OSBORNE

FONTHILL

Fonthill Media Language Policy

Fonthill Media publishes in the international English language market. One language edition is published worldwide. As there are minor differences in spelling and presentation, especially with regard to American English and British English, a policy is necessary to define which form of English to use. The Fonthill Policy is to use the form of English native to the author. Mike Osborne was born and educated in Britain; therefore British English has been adopted in this publication.

Fonthill Media Limited
Fonthill Media LLC
www.fonthillmedia.com
office@fonthillmedia.com

First published in the United Kingdom and the United States of America 2017

British Library Cataloguing in Publication Data:
A catalogue record for this book is available from the British Library

ISBN 978-1-78155-575-0

Typeset in 10pt on 13pt Sabon
Printed and bound by CPI Group (UK) Ltd, Croydon, CR0 4YY

Acknowledgements

Thanks go to Alan Anstee, Adrian Armishaw, Dr Gordon Barclay, Christopher Bird, Dr Colin Dobinson, Jeff Dorman, Julian Foynes, John Guy, and Dr Mike Heyworth for information or permission to use illustrative materials; thanks also go to Alan Sutton, Jay Slater, and Joshua Greenland at Fonthill Media for their support. Particular thanks, as ever, go to my wife, Pam, for her support—both practical and moral.

CONTENTS

Abbreviations

AA:	anti-aircraft
ADGB:	Air Defence Great Britain (from 1925)
APS:	Auxiliary Patrol Service (RN)
ARG:	Airfield Research Group
ARP:	air-raid precautions
ARS:	Aircraft Repair Shed
A/S:	anti-submarine
Bde:	brigade (four, later three, infantry battalions)
BEF:	British Expeditionary Force
BLC:	breech-loading converted (15-pounder field gun)
Bn:	battalion (600–1,000 infantry-men)
BOP:	Battery Observation Post (Coast Artillery)
CBA:	Council for British Archaeology
CID:	Committee for Imperial Defence
CIGS:	Chief of the Imperial General Staff
C-in-C:	commander-in-chief
Coy:	company (150 infantry-men)
CRE:	Commander Royal Engineers
cwt:	hundredweight (112 lb or 50 kg)
DAMS:	Defensively Armed Merchant Ships (DEMS in the Second World War)
DEL:	Defence Electric Light (CASL in WWII)
DLI:	Durham Light Infantry
DORA:	Defence of the Realm Act (1914)
EH:	English Heritage
FSG:	Fortress Study Group
GHQ:	General Headquarters
GOC:	General Officer Commanding

GPO:	General Post Office
GR:	Giorgius Rex (hence 'Gorgeous Wrecks' tag for VTC)
GS:	General Service (as in 'Belfast Truss' hangar roof)
HD:	Home Defence (Army Divisions & RFC Squadrons)
hp:	horsepower (equivalence in automobile engine)
HT:	horse transport
IWM:	Imperial War Museum
LCC:	London County Council
LG:	landing ground
LNER:	London North Eastern Railway
MO5:	Military Operations Department 5
M/S:	minesweeper
MT:	Motor Transport
NCO:	non-commissioned officer
OP:	Observation Post
OTC:	Officer Training Corps
Pounder:	designation of gun by weight of projectile (1 lb = 454 grams)
PH:	public house
PLA:	Port of London Authority
PWSS:	Port War Signal Station
QF:	quick-firing (gun)
RA:	Royal Artillery
RAF:	Royal Air Force (from 1 April 1918)
RAMC:	Royal Army Medical Corps
(R)AOC:	(Royal from 1922) Army Ordnance Corps
(R)ASC:	(Royal from 1918) Army Service Corps
RBL:	Rifled Breech Loader (Victorian cannon)
RCAHMS:	Royal Commission on Ancient & Historical Monuments of Scotland
RCHM(E):	Royal Commission for Historical Monuments (England)
RE:	Royal Engineers
REC:	Railway Executive Committee
RFA:	Royal Field Artillery
RFC:	Royal Flying Corps (to 31 March 1918)
RGA:	Royal Garrison Artillery
RHA:	Royal Horse Artillery
RMA:	Royal Marine Artillery
RML:	rifled muzzle-loader (Victorian cannon)
RN:	Royal Navy
RNAS:	Royal Naval Air Service (to 31 March 1918, FAA from 1938)
RND:	Royal Naval Division (later 63rd Division)
RN(V)R:	Royal Naval (Volunteer) Reserve

SNO:	Senior Naval Officer
Sqn:	Squadron (Cavalry or RFC/RNAS/RAF unit)
TDS:	Training Depot Station (RAF 1918–20)
TF:	Territorial Force (1908–1918)
USN:	United States Navy
VP:	vulnerable point
VTC:	Volunteer Training Corps
WAAC:	Women's Auxiliary Army Corps
WRNS:	Women's Royal Naval Service (Wrens)
W/T:	wireless/telegraphy

Introduction

In the years before war broke out, both the British military and the general public had become convinced that the country would be invaded by German troops, despatched by an envious and petulant Kaiser. A popular song of 1908, quoted in *The Perfect Summer*, asserted:

There'll be no wo'ar
As long as there's a King like good King Edward
There'll be no wo'ar
For 'e 'ates that sort of fing!

However, after Edward's death in 1911, people were less optimistic. Commentators have spoken of the country drifting or even sleepwalking into war, but a growing element of jingoism may have helped propel it forward consciously, underpinning the noisy enthusiasm of the crowds in Trafalgar Square, cheering as Asquith's ultimatum to Germany expired at midnight on 3 August 1914. However, as recorded by some of Richard Emden's witnesses, specific fears were to cause childhood nightmares, as Zeppelins landed to disgorge 'the Kaiser', whatever that meant, and to spirit them all back to Germany as captives. Fewer children pictured themselves as adventure-book heroes, defending their homes against the invading German troops rampaging through their villages. Invasion even became a yardstick by which other disasters might be measured; the British Government's failure to meet the demand for silver was seen by the Controller of Currency in India as constituting a greater blow to the Raj than Britain would suffer 'by a German landing in Norfolk'—this was in March 1918. Rumours of landings and attempted landings abounded: the sudden presence of 5,000 Scottish troops in Bristol in winter 1914–15 confirming some in their expectation of imminent invasion; the reported arrival of Russian troops (with snow on their boots), come to aid a desperate last-ditch defence; or news of German landings in the Wash with a German army already advancing on London.

However, an assault could take many forms. While it was the invasion of the country by a barbarian force—imposing its physical presence on the ground—that most exercised Britons in the early years of the twentieth century, when the threats finally materialised, they were in the shape of an invasion of their air-space; this resulted in aerial bombardment of towns and of the seas around them, causing the very real possibility of starvation. The imagined danger of Uhlan lancers perpetrating unspeakable atrocities on babies and nuns was replaced by death and destruction: haphazard, wanton, and random from the Zeppelin or cold, calculated, and targeted by the U-boat.

Unlike in the Second World War, the danger of invasion had to be taken seriously for the duration, right up until the final few months of the war. For the Germans, it was suggested, the terrible casualties that they must sustain in invading Britain would be no worse than another Verdun and might end the war at a stroke. Britain's largely untrained and unfit Home Army was not expected to be capable of dealing with much more than a raid, hence its notional strength throughout the war of half a million men.

This book is an attempt to explore an aspect of the Home Front in the First World War that is often overlooked. Two major initiatives of the CBA—the Defence of Britain Project in the 1990s (taking anti-invasion defences (mainly) of the Second World War as an achievable focus) and the current Home Front Legacy 1914–18 project—have both involved the community in recording material survivals from these two conflicts. I have tried to provide a narrative and a context for those elements that relate to the invasion that never was when the Kaiser could not make it.

Mike Osborne
May 2016

1
British Expectations of Invasion

Invasions of Britain 1066–1815

Despite the often repeated assertion that Britain has never been invaded since William the Conqueror in 1066, Britain's history is saturated with threatened, intended, attempted, or actual landings by imagined, potential, or real invaders. By 1100, there had been three serious incursions by the Danes, one of them in the company of Robert of Flanders. More serious, and reflecting the still-strong ties with France, was the invasion (albeit at the invitation of the Anglo-Norman barons) by the Dauphin, the future Louis VIII, in 1216, against King John, who appeared to be reneging on Magna Carta. In 1242, another French invasion was perceived as imminent and coastal towns were ordered to contribute ships for the royal fleet, eighty vessels being required from the now-vanished town of Dunwich in Suffolk. In 1326, Queen Isabella, widow of Edward II, landed with her lover Mortimer, backed up by a force of French troops. In 1336, Philip VI of France prepared to invade England in support of his ally David II of Scotland. Throughout the Hundred Years' War (1337–1453), intermittent French raids, such as the seizure of the Channel Islands by French and Genoese troops in 1338, were interspersed with more serious assaults. Plans for a French invasion in 1339 were discovered when Caen was captured in 1346. The Cinque Ports and their associated towns contributed a total of 105 ships to blockade the English Channel and to support the siege of Calais in 1347. In 1370, archers in four southern counties had been arrayed to counter a French attack on Southampton, but only in 1377, following the death of Edward III, did these constant pinpricks coalesce into something more substantial. A French fleet, untroubled by any English naval intervention, ravaged the south coast from Dover to Plymouth, landing troops to burn towns and carry away plunder. Eight years later, a combined

French and Scots invasion from Leith saw the refortification of castles such as Castle Rising (Norfolk) throughout the kingdom and was used to justify the building of Bodiam (East Sussex). In 1386, an army assembled to defend London against threatened French invasion. A French expeditionary force in support of Owain Glyndwr over-wintered in Wales in 1405–06. Reinforced by 2,500 soldiers, and with expectations of many more, they advanced as far as Worcester and only retreated when those reinforcements were intercepted at sea. The next hundred years witnessed a procession of usurpers, pretenders, and rivals for the throne, landing on our shores accompanied by armies of Burgundian, French, Flemish, and Swiss mercenaries.

Even, or perhaps especially, in the middle of those bitter civil wars (later dubbed the Wars of the Roses), the spectre of foreign invasion never went away. In 1458, a survey of the fortifications of the Isle of Wight was carried out by Osbern Mundeford, former Marshal of the Calais Garrison. In that same year, Sir John Fastolf had fired his artillery in defence of his castle of Caister (Norfolk) against a French raid. Yet the building of an artillery tower at Dartmouth in 1481 was driven by fears of enforced regime change, justified by the landing of Henry Tudor four years later, gathering local, mainly Welsh, support around a nucleus of French, Breton, and Scottish mercenaries. Once Henry was established on the throne and had subdued residual Yorkist resistance, England entered a period of relative stability, but the 1538 alliance between France and the Empire once more made invasion appear inevitable. Henry VIII mustered troops, mobilised his fleet, and initiated an ambitious and expensive building programme, encircling the coast from Hull to Milford Haven with a girdle of new artillery forts, designed by a continental engineer.

For the moment, the threat had been removed, only to be renewed in 1569 when the Duke of Alva, fighting against William of Orange in the Netherlands, expressed his intention of invading England. As a response, Elizabeth impounded Spanish ships and imprisoned Mary, Queen of Scots. The central period of Elizabeth's reign was characterised by a succession of events any one of which could have precipitated an invasion. Catholic plots and papal subversion were all aimed at the overthrowing of Elizabeth by armed force of one sort or another—invasion, assassination, or revolution; this culminated in the Spanish Armada of 1588, as troops from the Spanish Netherlands embarked in a large Spanish fleet with the intention of landing in southern and eastern England. The defeat of the Armada by a combination of the weather, the seamanship skills of the English sailors, large helpings of luck, and a lack of planning on the part of the Spanish did not altogether remove the threat. Expatriate Catholics continued to plot, and in 1592, Sir William Stanley planned for Elizabeth's assassination and for his regiment to form the nucleus of an invasion force supported by the Pope and led by the Duke of Parma. The activities of Stanley's men, mainly Irish, led to an increased fear of invasion into 1593, shortly to become still more acute in 1596 when the Spanish capture of Calais town and close investment of its citadel suggested that invasion across the Straits of Dover might be imminent. By 1599, fears that James VI of Scotland was planning a Catholic uprising aided by a Spanish fleet brought anti-invasion measures into force, with chains strung across London's streets and lanterns burned all night at every door. The Queen's vigorous response to the 1601 rebellion and subsequent execution of the Earl of Essex included activating the defences of London, as fears that a Spanish invasion of Ireland in support of Tyrone would escalate into a full-blown invasion of England. A dance named the 'Spanish Panic' was invented with frenetic double steps and leaps. In the weeks leading up to Elizabeth's death in 1603, security was tightened; the ports were closed, vagrants deported to the Low Countries, theatres closed; there was a ban on public gatherings; Catholics were imprisoned; the guards at Richmond Palace doubled; and the Crown Jewels were secured in the Tower of London.

Following the restoration of Charles II, a number of short wars with the Dutch saw foreign troops on English soil again. In 1667, during the Second Dutch War, 1,500 Dutch marines landed on Cottage Point, at Harwich, to attack Landguard Fort from the land-ward side, but were fortunately repulsed by Captain Darell's garrison.

More catastrophic for national morale was an extended Dutch raid on the Thames and Medway, which destroyed ships and stores, revealing the poor state of the defences of one of England's premier naval bases and the vulnerability of London to seaborne assault. In 1688, the Glorious Revolution brought William of Orange with an army of Dutch troops to Lyme Regis, although his forces contained so many turned prisoners-of-war that, for many, it was more of a homecoming than an invasion.

Knowing that his seizure of the Austrian Netherlands would provoke a declaration of war, Louis XV planned a pre-emptive strike on England in 1744 during the War of Austrian Succession. He assembled 10,000 troops outside Dunkirk aimed at landing in the Essex Blackwater and marching on London, while the French fleet from Brest would attack the British fleet in Portsmouth Harbour. The 1745 rebellion continued the possibility of a French invasion of southern England in support of an actual Jacobite invasion from Scotland, which penetrated as far south as Derby and caused a great deal of panic. The threat of a French invasion just would not go away. In 1756, camps at La Hougue, St Malo, Dunkirk, Calais, Dieppe, Le Havre, Grandville, and St Valery held 50,000 French troops poised for invasion, supported by fleets at Brest and Rochefort. In 1759, the Seven Years' War saw the French in process of building an invasion fleet in Le Havre, where some 40,000 French troops awaited embarkation—half destined for the Blackwater sailing from Ostend and the rest heading for the Clyde, from Brittany. As the French fleet took advantage of a break in the weather to escape the hitherto close British blockade of Brest, they were pursued by the British Channel Fleet under Sir Edward Hawke. On 20 November, he caught up with and destroyed the greater part of this French fleet in Quiberon Bay, making invasion impossible for the time being. After the end of the Seven Years' War in 1763, Louis XV, smarting from defeats in India and Canada, adopted a deliberate policy of ruses, decoys, deceptions, feints, and diversions to dissipate British superiority in the Channel and thus clear the way for an invasion.

It may have been Hawke's decisive action that led General Guy Carleton (later Lord Dorchester) to compose the memo which first set out the Blue Water principle in 1771. This put the responsibility for countering the invasion attempts of Britain's enemies firmly on the ships of the Royal Navy. This notion would dominate British defence policy for over two centuries, and has not entirely disappeared to this day. A recognition of this reliance on the Navy to keep Britain's island realm safe led to plans in 1777 for a combined Franco-Spanish invasion, 'The Other Armada'. As well as stepping up support for the Americans in their struggle for independence, a raid on Scotland, a simulated invasion of Ireland, and diversionary attacks on Gibraltar, the East Indies, and Minorca were all planned. These would ensure that the main attack by the French would find a British fleet weakened by having to respond simultaneously to all these threats. In August 1779, the Franco-Spanish fleet was sighted off Plymouth and a hasty attempt was made to improve the harbour's meagre fortifications. In the event, the seamen were hit by overwhelming sickness and then, forced to retreat, were scattered by a storm.

However, it was the French Wars (1797–1815) that would raise the probability of a French invasion to new heights. In 1797, four ships carrying the Black Legion made up of 600 French troops and 800 convicts under Col. William Tate, a septuagenarian Irish-American, left Camaret and attempted to land at Fishguard in Pembrokeshire. Diverted from the harbour by a single shot from the fort's gun, the force was landed on a beach nearby and left to fend for itself. A show of resistance from troops, volunteers, and civilians—especially the local women in their red shawls and tall, black bonnets—along with his men's indiscipline, persuaded Tate to surrender. Six days after sailing from Brittany, the Black Legion was being marched away to captivity, but the likelihood of invasion, especially now Napoleon Bonaparte had taken charge of the French effort, would only increase. After the collapse of the Peace of Amiens in 1803, Napoleon intensified his preparations for an invasion from the Channel ports across to England. The obvious thoroughness of Napoleon's preparations suggested a determination to carry through his invasion plans. Gathered together in Boulogne was a fleet consisting of over 1,500 flat-bottomed *praams*, sloops, pinnaces, corvettes, fishing vessels, *caïques*, and gunboats. The capacity of each type of vessel was meticulously quantified and an inventory of stores, munitions, and personnel recorded—down to the last sheep, bushel of oats, and tub of brandy. A total of 114,554 men, 12,000 horses, and over 1,000 guns would be landed on the Kent coast. At the same time, a second French invasion force, presumably aimed at East Anglia, was being assembled in the Dutch port of Flushing (now Vlissingen). Along with many larger vessels were 110 *schuyts*, each capable of transporting sixty to eighty men and armed with two 24-pounders. It was also understood that a third French flotilla was under construction in Antwerp. The invasion's timetable allowed for the balance of the French army, a further 50,000-plus troops to join the expedition in the Texel. However, the success of such an invasion was predicated on naval dominance of the Channel, and there was a suggestion of complacency surrounding Admiral Lord St Vincent's assurance to the Upper House: 'I do not say, my Lords, that the French will not come. I only say that they will not come by sea'. St Vincent had become a politician, but Admiral Keith, responsible for the defence of southern and eastern England, recognised the threat posed by a temporary and localised French dominance. He realised that this could be achieved by the escape from Brest of a strong French squadron, enabling an invasion fleet to establish a bridgehead on the Kent coast.

Nelson's crushing victory at Trafalgar would seem to have vindicated St Vincent's confidence as the French invasion effort soon dissipated. Subsequently, compounding Nelson's triumph, other naval victories would neutralise hostile fleets in Spain, the West Indies, and the Baltic, making an invasion even less likely. Additionally, the defences that would prevent its success were being put in place. Britain's south-coast naval bases were seen as being particularly vulnerable. The recent British expedition to La Rochelle in France, though ultimately unsuccessful, had shown how an amphibious landing could seriously disrupt communications, tie up large numbers of defending troops, and divert enemy troops from pressure points elsewhere. This experience influenced the fortification of Portsmouth, for instance, where the Duke of Cumberland, as military adviser to the cabinet, fully supported the construction of a fort on Eastney Point, named for himself. Large redoubts were constructed at Eastbourne, Dymchurch, and Harwich, and a chain of Martello Towers, carrying cannon and supported by detached batteries, was built around the south-eastern seaboard of England, from Seaford in Sussex to Aldeburgh in Suffolk. The Royal Military Canal in Kent provided an obstacle to an invading force and a means of transporting troop, while forts throughout the kingdom, particularly around naval bases, were strengthened and volunteer forces were raised. In the meantime, Napoleon embarked on an ambitious ship-building programme that might ultimately have challenged the predominance of the Royal Navy, which had peaked in 1808–09 with

113 line-of-battle ships. Fortunately for Britain, Napoleon was defeated on land, but the demonstrably successful Blue Water principle remained as the mainstay of defence thinking.

The Three Panics and Beyond: Scares and Responses, 1844–1907

The first of the trio of so-called 'panics' was triggered by a press leak. The Duke of Wellington wrote two memoranda in 1844 and 1845 expressing his concerns over the vulnerability of the English naval dockyards to attack by, particularly French, steam-powered naval vessels. These, he felt, could outmanoeuvre the hitherto invincible 'wooden walls' of England, upon whom so much defensive reliance was still placed. These new vessels were faster, more powerful, and, above all, subject to a much lesser extent to the influence of the weather. Worried by the lack of attention his warnings were receiving, Wellington wrote to General Sir John Burgoyne, the inspector general of fortifications. Only when parts of this private correspondence were published in *The Times*, to the anger of both men incidentally, was the public alerted to Wellington's hypothetical, but plausible scenario of a Franco-American attack on Britain. It was particularly his scepticism regarding the capability of the Royal Navy to respond in sufficient time to such a lightning invasion that created a degree of disquiet. As it happened, Louis Philippe was deposed in the 1848 Revolution and the fears abated.

The second cause for concern came four years later with the accession of Napoleon III, and the perceived possibility of a resumption of his uncle's ambitions. Palmerston fanned the flames by declaring that 50,000 French troops could be whisked across the Channel from Cherbourg in a single night, and that the Royal Navy would be entirely powerless to prevent this happening.

In 1859, the French launched an armoured frigate *La Gloire*, capable of firing the new explosive shells. As if this was not enough, there came the development of Cherbourg as a deep-water naval base, lying only a few hours steaming from Portsmouth, even nearer to Portland, and with the Channel Islands in its back yard. Together, these triggered the third panic event and unfortunately coincided with the Orsini affair in which the explosives used in an, albeit unsuccessful, attempt on the life of Napoleon III were found to have been sourced in London, causing fury across the Channel. Two immediate responses to the crisis, if crisis there were, came that year. The *Warrior*, Britain's first iron-hulled, armoured warship was laid down at the Thames Ironworks yard in Millwall as the latest move in what was becoming a naval arms race between Britain and France. The other development was the production of RBL artillery by Armstrongs, and further refined as the more effective RMLs.

All these factors came together to convince Palmerston's government of the need to render Britain's naval ports and arsenals proof against foreign attack, and a Royal Commission was appointed under the chairmanship of Major-General Sir Harry Jones, to inquire into the 'present state, condition and sufficiency of the Fortifications existing for the defence of Our United Kingdom ... and all work ... for the improvement thereof'.

Its remit included the south-coast ports from the Thames and Medway to Plymouth, and then Milford Haven and Cork. Interestingly, Wellington's memoranda had gone into a great deal of detail over the stretches of coastline linking the south-coast bases and the relative degrees of coast defence provision he deemed necessary, but strayed no further afield. Surprisingly, no mention was made in either memoranda or commission brief of the east coast, Liverpool, or Scotland, and it would appear that the traditional enemy, France, was perceived as the sole source of an invasion threat, and then only by the shortest route. The Royal Commission reported in 1860, recommending works costing a total of £11.85 million at ten sites. This sum included the fortifications themselves, nearly 4,000 guns (costing half a million sovereigns), and new barracks for over 30,000 troops. Burgoyne appended a generally approving note, resisting the 'did I not say this all along?' refrain. The works were completed by 1870, evaluated by a second Royal Commission as being well-executed and within budget, and evermore dubbed 'Palmerston's Follies' as, within a very short while, they were seen to be obsolete. The Royal Commission had rejected suggestions to ring London with a string of thirty forts to secure the metropolis against attack, preferring to restrict fortifications to the invasion coast. Twenty years later, renewed pressure succeeded in getting the government to establish the London Defence Positions (see Chapter 3).

Throughout these years, the alarms kept on sounding. The Fashoda Crisis of 1898–1900—a squabble over colonial boundaries—raised the possibility of war with France. The French Minister of Foreign Affairs Delcassé promoted discussion over an alliance with Russia to attack the British Empire, possibly with further support from Germany who at the time objected to the course of the Boer War. One suggestion was an invasion of mainland Britain from France, while the Russians invaded India, and French troops, stationed in Indochina, attacked Burma. The next decade saw many occasions on which petty irritations, misunderstandings and misrepresentations, dissonance between rhetoric and action, and blatant provocation could have led to physical conflict between any permutations of European power. In 1901, fear of a surprise attack by the French in the Mediterranean, possibly aided by Russian ships from the Black Sea Fleet, prompted worries about the strength of Britain's Mediterranean Fleet and the state of its base on Malta, with implications for the deployment of the Navy in home waters.

These scares generated a number of responses, both official and unofficial. In 1905, the National Service League, campaigning for compulsory conscription, formed; its president, Field Marshal Lord Roberts of Kandahar, had resigned from his post as C-in-C of the British Army. It enjoyed vocal support from Alfred Harmsworth (later Lord Northcliffe), the newspaper proprietor and founder of the *Daily Mail* (1896) and *Daily Mirror* (1903). Against the backdrop of a rumoured Anglo-German treaty, both men were concerned about Britain's apparent unpreparedness for invasion. She would have had little defence against a co-ordinated attack that might have brought a French invasion in the south of the country and a Russian one in the north-east. The League would have 200,000 members by 1914, but the Liberal establishment remained vociferous in its opposition. In 1913, Eddy Tenant, Lord Glenconner, was typical of his caste when, addressing the Liverpool Liberal Reform Club on the subject of Home Defence, he asserted that it was 'repugnant to the mental constitution of a freedom-loving people and the British nation would never stand it'.

At the same time, a further, unrelated initiative was the formation of the Legion of Frontiersmen, whose purpose was to gather intelligence in defence of the Empire. Following a defence debate in the House of Lords, the Government responded by commissioning General Sir John Owen to review coast defences at home and throughout the Empire. The Owen Committee reviewed the protection of home ports concentrating on their relative importance, especially to the national economy. The report categorised ports and set the extent of their fixed defences. Just as in 1860, the report excluded the area between the Thames and the Humber, and it would be several years more before evidence of reorientation toward a new foe might affect the disposition of coast defences.

Anxiety at home was matched across the Empire. In 1905, following her successful war with Russia, the strength of Japan's armed forces was increased and new naval bases built. This prompted fears of a Japanese invasion in Australia, and caused the creation of a dedicated Royal Australian Navy, mainly funded by the Australian taxpayer, and the maintenance of a standing force of 17,000 militia and volunteer soldiers. A proliferation of rifle clubs, some 325 in the state of Victoria alone, and a Junior Cadet organisation (with membership of 15,000 teenage boys) reflected feelings of insecurity at home and away. Back in Britain, an inquiry into the risk of invasion, chaired by Lord Esher, was followed the next year by Haldane's establishment of the Territorial Force (TF) in 1908 (see Chapter 2). Summers has described what she calls a British militarism that was as significant a force as its Prussian cousin, but it was based on a wholly different principle of voluntary service holding a strong appeal across all areas of the social and political spectrum, and which would lead to the instantaneous recruitment of a large citizen army in 1914.

In 1911, the German deployment of the gunboat *Panther* to Morocco, for the protection of German expatriates in an area of French influence, provoked the Agadir Crisis. Britain was preoccupied at the time with the passage of controversial legislation (the Parliament Bill in the Lords and the National Insurance Bill in the Commons), but Sir Edward Grey, the Foreign Secretary, communicated Britain's concern and diplomatic exchanges between Britain and Germany raised the possibility of hostilities. The Army and Navy were put on alert and the bridges on the South Eastern and Chatham Railway lines were guarded day and night. In the end, the Kaiser was given land in the Congo and in return recognised Morocco as a French protectorate, but remained unaware that, subsequently, Anglo-French discussions were held to plan a joint response to any future German aggression.

Scaremongering: The Literature of Invasion, 1871–1910

In 1871, at the time of the Franco-Prussian War, George Chesney, writing as a former RE officer, wrote *The Battle of Dorking: Reminiscences of a Volunteer*. Its accent was on the impact of technology and how countries were manoeuvred into war, featuring the invasion of an unprepared England and its defeat at the hands of Prussian armies. The choice of protagonist was, presumably, topical rather than especially prescient. In 1894, William le Queux (as in snooker), a hack journalist and novelist, under the patronage of Alfred Harmsworth, published *The Great War in England in 1897*, an account that included invasion and defeat. From 1900, both the British and Prussian press exacerbated latent paranoia by playing one off against the other, encouraging nationalism and whipping up xenophobia. In 1903, *The Riddle of the Sands*, by Erskine Childers, appeared to be describing a Prussian invasion of the east coast from North Sea ports in Germany. In the first decade of the twentieth century, over forty fictionalised accounts of German invasions were written and, sadly, published, but le Queux remained the master of the genre, if only from the point of view of churning out in quantity and scoring the highest fantasy quotient. On 14 March 1906, the first episode of his *The Invasion of 1910* appeared in serial form in the *Daily Mail*, describing a German invasion of East Anglia. Once landed, the route taken by the invading force was determined by Harmsworth, hoping to reinvigorate circulation of a flagging *Mail*. This explains the focus on non-strategic locations, where newsagents whose sales would be enhanced by local references might be found. An eventual British victory after the flight of the Government to Bristol may have reassured his readers, but a number of worrying elements should have raised some important issues. The formation of a plucky and clandestine resistance organisation, The League of Defenders may have prefigured the auxiliary units of the Second World War, but it should have alerted readers to the dangerous status of *franc tireurs*. The invaders were aided by large numbers of German troops living undercover in Britain—by implication, the 50,000 Prussian workers employed in the hospitality industry—and by the mass of socialist workers in the cities. Harmsworth's conscription agenda was furthered, the *Mail's* circulation was boosted by 80,000, and the book sold a million copies in twenty-seven languages. The German edition culminated in a Prussian victory. There were complaints in Parliament by MPs who argued that this form of literature harmed Britain's relations with her European neighbours by conditioning the population to accept the inevitability of war between Britain and Germany. Once unleashed, the juggernaut rolled on. Rudolf Martin, a retired Prussian civil servant, suggested at a public meeting in Berlin that 10,000 Zeppelins, each carrying twenty soldiers, could land overnight to capture a sleeping Britain. This prompted H. G. Wells to write *The War in the Air*, picking up on Rudolf's predictions of air-ships carrying out aerial bombing attacks on cities; New York would be destroyed in a matter of hours, and his follow-up, *The War of the Worlds*, was no less alarming. After the *Daily Mail* had reported Rudolf's suggestions to its readership, the British Government nevertheless decided no action to explore the military aspects of aviation was necessary at that time. Martin had also forecast the bombing of London and presented this threat as a deterrent to British aggression. Cartoons of Zeppelins bombing the British fleet immediately appeared in magazines, and this was before the German armed forces had ordered a single airship. Neither could the ostensibly respectable and responsible resist joining in the fun. In 1908, J. L. Garvin, editor of the *Observer*, admittedly part of Harmsworth's empire since 1905, was found to be the author of an anonymous article published in the *Quarterly Review* as 'The German Peril'; it warned of a possible German invasion supported by those 50,000 German waiters established in Britain. The German navy would cruise the Atlantic and Count Zeppelin would fly his new dirigible airships around Europe with impunity.

In 1909, Le Queux was back with *Spies of the Kaiser*, initially published in serial form. Its plot centred on the theft by German secret agents, many of whom were domiciled in Britain, of the plans of the new Rosyth naval base and dockyard, and of new British aircraft and submarines. This sat alongside his dozens of similar stories whipping up popular fears and anti-German sentiment after, in his telling, the British Army had been shrunk almost out of existence. Chapter 4 in *Spies of the Kaiser* describes 'How the Germans are Preparing for Invasion', while another chapter exposes a network of 5,000 German spies surveying the coasts of Yorkshire, the Humber estuary, the Wash, and East Anglia down to the Thames, locating suitable landing beaches. Hull is identified as a potential German bridgehead and base for reinforcement and resupply. Each of these German secret agents had been assigned a geographical area, and the task of systematically mapping vulnerable points and military installations and formulating detailed plans for their demolition or neutralisation, for simultaneous implementation on the eve of war. The 'novel's' final words ask: 'When will Germany strike?'

This peak year of 1909 witnessed an explosion of invasion-related events. A sub-Committee of the CID was set up to explore the factual basis of all these fantasies and, more specifically, a clutch of recent ones, which had their origin with Lt-Col. Edmonds, the director of MO5 at the War Office. The stories that Edmonds spread purported to confirm the existence of a secret and widespread network of German agents, preparing the way for an invasion. Most of these stories had little basis in fact and some were actually entries to a competition set up to publicise the launch of *Spies of the Kaiser* in the *Weekly News*. Edmonds was simply trying to justify his existence by inflating the importance of his department. Guy du Maurier's *An Englishman's Home* was a highly dramatised account of an invasion, but A. A. Milne's story for *Punch* was a spoof, borrowing Le Queux's style and characters, quite an achievement as Le Queux sometimes found it difficult to stick with the same hero for the duration of a whole novel. When he was in danger of missing a deadline for an instalment of a serial, he might insert a totally unrelated short story with different characters, written earlier and probably spiked. A full-length spoof novel by P. G. Wodehouse called *The Swoop! Or How Clarence Saved England* relates how a boy scout counters the assaults on Britain by the forces of nine different nations, including the armies of China, Monaco, and Russia, the Swiss navy, and the Mad Mullah. The extent to which the British public found it difficult to distinguish between supposedly fact-based revelations and their satirical imitations cannot now be known, but eventually the British Government was forced to deny rumours that 66,000 German soldiers were resident in Britain, had access to a cache in central London containing 50,000 rifles and 7.5 million rounds of ammunition, and awaited orders to seize the country. Despite these government denials, rumours persisted, especially after apparently genuine German invasion plans were discovered by accident. Citizens continuing to report espionage activities, particularly in the key coastal areas between the Isle of Wight and the Wash, included a Justice of the Peace in Lincolnshire. Warnings were printed in the *Daily Mail* regarding sightings of Zeppelins hovering over London. There were, nevertheless, attempts on both sides to redress the balance. A Berlin newspaper was moved to comment that irresponsible hallucinations, most likely inspired by party politicking, could easily produce in public opinion a destabilising prejudice against a friendly (German) nation, and in 1910, Ida Wylie published *My German Year* seeking to allay the fears of German aggression stoked up for its readers by the *Mail*. She portrayed Germany as a peace-loving country completely lacking in imperial ambition. By 1912, a marked increase in espionage trials had been recorded in both Britain and Germany. In 1913, F. W. Hirst's essay enumerating further 'panics', and universally panned by reviewers, cited rumours of brightly lit German airships hovering over British towns.

Anglo-German Attitudes

Throughout the sixty years leading up to the First World War, Anglo-German attitudes are characterised by ambivalence and confusion. As early as 1852, an account by Theodor Fontane offers harsh observations on Britain's tough mercantile climate, in which all foreigners are regarded with suspicion, but Prussians, especially, are seen as a threat to the overworked and underpaid English working class. Fontane was commissioned by a press agency to comment on national loyalty and the capacity of the English to resist a foreign invasion. His conclusion was that England was vulnerable and that once her outer defences were punctured, resistance would be futile against the power and persistence of Prussia. One possible source of the origins of Anglo-German antipathy was the German war of 1864 with Denmark over Schleswig-Holstein. Bismarck was particularly incensed by Britain's moral support for the Danes, but their refusal to commit militarily. From a position as Germany's mentor, Britain moved, over fifty years, to being perceived as a block to all her ambitions. Echoing Napoleon's earlier dismissive assessment, Britain was regarded by many influential Germans as a money-grubbing nation of shopkeepers and merchants, unreliable in her international dealings, arrogant, opportunistic in seizing colonies for herself, but quick to prevent others from acting similarly. Supreme hypocrisy was evident in such objections to other countries seeking to emulate what they, the Britons, had done. Of equal perfidy was her reliance on the Royal Navy to maintain her stranglehold on world trade. The ultimate example of 'Manchesterism' was Britain's sale of arms to Napoleon III during the Franco-Prussian War.

An Anglophobic German press promoted the expansion of the German Empire, and felt that they deserved the respect lacking from Britain. Reported Prussian atrocities during the Franco-Prussian War, which influenced British opinion, prompted the German press to publish similar stories about British soldiers' behaviour in the Boer Wars. The pro-German journal, *The Fatherland*, was published in the USA with articles by academics at Washington State and Harvard Universities. In an edition dated 10 August 1914, it included a poem:

...But thy great task will not be done
Until thou vanquish utterly
The Norman brother of the Hun,
England the serpent of the sea
The flame of war her tradesmen fanned
Shall yet consume her, fleet and field...

If the British and the Germans were indeed brothers, then they were subject to intense sibling rivalry. Germans were regarded by many Britons as backward, bellicose, and ill-mannered. The Prussians, stereotypically, were militaristic and statist. To the British working man, there were too many Germans employed in menial jobs in Britain, willing to work for lower wages than the natives and putting them out of jobs. Much of this predates by two decades the attitudes usually ascribed to Kaiser Wilhelm II and the Junkers caste, who were generally admiring of Britain. Britain sensed that German resentment of Britain was so strong that a war was far from impossible. Despite Bismarck's hatred of Britain, it was actually his political opponents who were more vociferous in wanting to win more colonies and to increase the German fleet. Later on, Kaiser Wilhelm II would be accused of being pro-British, guided by his English mother and grandmother, and aping British upper-class activities, such as sailing, and too proud of his British admiral's uniform. British 'supreme national self-confidence' was envied by Germans—particularly Bernhardi in 1912. German support for the Boers, with whom Germany had only a tenuous affinity, had antagonised Britain. The Kaiser was infuriated by Britain's 'unnatural' hostility to Germany based on what he perceived as envy and fear of German success.

Britain was regarded by Germans as 'contemptible' for maintaining such a tiny army, and for playing games instead of undergoing military training and duelling. Germany was regarded by liberal Britons as a police state. During the First World War, British POWs were shocked by the brutal and discriminating way in which they were often treated by German civilians and this may be explained by the way the two countries' news media had maintained their hate campaign for so long. British civilians were horrified by the atrocity stories regarding the German conduct of war, not all of which were necessarily fabrications, but appear not to have acted against German POWs to the same extent.

Prussian Challenges to Britain's Global Ascendancy

In his 1890 publication *The Influence of Sea Power upon History*, American A. T. Mahan described a struggle for global power between large fleets of battleships, and highlighted the planned invasion of Britain by Napoleon Bonaparte in 1805, which was thwarted by sea power. The Kaiser was a great admirer of Mahan's writing and became obsessed with building up German sea power, seeing it as the means of avoiding any future diplomatic clash with Britain, and furthering his own desire for the promotion of German prominence in the world. A *Weltpolitik*, a term first used by von Bülow, and little more than a neutral and vague aspiration in itself, could easily lead to a more aggressive bid for world domination, or *Weltmachtstellung*. By 1898, the Kaiser had put his support behind the faction led by von Tirpitz, which favoured a fleet of powerful battleships that could operate on the world stage, over the alternative of fast cruisers that might offer more flexibility in resolving localised colonial incidents. From the mid-1890s, von Tirpitz, for whom the 'most dangerous naval enemy at the present time' was England, established an Imperial Naval Office, which administered a long-term programme of naval construction backed by the Kaiser. In order to influence the formers of German opinion to finance this new fleet, he characterised it as being protective of German security. Unlike the British 'Blue Water' school, however, he saw a fleet of powerful battleships as the primary means of achieving victory through a strategic offensive to annihilate an opponent's forces at sea or, at the very least, to inflict crippling damage, fatally weakening an opponent. In reality, he had no time for those who saw sea power as a defensive element alongside coast defences. Nevertheless, from 1870 onwards, the approaches to the key German naval bases were provided with powerful coast artillery installations. Offshore islands—particularly Borkum at the mouth of the Ems and Heligoland, dominating the approaches to the mouths of the Weser and the Elbe, and the vital Kiel Canal—were strongly fortified, using 30.5-cm (12-inch) guns in twin turrets like those on warships, and a range of 24- and 28-cm (9.5- and 11-inch) guns. On the mainland, forts were either newly built or modernised at Cuxhafen, Wilhelmshafen, and Bremerhafen. Just as the 'bolt-from-the-blue' school in Britain saw the possibility of a surprise attack as an argument against Fisher's reserve fleet arrangements (see Chapter 4), so von Tirpitz feared a pre-emptive strike on his ships. Despite his ostensibly global preoccupations, the German fleet was really only suited to action on its North Sea doorstep and its Atlantic front garden. Quarters in the new German ships were cramped and, until they adopted oil over coal, their cruising range was limited. Moreover, the entire German battle fleet was permanently based in its north-western ports.

Von Tirpitz counted Britain, France, Russia, and the USA as Germany's most likely potential enemies. In 2002, some German naval papers came to light astonishingly revealing German plans for an invasion of the USA. The first dated from 1897 and consisted of detailed plans for attacks on the US naval bases at Norfolk, Newport News, and Hampton Roads, the purpose being to put pressure on the US to acquiesce to the establishment of a German naval base in the Caribbean. Plans were reworked several times over the next few years, and the next version was for attacks on New York and Boston using sixty warships and slightly fewer merchantmen to land 100,000 troops. There was a suggestion that a base in Cuba might be secured prior to this ambitious operation. The third version, in 1902–03, employed an existing US risk assessment to identify vulnerable points where troops might be landed to carry out a pincer movement on Boston. By 1906, the USA had assumed a new prominence in world politics and, believing that Filipino guerrillas would do their work for them, the Germans shelved their plans.

In 1901, the fraternal nations once more fell prey to misunderstandings. The Kaiser was present at Queen Victoria's death and attended her funeral, declaring his support for an alliance between the two Teutonic nations, Britain and Germany. However, the existing Triple Alliance with Austria-Hungary and Italy made it impossible for Britain to assume such responsibility for so much of Europe. This perceived slight and the ensuing irritation of his uncle, Edward VII, both upset the Kaiser.

Expansion of the German Empire, initially promoted by Bismarck and achieved through a combination of design and opportunism included Schleswig-Holstein, which was predominantly Danish; Alsace-Lorraine, mainly French; and East Prussia, which was largely Polish. Germany saw herself as having a 'mission east of the Vistula', and also in large areas of Africa. In 1904, a German naval base was built on the Shantung Peninsula at Kiaochow-Tsingtao. The costly, inept, and barbaric suppression of revolts in 1905–07 in German East Africa (Tanganyika), German South West Africa (Namibia), and German West Africa (Cameroon and Togo) did little to promote Germany's image as a civilising force.

Germany reciprocated Britain's fears of invasion, but to a far lesser extent. In 1904, joint naval and military exercises were held to test the defences in the event of a British invasion of the Baltic coast. Not quite as driven as Le Queux, 'Seestern' (in reality, a journalist named Grauthoff) in 1905 published *1906*, which foretold an Anglo-French naval assault on Cuxhafen and described an exchange of fire between German coast batteries and hostile warships attempting to bombard the coast. In 1909, the retired chief of the German general staff, Count von Schlieffen, author of the original 1905 thoughts on invading France through Belgium, published an article describing a war between the Central Powers and an alliance of France, Britain, Russia, and Italy, the latter still, at that time, a member of the Central Powers. The Kaiser expressed great enthusiasm for the idea, reading von Schlieffen's work aloud to his generals. As Max

Hastings, among others, pointed out, Schlieffen's suggested project was more of a concept than a detailed plan, a broad outline to be fleshed out in the prevailing circumstances of its implementation. Following this projected violation of Belgian neutrality, an amphibious British attack on northern Germany was anticipated, and von Moltke planned to station three and a half divisions there. The discovery of papers in the East German archives, referred to by Beatty, appear to suggest that the *coup de main* implicit in Schlieffen's plan for a short war was little more than a ruse to attract funding to the German military, as the Reichstag was more likely to invest in projections of potential, and instant, success. In reality, the generals were well aware that such a result was unattainable and that a war of attrition was unavoidable since they were denied the manpower to achieve the necessary local dominance.

The Arms Race between Britain and Germany

In 1884, there was an early indication that the relative levels of international naval power would become an issue. What F. W. Hirst described as his 'Fourth Panic' was the 'Two-Power Standard'. This was the policy adopted by Britain that the size of the Royal Navy should never fall below the level of the combined navies of any other two nations. The concern lay in the financial implications of such a policy when other nations were trying to match Britain's naval strength. In 1888, for instance, the naval estimates included £21.5 million to build eight battleships, thirty-eight cruisers, and twenty-two gunboats. In the same year, the Army received just £600,000. The Naval Defence Act of 1895 outlined a costly building programme that included fifty-two battleships over two decades. In Germany, Admiral von Tirpitz, encouraged by the Kaiser, was driving through a similar programme to inflate the German navy. In 1898, he secured the generous sum of 408 million marks, and in 1900, the Reichstag was coerced into passing a Navy Bill, laying out a twenty-year programme for the expansion of the German fleet. Tirpitz intended to outspend Britain and make it impossible, economically, for her to maintain the desired 3:2 ratio in capital ships, itself a significant erosion of the 2:1 ratio advocated by Admiral Fisher. In Britain, building continued, with over fifty submarines being launched in Vickers yards between 1901 and 1911. Germany launched fewer, but reckoned them higher quality.

Admiral Fisher had been appointed First Sea Lord in 1904, and the next year, the keel of HMS *Dreadnought* was laid down at Portsmouth. Completed and launched by Edward VII in 1906, she precipitated Hirst's fifth panic by rendering all other battleships obsolete at a stroke, and threatening the Royal Navy's superiority worldwide.

In 1908, the German navy became the largest fleet in the Baltic, and the USA sought to commission four additional first-class battleships 'to secure peace'. Congress would, however, sanction only two, which would bring the US fleet up to sixteen battleships that then embarked on a world cruise. In 1909, the Tsar overruled the veto of the Duma and pushed ahead with the construction of four *Dreadnought*-class battleships to British designs and to be built under British supervision. The Reichstag, meanwhile, debated the future size of the German navy and, in the absence of firm proposals from Britain for an Anglo-German arms limitation treaty, agreed to build three battleships and an armoured cruiser, bringing the German fleet up to ten large new battleships and three armoured cruisers by 1912. In Britain, a Naval War Council was set up in 1909, with the responsibility for the newly created Mobilisation Department. George V's coronation, in 1911, was marked by his Review of 167 Royal Navy vessels at Spithead. Britain and France agreed that the growth in the fleets of the Central Powers, through the construction of dreadnoughts by Austria-Hungary and Italy, made it sensible for the French fleet to assume responsibility for the Mediterranean, while the British looked after the English Channel, including the north French coast. German Army and Navy Bills were introduced in the Reichstag in 1912, proposing that the army should be increased to 544,000 men, and the navy would reach a target of forty-one battleships, twenty armoured cruisers, 144 destroyers, and seventy-two submarines by 1920. The justification for this was expressed as self-defence and the maintenance of peace. The bills were passed amid debate, which highlighted Germany's perceived vulnerability to an alliance of Britain, France, and Russia. Despite these pacific avowals, the German General Bernhardi's book *Germany and the Next War* asserted that if Germany were to assume her rightful place with a full share of the mastery of the world, then Britain, the enemy, must be defeated at sea, coining the mantra: 'World Power or Downfall'—('*Weltmacht oder Untergang*'). The next year, plans were introduced for increasing the size of the German army (now standing at 661,000 men) by a further 63,000 men every year, with a target of 5,400,000 men in 1937. The suggestion by Winston Churchill (First Lord of the Admiralty, 1912) that Britain and Germany might agree a 'Naval Holiday' received a favourable response from the German Chancellor, but was effectively sabotaged by the German naval leadership, presenting the initiative as a British plot to slow down German expansion plans. When Haldane visited Germany to discuss possible naval limitations, the Kaiser saw it as evidence of weakness on Britain's part and confirmation of the effectiveness of von Tirpitz's policy of forcing Britain to overspend. The newly opened Kiel Canal provided easy access for German warships from the Baltic through to the North Sea, a capability that had, presciently, been seen by Admiral Fisher as a crucial prerequisite for Germany's war with Britain.

The State of the British and German Fleets on the Eve of War

By 1913, there was a tacit German acceptance of their failure to achieve the goal of having two capital ships for every three British ones, a ratio Germany would never achieve. In 1914, the British Admiralty published comparative figures for the numbers of the major powers' capital ships, including those under twenty years old, some of them, of course, pre-dreadnoughts, and new builds that were already afloat: Britain had fifty-eight; Germany, thirty-five; the USA, thirty; France, twenty-one; Japan, seventeen; Austria-Hungary, fourteen; Italy, nine; and Russia, eight. Britain had thirteen more battleships under construction and four more scheduled. Churchill declared the Government's intention of maintaining a 60 per cent superiority over Germany in capital ships—a ratio of 8:5. Churchill was still working with Grand Admiral von Tirpitz to curb mutual naval expansion, and was invited to Kiel in June, a visit vetoed by the Foreign Secretary. Even as late as the opening of the Kiel Canal, German and British naval officers were still subscribing to the notion that they were the 'two white nations'—natural allies, superior to others—and the German navy continued to model itself on the Royal Navy. When war broke out in 1914, Britain had twenty-two dreadnoughts and ten more under construction, against Germany's fifteen and six, respectively, and nine battlecruisers to Germany's five. Additionally, many of the Royal Navy's forty-two pre-dreadnoughts were still afloat and capable of being active in coast defence or bombardment, or as port guard ships.

Battle Plans of the European Alliances

A total lack of co-operation between the Admiralty and the War Office existed, there being no place in a staff officer's lexicon for the words 'liaison', 'co-ordination', or 'joint'. The only matter on which the two institutions agreed was the determination to conceal from their political masters the 'frocks', any plans they might have made, or strategic thinking they might have undertaken. This was perfectly exemplified by the secret meeting of the CID called by Asquith in August 1911 at the time of the Agadir Crisis. Asked for their respective departments' plans in the event of war with Germany, Major-General Henry Wilson, Director of Military Operations at the War Office, presented a well-prepared and thoroughly professional appreciation. This covered possible German invasion scenarios involving Belgium and France, with some indication, based on recent discussions with his French opposite number, of how the BEF might be deployed and in what strength, if it came to it. Admiral Sir Arthur Wilson, First Sea Lord at the Admiralty, on the other hand, unaware that his staff was already in discussion with the War Office, admitted that he had not really thought about how the Navy might deliver the BEF safely onto French soil. He then went on to explain that once his fleet had disposed of their German opposition, a better idea might be to deliver the BEF to Germany's Baltic coast to threaten Berlin, a notion apparently occurring to him on the spur-of-the-moment, but interesting in light of von Moltke's awareness of the possibility. Following this Wilson *v.* Wilson event, Asquith, with some help from Churchill, decided that the War Office plans would determine British strategy in the countdown to war. Britain's vague promise to protect Belgian neutrality was thus accelerated along its course of becoming a firm commitment to act as France's ally in a European war. This failure to explore alternative options would have fateful consequences for all sections of the British Army in the early months of the war. In 1912, Churchill set up a Naval War Staff to formulate appropriate policy for the conduct of naval operations in wartime, and to avoid a recurrence of the prevailing situation where all Admiralty plans resided in the head of one man, the First Sea Lord. A chain of seaplane bases was being constructed around the British coast, as aircraft were finally being designed with military applications in mind.

Austro-Hungarian plans envisaged a quick defeat of Serbia, followed by a concentrated attack on Russia. This was mirrored by Germany's plans for France and Russia, but Italy's initially neutral stance and then her defection from the Central Powers to the Allies threw an added strain on Hapsburg armies. Neither of Austria's military leaders—Conrad von Hotzendorf, her strategic mastermind, nor Oscar Potiorek, who led the invasion of Serbia in 1914—had any experience of actual warfare. They further failed to anticipate that Britain, her former ally, would be aligned alongside France and Russia. While those old enemies might now be allies, Britain's anxieties over Germany's plans for an adventure across the North Sea continued to dominate.

2

Britain's Defence Strategy Prior to the First World War

As an island nation, Britain enjoyed a sense of security denied its neighbours in continental Europe, and diplomatic initiatives were usually preferred to military action in bolstering those natural defences. The Congress of Vienna had set up the union of Holland and Belgium as a buffer between France and Prussia, but it also benefited Britain by depriving the French of the Scheldt estuary as a springboard for invading England. The maintenance of the English Channel as a physical barrier to invasion can be seen in the opposition to a Channel Tunnel in 1882, when work was abandoned after Parliament and the press voiced fears over national security. Later, Harmsworth was disgusted when his generous prize, awarded for the first powered flight across the Channel, went to (of all people) a Frenchman. The way lay open, he trumpeted, for aerial invasions to breach Britain's defences at will.

Defence Against Invasion: Policy and Practice, 1905–1914

A lack of an agreed and clearly presented defence strategy had come about owing to a number of factors. First was the predominance of the 'Blue Water' school of thought in the Admiralty, in the Government, and among the general public, which for long refused to countenance the remotest possibility of a successful invasion of Britain by France, Russia, Germany, or any other nation. This, in turn, led to an obsessive determination to increase the strength of the Royal Navy that, at a time when other priorities controlled the budget, led to a concomitant neglect of the army. All this was taking place at a time when domestic issues dominated the political agenda to the extent that the only external concerns appeared to be India and Ireland, and the Foreign Secretary from 1905, Sir Edward Grey, had only set foot on alien soil once in his term of office, and then only for a short trip to France.

Was Invasion Likely or Possible?

The answers to these key questions concerning either the probability or the feasibility of invasion were all to do with timing, and attempts were made to resolve the problem by simple arithmetic. In the event of war, the Royal Navy's Grand Fleet would be based mainly at Scapa Flow in the Orkney Islands, with squadrons of capital ships at the new base of Rosyth in the Firth of Forth and at Invergordon in Cromarty Firth. The crucial factor affecting this basis for Britain's defences was the time it would take them to reach the invasion beaches, likely lying far to the south. The Navy suggested the Fleet would require thirty-two to thirty-six hours for such a move. Discussion between the politicians and the military concluded that no foreign power could contemplate an invasion force of fewer than 70,000 men, a figure arrived at, not as an estimate of the minimum size for a force to be effective, but as the maximum that might practicably be conveyed across the water. This more or less arbitrary figure was based on a reckoning that the Germans might be able to assemble a fleet of 200 transports and that they would need to effect the crossing and establish a bridgehead of some strength in no more than two days. These figures soon took on a life of their own as the basis for defence planning, and between 1904 and 1913, exercises were regularly held to test their validity. In 1904, the Army staged an invasion to test the defences. The Guards Brigade, under Francis Lloyd (later GOC London District), was based in Aldershot. It embarked at Southampton and was put ashore at Wivenhoe, fighting a simulated battle across Essex, prior to re-embarking at Clacton for the return to Southampton. The 1908 Naval Manoeuvres ended with troops evading the Navy and landing near Wick, in the far north of Scotland. Doubts had surfaced earlier, when, in 1907, Colonel Hickson had written an article expressing scepticism over the Navy's ability to provide complete immunity from invasion. After the inquiry by Lord Esher's CID, Colonel Repington, military correspondent of *The Times*, used the occasion to suggest that the Royal Navy was unlikely to be able to fulfil its obligations. Admiral Fisher, the First Sea Lord, had recently written a paper reasserting his navy's fitness for the job, and Repington had attempted to have him excluded from the inquiry. In the 1912 Manoeuvres, a 'German' fleet evaded the Navy to land a force of 28,000 troops in the Humber Estuary. This result was explained away as due to extraordinary circumstances and to be disregarded.

The Army Manoeuvres of 1912 were held in East Anglia when Haig commanded the Red Army, mainly consisting of his regular command based in Aldershot. The Blue Army, under Grierson, was more of a scratch force of regular infantry, but yeomanry cavalry and TF cyclists from the Volunteer TF also filled the ranks. Both armies were provided with aircraft, but Grierson's carried out effective reconnaissance missions that led to his overall success. Haig later informed his staff that reconnaissance was the job of the cavalry and that aircraft would never usurp that role. The notion that aircraft might patrol the coast and give warning of approaching invaders seems not to have occurred to the War Office at all, and was only just entering the consciousness of the Admiralty. Challenging Fisher's unshakeable certainty that the Fleet could meet its timetable were concerns over recent advances in mines and submarine warfare. Sceptics thought that an invader would use every possible method of preventing the Fleet's smooth passage down the east coast, and that the invader's troops, supplies, and equipment being landed on the beaches of eastern England would have a great deal more grace than the Navy's thirty-six hours.

Once the war had started, a range of possible scenarios was generated. There was speculation that a full-scale invasion was unlikely so early in the war, but disruptive raids by forces of more than 20,000 men were possible. Fresh estimates that Germany had sufficient shipping to transport an invasion force of 195,000 to land on the east coast suggested the possibility of a 'Gamblers Throw' to finish the war early, particularly if Russia or France were to be knocked out, so Britain's need to keep the war on the continent became a priority. Another fear was that, as Home Forces were steadily depleted to make up early losses in France and Belgium, the Germans could protect an invasion fleet with mines and submarines to land 100,000 men on the east coast before the Grand Fleet could arrive. By 1915, Lt-Gen. Kiggell, Director of Home Defence, was of the opinion that the Germans might even risk a naval defeat to effect a landing since no more men would be lost in overcoming British resistance than would be sacrificed in a two- or three-day battle on either continental front.

One further factor was Ireland. Many Irishmen enlisted in the British Army, more from the south, proportionately, than from Ulster. Those taken prisoner in the early battles of 1914 were hived off to a special POW camp where attempts were made to recruit them into Sir Roger Casement's Irish Brigade. This proved to be a dismal failure with only fifty-two men volunteering out of a total of 2,500 POWs. However, although both nationalist and unionist leaders had declared a cessation of hostilities for the duration, the importation of arms into Ireland and the build-up to the misconceived Easter Rising of 1916 highlighted yet a further cause for concern.

Defence Policy and Resources

The words of 'Ye Mariners of England', written in 1800 by Thomas Campbell, neatly summed up Britain's defence policy:

Britannia needs no bulwarks
No towers along the steep

This default position was reinforced by the allocation of funds. Between 1895 and 1914, a staggering 40 per cent of Government spending went into defence, with a double share going to the Navy. In 1906, the Liberals secured victory in the General Election off a manifesto offering 'Peace, Retrenchment and Reform' and promising a significant cutback in military expenditure. The factor of the German challenge to Britain's dominance of the global seas was used by the Royal Navy and politicians, such as Sir Edward Grey, to enlarge the Senior Service. This meant that any cuts would be at the expense of the Army, and they would bite deep. Among the more surgical proposals made by Haldane, the Secretary of State for War, was a reduction in the strength of the Guards by disbanding three battalions from the Scots and Coldstream Guards. The Guards Brigade at Aldershot should henceforth comprise just two battalions of Guards and be made up with two battalions from line regiments, becoming the 1st Infantry Brigade. In the introduction to Ian Hamilton's *Compulsory Service*, Haldane expressed his broad principles of defence against invasion:

> A first line army for home defence we do not want. The first line here is composed of the divisions of the fleet in Home Waters and the flotilla of destroyers and submarines which guard our coastline ... the Defence Committee (proposes) to raise and train a citizen force which will be greatly superior in numbers to any force that can slip through.

Haldane went on to say that if conscription into the Regular Army were to be brought in, its cost would be wasted and would be better spent on the Navy.

Writing in the *RE Journal* in 1907, Colonel Hickson of the Royal Engineers took the opposite view. He restated the role of coast defences in preventing an enemy landing, suggesting the construction of a continuous chain of coast batteries, at roughly 10-mile (16-km) intervals, to link the defended ports and deny the enemy easy access to the invasion beaches. It was calculated that such a level of defence would demand an impossibly inflated Regular Army of thirty divisions to man the chain stretching the 400 miles (640 km) from the Nore to the Lizard, from Kent to Cornwall. The British Army of 1914 consisted of six regular infantry divisions, three of cavalry, fourteen more in the TF, plus the Reserve. The response of the CID was to maintain a home army only large enough to ensure that no foreign power could invade with a force of up to 70,000 men. By 1913, when Haldane's citizen army had been in existence for five years, an inquiry into an invasion of Britain concluded that two of the BEF's six infantry divisions should remain in Britain until TF divisions could be brought to a higher degree of readiness. Concerns also centred round the TF's efficiency. In 1913, it stood at only 80 per cent of establishment with 80 per cent of that strength having served four years or less. Furthermore, fewer than 10 per cent stated their intention to volunteer for service overseas, and in the 1912 TF Exercises, only 60 per cent (155,000 men) had attended their annual camps for the full fifteen days. Politicians argued that the TF should number at least 500,000–600,000 men, but despite the arguments for ensuring adequate numbers at home to defend against invasion, the Royal Navy continued to be trusted in the vanguard.

The Role of the Royal Navy: The Blue Water School

This doctrine, which maintained that no foreign invasion could succeed while the Royal Navy ruled the waves, enjoyed a long history—from the 'wooden walls' of the Athenians, through the defeat of the Spanish Armada, to Earl St Vincent's assertion in 1803. It was the contention of Admiral Sir John 'Jackie' Fisher, First Sea Lord since 1904, that, providing the Royal Navy was enabled to maintain superiority over foreign navies, it would always retain the capability of defending Empire and homeland alike. His new navy was designed to withstand a range of threats. The powerful, all big-gun *Dreadnought*-class battleships were designed to be dominant in a fleet action against any extant comparable force. The new, fast, but less heavily armoured battlecruisers could fulfil a number of roles from scouting ahead of the main fleet to hit-and-run raids, and were powerful enough to deal with any single vessel they might meet along their way. Cruisers, both armoured and light, could patrol the sea-lanes and show the flag in remote corners of the Empire. Fleet destroyers would escort the battle fleet in its main role of seeking out and destroying that of the enemy. Much of this was out in the open, but Fisher was more secretive about his planned 'flotilla defence'. This was a dispersed deployment of large numbers of submarines, destroyers, and coastal torpedo-boats around the coast, on constant patrol to provide advance warning of enemy sailings and to deter the German fleet from braving the North Sea. He avoided too much explanation of this strategy in order to maintain an advantage over the (putative) enemy across the water.

Fisher's Reform of the Royal Navy

In 1904, on taking up his new appointment, Fisher recognised the financial constraints that would be placed on the Royal Navy by a Liberal Government seeking to fund Lloyd George's social welfare programme, and immediately embarked on a sweeping programme of reform. He quickly reorganised officer training, bringing in a common entry and education system for executive and engineer branches designed to raise the status of the engineer officers who hitherto had not been considered as gentlemen by their often aristocratic colleagues, but were nevertheless vital to the efficient operation of technologically sophisticated ships. More fundamentally, he set in train a policy of improving the quality of the ships themselves and the performance of their crews. Defence spending fell in 1904, only regaining previous levels in 1911, but cuts effectively impacted only on the Army, as naval expenditure on capital ships soared after 1906. Nevertheless, Fisher was forced to make significant efficiency savings to fund the dreadnought programme. He set about scrapping or mothballing over 150 obsolete vessels in order to free up personnel to man this new breed of battleship, and pushed forward the use of oil-fired turbines to replace coal-burning boilers. He also reorganised the distribution of the Navy in home waters by creating a Reserve Fleet, composed of vessels manned by 'nucleus crews', cadres of key personnel, familiar with the workings of their ships. These would be brought up to full strength for periodic manoeuvres at sea or, in the event of war, for full-scale naval mobilisation, by drawing on personnel from naval barracks and a central pool of reservists. This proved to be an extremely cost-effective way of reducing manning costs while maintaining the maximum number of available ships.

Fisher's reforms inevitably met with opposition from the essentially conservative officer corps of the Royal Navy. One particularly vociferous opponent was Lord Charles Beresford, the admiral commanding the Channel Fleet by 1907, whose life in the Royal Navy had been punctuated by regular official reprimands, but who had survived by becoming a popular hero and by regularly entering Parliament to oppose the Government. Much of Beresford's support came from the Imperial Navy League, set up in 1896 to focus public awareness on British dependency on the sea, and on the consequent need for a strong navy. Despite the Admiralty's demonstration that on any given day, the strength of the Royal Navy was equal to anything that Germany or any other power could mobilise, a campaign was mounted by Beresford, his political sponsors, the League, and a number of newspaper proprietors to undermine and discredit the Board of Admiralty generally and Fisher in particular. Asquith, the Prime Minister, held an inquiry at Cabinet level that exonerated Fisher and the Board and showed Beresford to be an insubordinate incompetent, a deceitful and vindictive operator, and a self-seeking rogue, but declined to publicise these findings. Asquith felt he was being squeezed between his own supporters who wanted to reduce military expenditure year on year, and those pressure-groups—such as the League and its off-shoot (the Imperial Maritime League), supported by the blue water armchair admirals—who played on public fears of foreign aggression to lobby for an ever-expanding Royal Navy. He therefore sought to minimise friction and controversy where the Navy was involved. Fortunately, most of Fisher's work had been completed, but apart from enjoying the King's approbation, he was denied the credit to which he was clearly entitled. The one positive to emerge from the Asquith inquiry was the suggestion that a strengthened Naval War Staff would provide a focus for the development of naval tactics and strategy both for senior naval officers afloat, and for the political and professional members of the Board of Admiralty.

The *Dreadnought*-Class Battleships

Dreadnoughts were designed to use the new steam-turbine engines of Sir Charles Parsons, also to be used by Cunard for passenger liners such as the RMS *Lusitania*. The Battle of Tsushima, at which the Russian Fleet had been destroyed, had shown the dangers of fast torpedo-boats getting among capital warships. One solution was to create battleships with a main armament wholly of big guns that could prevent any enemy vessel from getting within torpedo range. Through his efficiency savings, Fisher was able to stretch the budget enough to begin the construction of a completely new class of battleship. The first of these was laid down in late 1905 in Portsmouth Dockyard and, remarkably, within twelve months, *Dreadnought* was undergoing sea-trials prior to her final fitting-out. She had ten 12-inch guns in five turrets, five 18-inch torpedo tubes, and over two dozen 12-pounder anti-torpedo-boat guns mounted singly around her decks. Thick armour protected her turrets and decks, and for later vessels of her class, this was extended. She could cruise at 21 knots and had a crew of 700–800 men. Four new ships were built each year. Portsmouth and Devonport Dockyards built eight and five respectively; three more came from Barrow-in-Furness, with one each from Millwall and Birkenhead; and yards in the Tyne and the Clyde contributed a further six each, making a total of thirty ships available to the Royal Navy by the end of 1914. More were laid down in 1915–16, for completion through the war. Alongside these battleships, a new class of armoured battlecruiser, the *Inflexible*-class, was built from 1906. These were given eight 12-inch guns in four turrets and thinner armour, giving them a speed of 25 knots, but making them more vulnerable under fire, as would be discovered at Jutland.

Alternative Naval Strategies

Fisher's policies were not without their opponents. Proponents of the *Jeune École* saw the dreadnoughts as a waste of resources, which confined the Navy to a single type of operation: the Fleet Action. They preached the value of fast cruisers to maintain the freedom of the seas, which formed the lifeblood of empire, and to keep safe the seaways used by the world's commercial shipping. Cruisers could raid their enemies' commerce and support small colonial actions. Britain's far-flung empire provided the web of naval bases, coaling stations, and telegraph junctions through which imperial hegemony was maintained, but this network would become vulnerable to attack in times of war, requiring the protection of the very ships it was meant to sustain. In fact, the 1909 Review of coast artillery defences throughout the Empire recognised that the increase in the size of foreign navies—specifically those of Germany, Japan, and the USA—might result in a temporary loss of local naval superiority off imperial ports and harbours. Fisher remained impervious to these arguments, regarding the winning of set-piece battles as the supreme naval aspiration.

Regardless of this question of what sort of ship should make up the Navy, there was scepticism regarding its ability to mobilise efficiently, given Fisher's introduction of the Reserve Fleet system. This argument was put forward by those who believed in the 'bolt from the blue' scenario, being a sudden strike by an enemy eschewing the formal niceties of declaring war. An extension of this argument, put forward by several senior officers, including Lord Charles Beresford, criticised what they saw as a lack of concise war plans in the Admiralty. In other words, the Royal Navy was unprepared for war. Several of those officers, including Beresford himself, had found themselves with shrunken commands as a consequence of Fisher's creation of the Reserve Fleet. Others, the (bosun's) whistle-blowers, strove to increase naval spending by calling into question the Navy's efficacy. Fisher, however, remained confident that war would be preceded by diplomatic processes, providing ample time for last-minute planning and orderly mobilisation.

The Regular Army and the Territorial Force: Roles, Organisation, and Modernisation

British troops, whose tactics of close-order volley firing had hardly changed since the French wars, were outfought and outmanoeuvred in the South African wars by Boer *Kommandos*. The Boers' marksmanship, mobility, and fieldcraft all contributed to force the British to employ the sledgehammer of overwhelming force to subdue them. These setbacks to Britain's imperial prowess encouraged German thoughts of offering a future challenge. The bitter experience of the Boer War, however, ensured that the British Army would fight future wars using entirely different tactics, and its training would henceforth be geared to consolidating those changes implicit in the evidence presented from October 1902 to the Elgin Commission. The implementation of these changes, however, was predicated on a fundamental reorganisation of the War Office. A trio of reformers—Lord Esher, Admiral Fisher, and Sir George Clarke (soon to be first secretary of the new CID, set up in 1904)—made recommendations in the light of the Elgin findings. The post of commander-in-chief was abolished and an Army Council was set up under the CIGS. This brought together all the disparate branches, such as the Royal Ordnance, as directorates of a single, integrated body. The establishment of a General Staff with three directorates to control training, operational planning, and staff work brought some order to a hitherto haphazard and disjointed series of processes. Esher also insisted that these staff functions should be replicated in the GHQ structure, which would run the BEF, establishing distinct and consistent chains of command right down to unit level.

Despite attempts by Haldane to establish definitive roles and purposes for the Army as a way of prioritising defence spending, no real progress was made in the strategic planning that ought to have underpinned the *Entente Cordiale*, the treaty with France, of 1904. The Royal Commission on Militia and Volunteers of 1904, under the Duke of Norfolk, judged the militia and volunteer forces incapable of carrying out an effective defence of the country in the event of invasion. Haldane persisted with a reorganisation of the Volunteer Force, and in 1907, he formed the County Territorial Force Associations as the prelude to radical reform. In 1908, the Yeomanry and Rifle Volunteers were combined into the Territorial Force; the Militia became the Special Reserve, usually a regiment's 3rd Battalion, intended as a way of replacing battle-casualties; and the old volunteer battalions were now numbered in sequence, generally as the 4th and 5th Battalions of their parent regiments of the line. Yeomanry regiments were given stronger ties to regular cavalry regiments, particularly for the purposes of training. The TF was organised as a regionally based home defence force in fourteen divisions, each with cavalry, infantry, artillery, engineers (including signallers), service corps, and medical services. Potential officers could be supplied through units of the Officer Training Corps, with school-based junior corps and senior ones attached to universities. In 1909, the TF peaked at 270,000, but it had declined to 246,000 by 1913, 66,000 below establishment, although it began to recover. In 1914, the Regular Army numbered 247,432; there were 145,347 reservists; and just short of 270,000 Territorials. Compared to other European countries, most of which employed conscription, Britain's Army was tiny, but Haldane had fashioned a professional core, a viable and trained reserve, and a semi-trained, but more-focused home defence force. In late 1914, TF battalions would be considered eligible, so long as they had a 60 per cent complement volunteering for overseas service. The residue was to form the nucleus of second-line battalions, filling in for their first-line units deployed overseas, training recruits, and providing drafts to first-line units.

New Directions in the Army

Battlefield tactics were to be dictated by the twin imperatives of firepower and manoeuvre, and a dawning recognition of the sheer force of modern weapons, particularly artillery and machine guns. The infantry's essential skill set could be summarised as marching, shooting, both volleys and individual aimed shots, and fieldcraft. As the War Office began to internalise new imperatives, appropriate officers were placed in key posts, the command of the School of Musketry at Hythe being one of them. He and his successors, all men who had experience of fighting in South Africa and who had also learned from observation of the Russo-Japanese War, evolved a doctrine of rapid fire, tailored both to the expected conditions of a European battlefield and the known behaviours of German troops under fire. The standard rifle of the British Army, the .303-inch SMLE, was the perfect weapon with which to develop this rapid fire technique that aspired to a consistent rate of fire of fifteen aimed shots per minute. Fire control was devolved to platoon commanders, creating far more flexibility, and the reorganisation of the battalion into fewer, but larger companies (made up of fixed platoons under their own officers and NCOs) made the new tactics more achievable. The subaltern would become the key component in this new system. Right up to the outbreak of war, the role of the cavalry had been hotly debated between those who saw the cavalryman with his lance and sabre as some sort of successor to the knights of old and those for whom he was an anachronism, better employed as a mounted infantryman. Beyond the distinct tasks of reconnaissance and manning outlying picquets, there would be little (at least in Europe) for the cavalry to do in their traditional role, and once they had been equipped with the same rifle as the infantry and some horse-drawn machine guns, their only advantage would be increased mobility and freedom of manoeuvre. The introduction of rifled QF guns enabled the Royal Artillery to adopt a similar approach to the infantry, smothering the enemy with rapid-fire shrapnel bullets from exposed positions close to the front, providing what the training manual described as 'intimate support to the infantry'. Innovations such as aerial reconnaissance and wireless communication were still to be fully exploited, but their potential had come under scrutiny. Many of the Army's practices and tactics would prove inappropriate to the battlefields of France and Flanders, but at the very least, the Army had begun to acknowledge that thought, reflection, and professional debate were acceptable behaviours for its officers.

The Military on the Eve of War: Expectations, Preparations and Roles

From 1906, secret, but deniable talks between British and French general staff officers were sanctioned by Sir Edward Grey. These talks were soon extended to include the Belgians, and close contact between British and French staff colleges was established. All this behind-the-scenes co-operation led to more formal joint meetings between French and British general staffs regarding contingency plans for the defence of Belgian neutrality and the possible deployment of a BEF. In order to facilitate forward planning and preparedness in the event of war, the CID compiled a war book of plans and updates, to which departments might refer. However, the CID never resolved the fundamental questions regarding the relative responsibilities of the Army or the Navy in waging a war against, most probably, Germany or in protecting the homeland. *Pro forma* orders were prepared for instant issue on the outbreak of war, enabling swift mobilisation, despatch of the BEF to France, and deployment of TF divisions to home defence war stations, although it was expected that the TF divisions would require six months' training before they were fit even for home defence. The war book had been recently revised in 1914, but procedures were still unclear to some ministers. Lloyd George later admitted that for the eight years prior to the outbreak of war, little time had ever been devoted by the government to questions of foreign policy let alone strategy.

Mobilisation and the Outbreak of War

In July 1914, over 150 of the Royal Navy's vessels, including fifty-two battleships, were assembled at Spithead for George V's inspection and royal review. As the war clouds gathered, Churchill as First Lord of the Admiralty ordered a test mobilisation on 27 July, following the latest procedures laid down in orders of 1912. Having held elements of the Home Fleet at Portland for a week, the Admiralty ordered the capital ships to the fleet anchorage at Scapa Flow once war had been declared. A degree of confusion attended the mobilisation as ships involved in the annual manoeuvres were manned by crews, which contained men due to serve on other ships in wartime, and many reservists, who responded to the summons in far greater numbers than expected, were temporarily sent home. Contrary to the warnings of the Beresford set, there was an over-provision of men. Personnel of the RNR included coastguards, merchant seamen, and trawler men, the RNR Trawler section having been formed in 1910, all reporting to their home ports. The RNVR had been formed in 1903 with bases on the Thames, the Clyde, the

Tyne, in Bristol, Edinburgh, and Hove, and most duly arrived to sign on. The Thames Division's drill hall in a converted warehouse in Commercial Road, Lambeth, served as a naval recruiting office. An embarrassment of sailors was partly the result of converting ships from coal to oil, thereby making many stokers effectively redundant. One solution was the formation, from these surplus personnel, of the Royal Naval Division. A depot was established at the Crystal Palace in south London from which men were despatched to tented camps at Walmer and Betteshanger in Kent. After a mere six weeks' training, the division was deployed to defend Antwerp. On their return, the depot was moved to Blandford in Dorset, and Crystal Palace became the reception centre for the RNVR and the RNAS.

While the big ships sailed north, the Admiralty implemented the procedures it had prepared and rehearsed. The Port Defence Flotillas, comprising old destroyers and torpedo boats and now renamed Patrol Flotillas, redeployed from their south coast bases to their east coast war stations: the 6th Flotilla from Portsmouth to Dover; the 7th from Devonport to Immingham; and the 8th and 9th from the Nore to the Tyne and the Forth respectively. The other key element of Fisher's policy was the deployment of submarine flotillas to the east coast ports. Depot ships ranged from the battleship *Bonaventure* in the Tyne to the purpose-built *Alecto* at Great Yarmouth, as the submarines moved into their new home ports from Scapa to Harwich. Enemy submarine cables were dredged up and cut by the GPO's cable ship *Alert* off Dover, and cables to neutral countries were patched into the British network. Enemy merchant ships were seized and neutrals informed of the blockade of enemy ports. Most importantly for the safeguarding of the BEF's shipment across the Channel to France, the Straits of Dover were sealed by the Navy, but there was no guarantee of protection for shipping crossing the North Sea to Antwerp. It may have been a product of the general expectation that it would be a short war that caused the Navy to shut down its training facilities and to deploy the instructional staff to sea duty, but it quickly became apparent that training would form a large part of future naval activity. Shore establishments would soak up large numbers of personnel, and this prompted the formation of the WRNS. It was also soon regretted that so many trained sailors had been reassigned as infantry in the RN Division, which the Army declined to relinquish.

Urgency also attended the Army's mobilisation. On 27 July, Reserve officers with roles in the BEF were recalled to their units and guards were placed on VPs. On 29 July, the 4th Battalion, Royal Fusiliers, returning from machine-gun firing practice on the ranges in Dorset to their barracks at Parkhurst on the Isle of Wight, were ordered to place sentries in the Palmerston forts as an anti-invasion precaution. On 30 July, the 4th (Reserve) Battalion, Warwickshire Regiment, arrived to relieve them as the Fusiliers, part of the

9th Infantry Brigade in the 3rd Division of the BEF, would be embarking for France immediately upon the declaration of war. Inhabitants of the island felt particularly vulnerable and imminently expected an invasion in Sandown Bay. Though the Cowes Regatta had been abandoned and yachts were banned from the Solent, several having to be reminded with warning shots from patrol boats, some islanders ensured that their boats remained available for a precipitate evacuation to the Beaulieu River.

On the outbreak of war, haphazard measures were taken to defend the coast. For example, the 7th (Reserve) Battalion, Royal Fusiliers, was at a Felixstowe training camp, on outpost duty on the seashore, guarding 200 yards of esplanade with no troops on either side, preparing to repel an invasion. They soon received a recall to London to guard VPs. The reserve battalions of line regiments were sent to their war stations as garrison battalions in the defended ports, with base parties manning the regimental depots. Many TF units were on their annual camps, so they were sent home with orders to report to their local drill halls. They were then deployed to their war stations, many of them on the east coast. Police were instructed to pay special attention to foreigners and to watch out for suspicious movements. In the first month of the war, Parliament had passed the Aliens Registration and the Defence of the Realm (DORA) Acts. The War Office commissioned the ordnance survey to produce a set of maps at 2.5 inches to 1 mile (1:25,344) for home defence purposes, probably based on maps produced in around 1911 for the annual manoeuvres. That for East Anglia was extended south of the Thames and retitled *Map of the Eastern Counties*. One sheet, for example, covers Suffolk and northern Kent. It was eventually extended to include the coast from Cromer to Dover, and inland as far as London, the expected invasion coast and the focus of any invader's ambitions.

3

Britain's Anti-Invasion Defences in the First World War

Despite the general antipathy to the principle of Coast Defence evinced by politicians and the military alike, and the consequent financial starvation of that sector, there had nevertheless long been strong pockets of fixed defences around Britain's coasts. The threat of invasion from Germany from the early 1900s then prompted a general reorientation, which shifted the focus to the east coast. War brought anxieties that an invasion or a raid in strength might threaten London, introducing a need for in-depth defences inland from the coast. This chapter will examine the nature of those various layers of defence.

The Coast Defences 1900–1914: Defended Ports and Fleet Anchorages

Successive inquiries from the 1860 Royal Commission onwards identified the major naval bases as the priority areas for receiving fixed defences. In 1905, the CID set up an inquiry under the chairmanship of Sir John Owen to investigate and report on the protection of home ports. The Committee approached the problem by consulting the Admiralty in order to estimate the amount of force an enemy might commit to an attack on a specific port, and then to decide the level of armament that might suffice as a deterrent. Class 'A' ports, such as Portsmouth, Plymouth, Pembroke Dock, or Chatham, might be expected to attract the attentions of enemy battleships, and so would be provided with sufficiently heavy armament to deter such force. Ports in Class 'B', liable to attack by armoured cruisers, would receive less protection, and Class 'C', described as commercial ports and deemed to be potential targets for only lightly armoured cruisers, would receive least of all. In 1905, the responsibility for the maintenance and operation of the submarine minefields hitherto maintained by the RE miners of the militia or the volunteers, had been handed over to the Admiralty. The majority were then scrapped, along with the wire-guided Brennan torpedoes that had been installed in eight sites in Britain, Malta, and Hong Kong. Not only was bombardment from heavy guns offshore a real threat, but also assault by small, fast torpedo-boats that might rush the harbour entrance and cause havoc among ships in an anchorage. Although the Admiralty had discouraged the use of booms and anti-torpedo netting, unilateral decisions to disregard this policy were made and their use subsequently became universal. There remained, however, a vital need for light quick-firing (QF) guns to engage raiders and destroy them before they might penetrate an inner harbour. After the Japanese success against the Russians at Port Arthur, the practice of sinking block ships in a harbour entrance to bottle up an enemy fleet, thereby rendering it more vulnerable to bombardment, also merited attention. The Owen Committee assessed the perceived vulnerability to attack, the weapons available to the defence, and those likely to be used by an attacking force, to produce an optimal level of armament for each defended port in each of the three classes. Recognising that new weapons demonstrated far better performance in terms of range, accuracy, and both weight and speed of fire, the old RBL and RML guns were mainly scrapped, effectively reducing the defences of many ports. Although the Owen Committee employed the familiar 'leaner but fitter' justification for the cuts, many felt that the nation's shores were no more secure as a result of the exercise. Owen's reduction of the number of batteries by a third, and the guns mounted by just under a half, may not have been welcomed by all, but his scrapping of three-quarters of the types of guns then in use was generally seen as beneficial, rationalising training and both the supply and the production of ammunition. New weaponry made it possible for coast batteries to cover much wider expanses of sea with fewer, more effective guns, so it was quite sensible to scrap the old Victorian muzzle loaders even if, as Peter Kent has suggested, they could have been devastating at close range as gigantic blunderbusses.

After Owen's reorganisation, just four types of gun remained in use generally: the 9.2-inch, the 6-inch, the 4.7-inch QF, and the 12-pounder QF. The 9.2-inch Mark X BL guns were usually emplaced in pairs, in open concrete emplacements served by underground crew shelters, and magazines with separate compartments for shells, cartridges, and fuses, stocked by shell hoists. Shells were raised up to the guns from the magazines by band or ladder lifts. Close by were the Battery Observation Post (BOP), with its depression range-finding (DRF) instruments, and the position-finding (PF) cells, which fed information to the guns' controllers. Flanking the emplacements were the searchlights, known as Defence Electric Lights (DEL), with their engine-rooms housing generators. These heavy guns had a range of about 29,200 yards or 16 miles (26 km) and fired a shell weighing 380 lb (172 kg). Their primary purpose in defence of a port was fending off enemy capital ships in the counter-bombardment role. Given that the likelihood of being hit by incoming fire from unstable platforms out at sea was low, then open barbette positions were quite acceptable, especially since, seldom having a sight of their target, they could be located out of sight themselves. If a lucky shot were to come perilously close, it might well be deflected over the gun by the sloping concrete apron in front of the gun pit. The battery's offices, workshops, living accommodation, and messes were grouped a short distance away.

The 6-inch Mk VII BL gun, on the other hand, was a weapon of interdiction, whose primary task was to engage attacking warships or troop transports. It was emplaced in a very similar manner to its heavier cousin, sharing most of the same features but on a smaller scale. It fired a projectile weighing 102 lb (46 kg) to a maximum range of 12,000 yards or 7 miles (11 km). Clever siting could ensure that targets much closer inshore might be engaged as well. The QF guns were intended to prevent enemy torpedo-boats entering an anchorage so were sited to cover entrances. An ideal place for them (the smaller 12-pounder guns especially) was on the end of a mole or breakwater where there was good, all-round visibility and unobstructed fields of fire. It was vital that there should be illumination of those areas covered by the QF guns, either by free-roving searchlights or those in emplacements with slits in their forward walls concentrating their beams onto fixed areas of water. With the guns pre-ranged, the target could be engaged instantaneously on entering the fixed, or 'sentry', beam. The majority of the new batteries constructed between 1905 and 1914 were equipped with either 9.2-inch or 6-inch guns, but there were plenty of QF guns and some of the older 6-pounder QF guns remained in service. A memorandum issued by the CID in 1911 noted the general need to defend coast artillery batteries against attack from the land, either by raiding parties landed to silence the battery or by larger forces carrying out a general assault on the port. Also reiterated in the same document was the specific danger posed by an invasion force coming across the North Sea from Germany, with the coast between the Humber and the Thames as the likely target, but also the possibility of an attack on Kent or Sussex or both. The size of such a force was set at the magic figure of 70,000 men, now, apparently, the accepted upper limit.

The Owen Committee, reporting at the end of 1905, was understandably oblivious to the slowly emerging threat from Germany. On the east coast, the port of Harwich had its defences downgraded to Class 'C' to reflect its low military importance, and the Humber, also Class 'C', lost most of its guns. In the north-east, Tynemouth retained its 6-inch guns and Sunderland was equipped with new ones. The Hartlepool batteries were rearmed, but Tees-mouth had to settle for an existing 4.7-inch battery. Elsewhere, around the coast, improvements were patchy: at Crosby (Mersey) and Barrow-in-Furness,

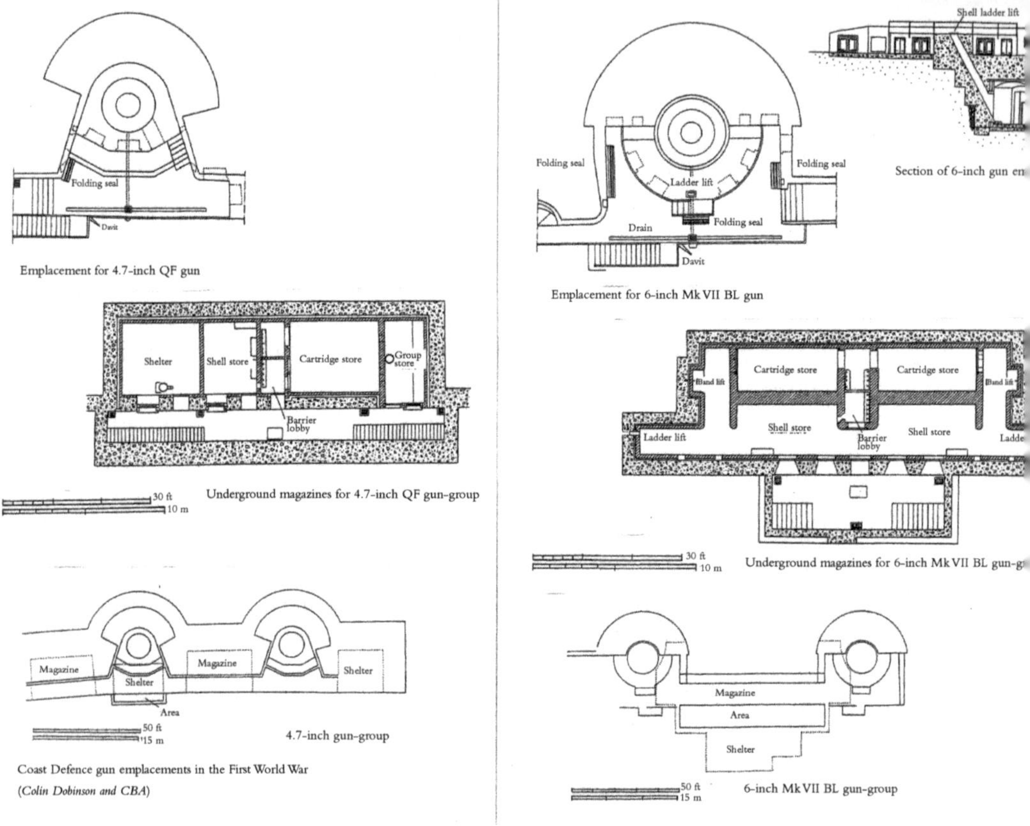

Plans of 6-inch and 4.7-inch battery layouts. (*Colin Dobinson and the CBA*)

the go-ahead to complete planned 6-inch batteries was given; Dover and Portland were both permitted to improve their anti-block-ship defences and to reorganise the guns in their various batteries; but the defences of the Bristol Channel were scrapped entirely, when Steep Holm, Flat Holm, and Brean Down were all disarmed. The guns from St Mary's in the Scilly Isles were redeployed to Plymouth. In Scotland, as Gordon Barclay records, there were defences in place prior to 1914, in the Clyde and the Forth, at Cromarty Firth, Dundee, and Aberdeen, but, while the Royal Navy had settled on Scapa Flow as the main anchorage for its Grand Fleet and the preliminary planning had commenced in 1912, there were still no coast defence batteries in place there on the outbreak of war. The defences of Welsh ports were confined to Milford Haven, Cardiff, Barry, and Swansea. Lough Swilly, Lough Foyle, and Belfast Lough in the north of Ireland were defended, as were Queenstown and Berehaven in the south.

The coast defence guns and searchlights were generally manned by regular gunners of the RGA, whose companies were scattered around the coast of the British Isles and based on Defended Ports. Some ports had RGA units of the TF, descendants of the old volunteer artillery batteries. The regular Fortress

Engineer units of the REs were similarly aided by RE (Defended Ports) units of the TF. As there were insufficient regular RE units to man every defended port, a wider coverage was achieved by combining detachments from five regular Fortress Companies into the Coast Battalion based in six different ports.

Class 'A' Defended Ports in England

Portsmouth, as spiritual home of the Royal Navy, was the most heavily defended port on the eve of war, and it is evident that, despite Owen's reductions, its armament was still impressive. Although all the old RMLs at Hurst Castle and on the sea forts had been removed by summer 1914, there remained thirteen 9.2-inch, two dozen 6-inch, nine 4.7-inch, and seventeen 12-pounder guns. These were scattered in eight batteries covering the Needles Passage and Sandown Bay; two batteries and three of the four sea-forts guarding Spithead; and five batteries closer in. Three of the 9.2-inch batteries had only opened between 1901 and 1906, but around a dozen 12-pounders had been redistributed, mainly in the inner defences, by 1916. The most notable additions during the war were the two batteries, each with two 12-pounders at Stone Point on the mainland, and at Egypt Point on the Island, covering the new anti-submarine net that sealed the westerly passage into Southampton Water. The Calshot defences were disarmed in 1914, but the boom itself, opposite the castle, continued to operate, although the guns had been removed from the dolphins. Fort Cumberland acquired one of the new 15-inch (380-mm) howitzers, commissioned by the Admiralty from Coventry Ordnance Works in 1915, to train RMA gunners. Also manned by Royal Marines were two 6-inch howitzers, mounted in Lumps Fort and capable of pouring showers of deadly shrapnel onto the adjacent beaches. Southsea Castle, Forts Cumberland, and Blockhouse, along with all the later forts and batteries, were integrated into a defended perimeter that took in the naval dockyard, the several barracks, the harbour, and the various training and supply depots. The old Royal Commission-era land forts had long been disarmed but continued in use as barracks, depots, and training facilities. The garrison, seldom less than 25,000-strong and often up to twice that strength, included the Hampshire Regiment's depot staff and recruits at St George's Barracks, Gosport; the permanent staff of No. 3 RA Depot in Hilsea; at least five battalions of reserve or home service troops on permanent garrison duty; the Royal Marines at Eastney; sailors awaiting postings in HMS *Victory*, the naval barracks; companies of regular Fortress Engineers at Gosport, as well as TF engineer units; the regular RGA gunners; and the eight companies of the Hampshire RGA (TF). HMS *Hermione*, a twenty-year-old cruiser, served as guard ship at Yarmouth, Cowes, and Southampton Water at different times.

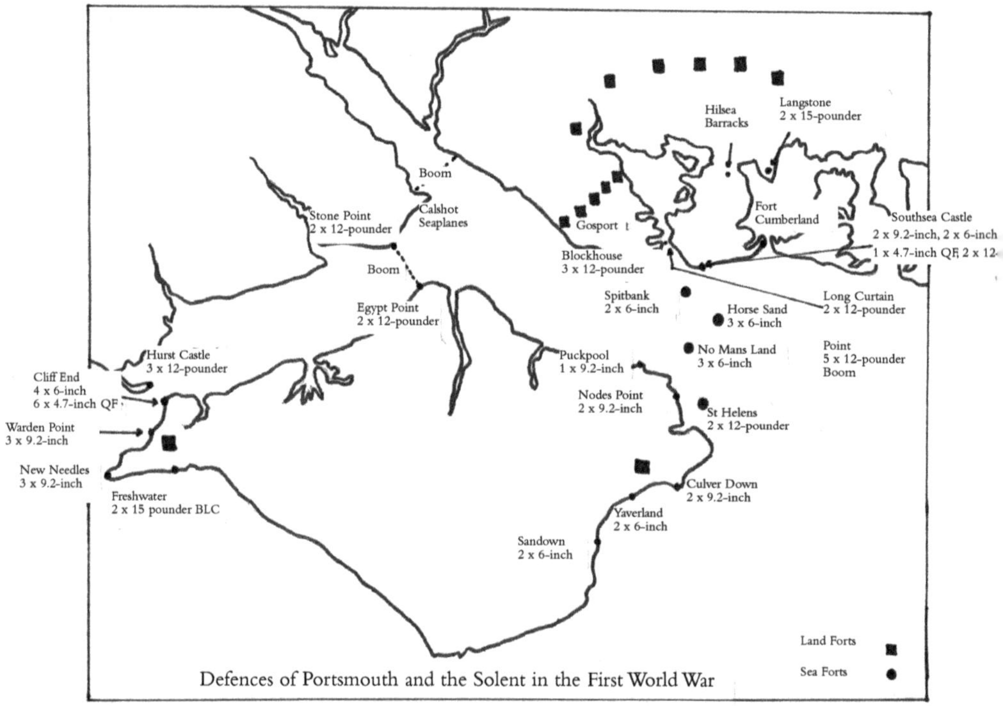

Sketch-map of Portsmouth's defences in the First World War.

The Royal Commission had combined the Thames and Medway defences into one integrated system that comprised the riverside defences of the Thames with one fort, Coalhouse, on the left (Essex) bank, and three on the right (Kent) bank; the sea defences of the Medway at Sheerness and Grain; and Okeham Ness, where forts on the islands of Hoo and Darnet, a little way downstream from the Tudor Upnor Castle, would bar the approaches to Chatham Dockyard. The report included details of the discussion of the landward defences of both Sheerness and Chatham, as well as those of London that never got off the ground. Owen, however, chose to separate the two elements. Chatham remained a strongly fortified Class 'A' dockyard and naval base, while London was assessed as a Class 'C' commercial port, theoretically no more vulnerable to enemy attack than Newhaven or Sunderland. By 1914, the Thames defences consisted of four 6-inch guns at Coalhouse Fort and four 12-pounder QF guns at the School of Coast Artillery at Shoeburyness, diagonally opposite which was Slough Fort with two 9.2-inch guns. During the course of the war, Shoeburyness and Cliffe Fort each gained a pair of 6-inch guns, with two 12-pounders going to Thames Haven, but the armament of Coalhouse Fort was halved, and Cliffe's 6-inch guns were later exchanged for a pair of 4-inch QF. The Medway approaches to Chatham remained heavily fortified with large numbers of guns, including four 9.2-inch and six 6-inch in eight discrete batteries, mainly clustered at the river-mouth at Grain and Sheerness, where pairs of QF guns covered the ends of the boom that, from 1915, stretched from Grain Tower to Sheerness. Just as the war was drawing to a close, two more batteries were added, one of two further 9.2-inch guns at Fletcher Battery on Sheppey and a pair of 6-inch guns at Whitehall Farm on Grain. The majority of these guns were emplaced in the standard open gun pits with underground shelters and magazines, but adjacent to Garrison Point Fort at Sheerness, Centre or Martello Battery consists of two circular concrete towers each mounting a 4.7-inch QF gun, with the BOP in the third, square tower behind. Grain Tower, one of several Martello Towers built around 1855, had always mounted cannon, but was remodelled in 1912 to carry two 4.7-inch QF guns, taken from the adjacent Wing Battery. Thames and Medway Garrison included ten reserve battalions dispersed to Tilbury, Gravesend, and the Isle of Grain; between Sittingbourne and Maidstone; at Chatham and Gillingham; at Queenborough and Sheerness; and at Leysdown, Minster, and Eastchurch on the Isle of Sheppey. At Sheerness, there was a RE Fortress Company and four RGA companies, with a fifth at Shoeburyness.

England's third Class 'A' port was Plymouth/Devonport, with a major naval base and dockyard. Plymouth Sound had been provided with a wide range of fortifications over eight centuries and was one of the Royal Commission's primary areas of focus as the harbour, fleet anchorage, naval dockyard, victualling yard, and arsenal all contributed to its importance. The Royal Commission built a great ring of eighteen land forts as well as updating the coast defences, stretching from Whitsand Bay, across the Rame Peninsular, across the Sound, to Staddon Heights and constantly improved into the twentieth century. By the time of the Owen Committee's appraisal, there were twenty-six coast defence batteries mounting ninety-three different guns of nine different types—ranging from the 12-pounder QF to a 13.5-inch BL, the only one ever emplaced on Britain's coast. Plymouth was probably the place that benefited most from Owen, in that new developments and improvements already underway were allowed to continue, while obsolete weapons were discarded. Only at Whitsand Bay, on the western side of the Rame Peninsular and the sole battery commanding the south-western approaches, were three 12.5-inch RMLs allowed to remain, but only on the understanding that they would be replaced by 9.2-inch guns. They never were, but elsewhere, some four dozen other RMLs were summarily scrapped. Rationalisation left the entrance to the Sound commanded by the six 9.2-inch Mk X BL guns of Penlee Point and Renney Batteries with two more at Rame Church Battery. Level with the breakwater, a defence line clustered two 6-inch Mk VII BL and a pair of 4-inch QF guns at Fort Picklecombe with two more 6-inch guns at Watch House Battery above

Fort Bovisand with its four 12-pounder QF guns. Also on the eastern heights, between Bovisand and Renney, Lentney Battery would come on stream with a further pair of 6-inch guns in 1916. Just to make absolutely certain that no boom-buster might get through into the inner harbour, Drake's Island had three more 6-inch guns along with six 12-pounders, while the final narrow channel into the Dockyard area—between Garden and Devil's Point Batteries—was sealed by four batteries mounting no fewer than fifteen 12-pounders. Beyond a few minor adjustments to armaments during the course of the war, the only significant change was the reinstatement of Grenville and Hawkins Batteries on the eastern side of the Rame. Grenville was re-equipped with three more modern 4.7-inch guns, while Hawkins received a pair of 9.2-inch High Angle guns. These performed the same function as had its old RMLs, but now more effectively, reflecting the improved state of all Plymouth's defences. Plymouth Garrison consisted of seven reserve battalions, and four companies of the RGA with their depot in the Citadel. Based in Devonport was the RGA (TF) along with a RE Fortress Company, and the Mutley militia barracks housed the Devonshire Fortress Engineers (TF).

Defences of Plymouth and Devonport in the First World War

Sketch-map of Plymouth's defences in the First World War.

Class 'B' Defended Ports in England

From mediaeval times, Dover was regarded as the gateway to England—a status underlined by Roman and Saxon forts, Norman castles, Tudor blockhouses, and extensive Napoleonic-era fortifications. The Royal Commission improved on the strength of existing works and added new ones on the Western Heights and behind the castle. By the early twentieth century, Dover's importance lay in its naval use as a base from which to secure the Straits, the entrance to the English Channel from the North Sea, and to monitor the movement of shipping through to the Atlantic. To protect the anchorage from enemy bombardment, there were, from 1900, two batteries armed with 9.2-inch Mk X BL guns. Citadel Battery on the Western Heights mounted three, subsequently reduced by 1914 to two, and Langdon Battery, above the White Cliffs, retained three 9.2-inch guns, along with two 6-inch Mk VII BL. The Owen Committee strongly recommended the installation of QF guns, both to defend against fast torpedo-boats, and to prevent the insertion of block-ships into the harbour entrances. Three new batteries were proposed to hold seven 12-pounder QF guns. Two were located, one each side of the South Breakwater-Pier Extension entry point, and a third was placed on the Eastern Arm. By the end of the war, Knuckle Battery, on the top end of the South Breakwater, had been armed with two 4-inch QF guns. Both entrances to the harbour were obstructed by booms and block ships, but there still remained a concern that the heavy guns needed to stop a large vessel smashing through; however, the booms were not in the appropriate place to achieve this. In the early 1880s, the Admiralty Turret had been built on the Admiralty Pier. Constructed of masonry, iron, and concrete, it contained two monster 80-ton 16-inch RML guns, the biggest ever mounted for coast defence. By 1902, however, they had been declared redundant, but were too big to remove; they remain, to this day, sealed within their turret. This nevertheless remained the optimal place for a pair of 6-inch guns, so Pier Turret Battery was constructed on and around the old turret. As well as the guns in these fixed defences, the port was protected by those of the light cruiser *Attentive*, base ship for the Dover Patrol; of *Surprise*, a steam yacht hired for the duration of the war; and of *Surf*, depot ship for the Rear Admiral (Controlled Minefields). The gunnery trials gunboat *Drudge*, with a single 9.2-inch gun, was also around into 1915, when the gun was removed and poor *Drudge* was sold.

A number of specialist regular and TF units manned the guns and searchlights. The Fortress REs and the Cinque Ports REs (TF) at their Bench Street drill hall saw to the DELs. The guns were manned by two RGA companies, who were joined by the Kent RGA (TF) having transferred their HQ from Sheerness to Dover in 1914, and the garrison consisted of six reserve battalions. Both the castle and the Citadel on the Western Heights contained barracks for the garrison, and there was an Admiralty lookout post on the edge of the cliff inside the castle. Tunnels in the cliffs served as offices and stores.

The defences of Portland and Weymouth were updated by the Royal Commission and consisted of casemated works at the Nothe Fort in Weymouth and the Verne Citadel on the Isle of Portland. The approaches were still dominated by two sixteenth-century Henrician forts, as well as the East Weare batteries on the Isle. The anchorage was protected by breakwaters on which had been constructed five batteries, four mounting anti-torpedo-boat 12-pounders, while the Breakwater Fort mounted heavy RMLs as well as two 12-pounders. The Owen Committee, recognising the importance of the naval base, recommended measures against block ships and a rearrangement of the heavy guns. In fact, the distribution of the basic counter-bombardment weapons hardly changed with six 9.2-inch guns in three batteries, two crossing their fire over Weymouth Bay, and the third covering the western approach up the Channel. The biggest increase came in the weight of fire available to defend the entrances to the inner harbour. The Nothe Fort mounted three 6-inch Mk VII BL guns with three more in one of the East Weare batteries, singles on Breakwaters 'B' and 'C', and two more in the Breakwater Fort (ten in all), and ten 12-pounders on the breakwaters. Apart from the disarmament of the Nothe in 1916, this layout remained more or less intact for the duration. The guns were manned by three regular RGA companies and the Dorsetshire RGA (TF), with a RE Fortress Company to run the searchlights aided by a detachment of the Wiltshire Fortress Engineers (TF), based in Swindon, but designated as coast defence troops. The garrison included two reserve battalions at Wyke Regis and a third in Weymouth until 1917.

Class 'C' Defended Ports in England

Barrow-in-Furness had become a military target when the Vickers Maxim Company took over the shipbuilding yard in 1897, building four of the *Dreadnought*-class battleships. A battery was proposed for the northern end of Walney Island, mounting a single 9.2-inch and two 6-inch guns. However, the 9.2-inch gun was deleted by the Owen Committee, substituting a third 6-inch gun that never materialised. Early in 1915, one of the few new batteries to be built during the war was opened at the southern end of Walney Island. This was the Hilpsford Battery of two 4.7-inch QF guns. The garrison comprised two companies of RGA (TF) and a reserve battalion of infantry.

Although the defences of the Bristol Channel had been abandoned by the Army in 1901, the war brought a realisation that shipping was vulnerable to attack unless afforded some protection by coast artillery. Portishead Battery, below Bristol, mounted two 6-inch BL guns in 1903, but had been closed by Owen. It was rebuilt and, along with Hayle Battery (built on the north Cornish coast to defend the explosives factory), opened around 1915—each of them armed with two 12-pounder QF guns.

Despite the historical importance of Carrick Roads as one of the most extensive deep-water anchorages in Britain, Owen classed Falmouth as a merely commercial port. Pendennis Castle was an important establishment for the RGA, with a new barracks opening in 1902; this was occupied until 1911 by the 105th Company, RGA. The Castle also contained—tacked onto the Henrician keep—the HQ of the Devon and Cornwall Miners Militia. The RE successor unit to the submarine miners had their depot in Bar Road, down by the harbour. The Roads were defended by batteries of heavy guns in the Castle and at St Anthony's Head, while lighter QF guns were mounted at Crab Quay, site of a much earlier battery below Pendennis, and also above St Mawes Castle on the opposite side of the water. Owen discarded the 12-pounder batteries and upgraded the others to a pair of 6-inch Mk VII BL guns at Pendennis, and a second pair at St Anthony's Head, which remained operational only for the first few years of the war. However, Falmouth's status as a defended port manifest in its interservice operations, suggesting some protection against raids was merited. Two 4.7-inch guns were lodged in the castle in 1907 for tactical deployment in the heavier guns' blind spots. All the guns were manned by the Cornwall RGA (TF), and No. 18 Company, RE Fortress Engineers, operated the lights. The infantry garrison was supplied by a reserve battalion of the Rifle Brigade.

In common with many other east coast ports, Great Yarmouth and Gorleston, while selected by Admiral Fisher's planners as a flotilla base, had never been properly fortified and were completely absent from Owen's deliberations. As a response to the German bombardment of Great Yarmouth and Lowestoft in November 1914, just one 4.7-inch gun was emplaced on Gorleston Cliffs on an open platform with a magazine linked to two subsurface crew shelters.

Harwich had also been ignored by the Royal Commission, but Landguard Fort, on the Felixstowe side, had subsequently been given a bombproof caponier and granite casemates in the 1870s. Twenty years later, heavy guns were mounted to command the entrance to the Haven both flanking the fort and on the opposite side at Beacon Hill. These were supplemented by a pair of 4.7-inch QF guns at Darrells Battery, but the defences were downgraded by Owen to reflect what the Committee perceived as its diminished role. By 1914, there were only a pair of 6-inch Mk VII BL guns in Beacon Hill Fort and another pair in Landguard's right battery. The reorientation exercise precipitated by fears of Germany's expansionist ambitions caused a rethink as Harwich regained its status as an important naval base. Beacon Hill's two 4.7-

inch Mk IV QF guns, an unauthorised installation of 1911, were legitimised, with a further brace being restored to an improved Darrell's Battery. In 1915, a completely new counter-bombardment battery was built north of Felixstowe, opening as Brackenbury Battery, with two 9.2-inch Mk X BL guns and their accompanying DELs. The floating HQ of the Senior Naval Officer, HMS *Hercules*, a *Dreadnought*-class battleship, provided extra firepower for a while. The batteries were manned by a Regular Army RGA company and they were supported by the Essex and Suffolk RGA (TF), with their HQ in Dovercourt, and a detachment in the Felixstowe drill hall. Lights were operated by a company of RE Fortress Engineers. The garrison included four reserve battalions, with a Garrison Battalion of the Suffolk Regiment raised in 1916 specifically for duty in Harwich.

The Humber Estuary provides a classic illustration of how improvements in both weapons and gunnery enabled defences to be pushed further and further away from what was being protected—in this case, Hull Docks. The Henrician blockhouses (close to the medieval centre) were supplanted by Paull Fort, which, in turn, was replaced by batteries further downstream,

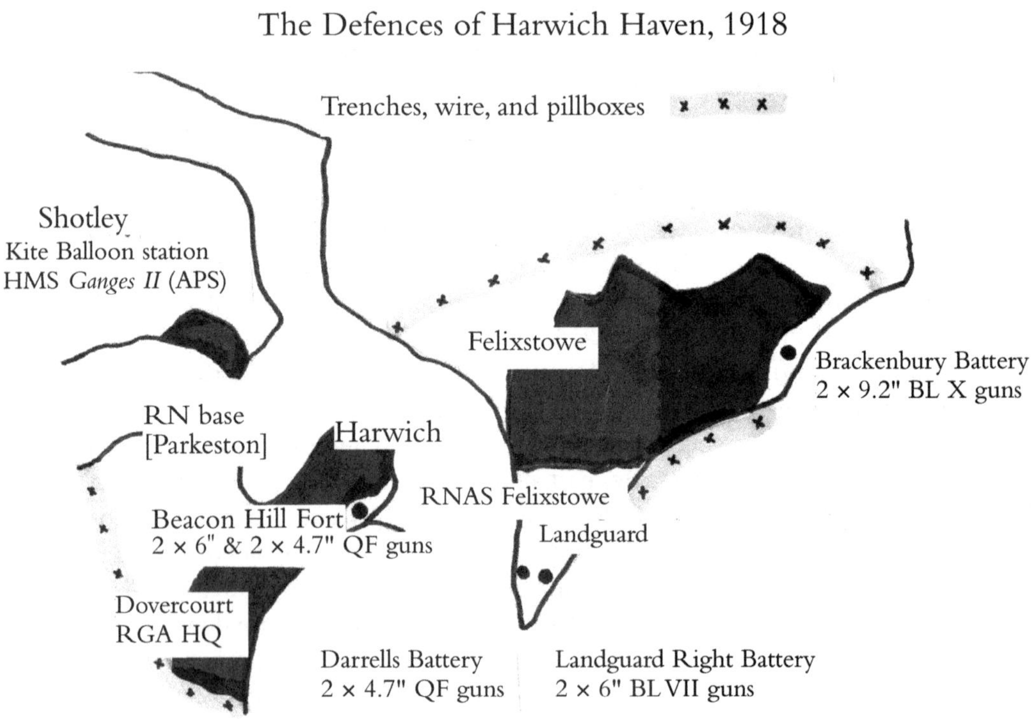

Defences of Harwich Haven in 1918.

until the defences were finally placed on the coast—some 20 miles (32 km) away. It was these Humber defences that would change most dramatically both immediately prior to and during the war. Owen had suggested that the existing battery at Paull Point, with its submarine-mining depot and pier beside it, was adequate to defend the port. Paull Fort, a Victorian work, had been rearmed in 1904 with three 6-inch Mk VII BL guns, along with three DELs joining a pair of older established 4.7-inch QF guns—but Owen had these QF guns removed.

The emerging threat from Germany, however, soon prompted the Admiralty to earmark the Humber as a conveniently placed naval base and—especially after an exercise in 1911 revealed how ineffectual the examination service was—showed concern for the paucity of defences. A building programme was quickly put in place, with a start being made on a pair of 6-inch batteries downstream from Paull at Sunk Island on the left bank and Stallingborough on the right. Both these new batteries were enclosed within banks and moats defended by blockhouses and unclimbable fences. To gain as much dominance over the river as possible, the guns were mounted on 40-foot-high (12-metre-high) concrete towers with flared tops forming platforms for the guns and their expense magazines. While these batteries were being built, old pre-dreadnought *Majestic*-class battleships were stationed in the Humber as floating batteries. HMS *Albion*, for instance, was moored above Killingholme for a time. A combined PWSS and fire-control post was built behind Sunk Island Battery. Once both these batteries were considered ready for action in May 1915, the three 6-inch guns from Paull Fort were redeployed to Inchkeith Island in the Forth, and a battery for two 12-pounder QF guns, on 26-foot-high (8-metre-high) towers, was built at Killingholme, midway between Paull and Stallingborough. The next project was the fortification of Spurn Head, with two 9.2-inch Mk X BL guns and six 4.7-inch QF up and running in 1916. Next came Fort Godwin at Kilnsea with two more 9.2-inch guns, but the construction of Green Battery on Spurn Point brought a rearrangement. Spurn Point Battery was split between one battery, with two 4.7-inch guns and another with two 4-inch guns, while the two 9.2-inch guns went into the adjacent Green Battery. The final development in the Humber defences was completed too late for service in that particular war. The two sea forts of Bull Sand nearer to the Yorkshire bank and Haile Sand on the Lincolnshire side were designed to carry, respectively, four 6-inch Mk VII BL guns and two 4-inch QF guns, all with accompanying searchlights. Bull Sand with its four storeys was larger than Haile Sand's three. The guns were mounted on the upper decks, with searchlights in sponsons attached to the forts' sides. The Spurn Head batteries were contained within a perimeter wall, with blockhouses accessed by a light railway. Permanent barracks were built, but proved inadequate for the garrison, many of whom lived in temporary huts. The guns were manned by the East Riding RGA (TF) and the lights by the local RE Fortress Engineers (TF), with their HQ in Hull. Part of the company of Fortress REs was based at Paull Fort. The Humber Garrison was probably the one that covered the largest area, extending from Hornsea and Withernsea (where two reserve battalions were based) over the water to another in Grimsby. Cleethorpes, Humberstone Fitties, and Riby held two reserve battalions of the Manchester Regiment, processing recruits, while the 2/1st Northern Cyclist Battalion patrolled the area around Skegness and, later, Burton Constable. Four reserve battalions were stationed in Hull and Grimsby and four 15-pounder field guns were assigned to mobile forces in the garrison. HMS *Victorious*, a pre-*Dreadnought* battleship, was serving as guard ship and HQ of the Senior Naval Officer in 1914. Immingham naval base's anti-submarine defences were tended by HMS *Wallington*, a boom defence vessel launched in 1907, later renamed HMS *Sheraton*.

As England's second port, the Mersey was regarded as particularly important by Owen, but, still, only low-level protection was recommended. The argument was because of the geography: enemy vessels would be forced to sail in line ahead, thereby making themselves vulnerable to the fire of QF guns, apparently obviating the need to mount heavier ordnance. Fort Perch Rock exchanged its three 6-inch hydro-pneumatic guns for three new Mk VII BL guns; the new Crosby Battery, opened in 1907, was given three more. Seaforth Battery was re-equipped with a pair of 4.7-inch QF guns, while Liscard Battery was shut down and its old RML guns scrapped. The Mersey garrison comprised reserve battalions at Birkenhead, Great Crosby, Hightown, and Litherland. Two Electric Lights companies of the Lancashire Fortress Engineers (TF), from the Tramway Road drill hall in Aigburth, manned the searchlights, and gunners of six companies of the RGA (TF), from Low Hill and Seacombe, manned the guns.

By 1870, Newhaven Fort had been modernised outside the remit of the Royal Commission, receiving new armament, mainly RMLs and some mortars; however, by 1902, these were obsolete and had been replaced by two 6-inch Mk VII BL guns, a pair of 12-pounder QF guns, and four Maxim guns for close defence. The Owen Committee saw the QF guns as unnecessary, but recommended that the rest should stay. Although the fort had served as a RGA Depot, there was no resident regular company, so the guns were manned by the Sussex RGA (TF), based in Brighton and Lewes, who replaced the depot staff in 1914. Two 90-cm (35.4-inch) searchlights were operated by a small detachment of the RE Electrical Engineers (TF) from their Westminster base, working continuous six-hour shifts.

In 1913, nearly 50,000 troops were landed at Sunderland and Blyth in an exercise that vindicated those sceptical of the Blue Water School's claims. Even if capable of locating an invasion force, the Navy was nevertheless vulnerable

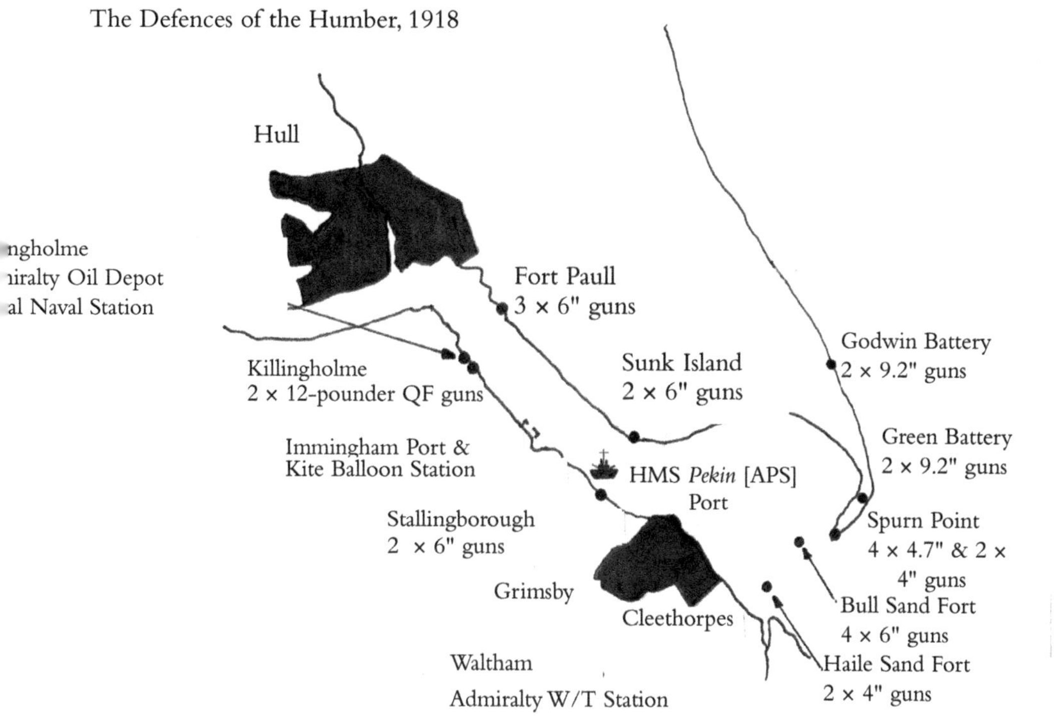

Above: Defences of the Humber Estuary in 1918.

Below: Humber Estuary: planned elevations of the two sea-forts that were not fully operational until some time after the end of the war. (*Jeff Dorman*)

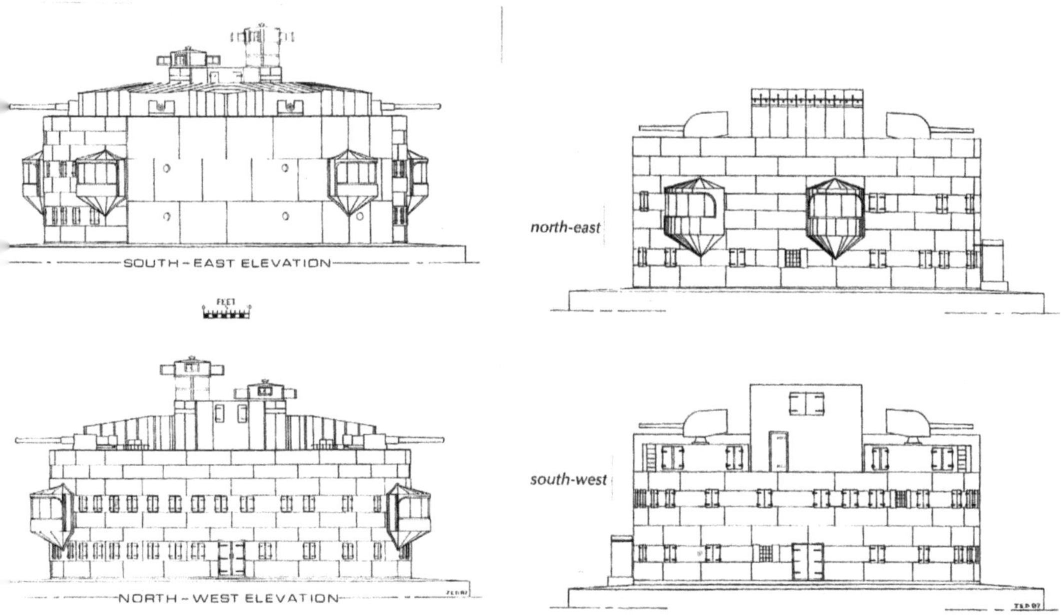

e Humber Estuary Sea-forts, 1918 (*Jeff Dorman*)
ll Sand Fort (left) and Haile Sand Fort (right)

to submarines and mines. Sunderland had been undefended until the Owen Committee recommended the construction of two 6-inch batteries. Nothing was done, though, until well into the war when Roker Battery on Abbs Point was built for two 4.7-inch QF guns. From 1916, there was a 9.2-inch rail gun on a siding in Blyth to defend the submarine base. This was replaced by a battery, known as Fort Coulson, mounting two 6-inch QF guns in the usual arrangement of open gun pits with underground magazine, defensible DELs, and a fire-control tower.

The mouth of the Tees, marked by the North and South Gare breakwaters, was defended by a battery on the South Gare, next to the submarine-mining station in its defended compound. In 1902, there were two 4.7-inch and a pair of 12-pounder QF guns—the latter removed after Owen's reassessment. There were more substantial defences at Hartlepool to the north; here, there were three 6-inch guns, one—a Mk VI BL in the Lighthouse Battery—upgraded by 1914 and two Mk VII BLs in the nearby Heugh Battery. After the German bombardment (see Chapter 7), a new battery was built on what is now Pilot Pier for a single 4.7-inch gun and two new counter-bombardment batteries were begun. Pasley Battery, at Coatham, and Palliser Battery, at Hart Warren, each mounted a single 9.2-inch Mk X BL gun, but neither was completed before the war's end.

Tyneside was home to shipyards that were vital to the war effort, so had long merited the protection of coast defence batteries. The port was the source of convoys of colliers supplying London and the south, which made it a tempting target for raiders. Therefore, it is somewhat surprising that the Owen Committee awarded it only the status of a commercial port. Successive inquiries throughout the last decades of the nineteenth century had recommended the installation of counter-bombardment guns at the mouth of the Tyne. However, only in 1905 had these finally come to fruition when Frenchman's Point Battery opened with one 9.2-inch Mk X BL and, joining the three already mounted in Tynemouth Castle and Spanish Battery, two 6-inch Mk VII BL guns. Owen, however, decided that the newly opened Frenchman's Point Battery was unnecessary and relegated it to a practice role. An extra 6-inch gun was added to Spanish Battery, but the QF guns at Clifford's Fort, the Castle, and Spanish Battery were all scrapped. Thus, in 1914, the Tyne was defended by only the two remaining 6-inch batteries.

In 1916, Frenchman's Point was reactivated and Tynemouth Castle gained its own 9.2-inch gun, but this was still considered inadequate. Early in the war, the *Majestic*-class battleship HMS *Jupiter* had served as guard ship in the Tyne, and she was succeeded by her sister-ship HMS *Illustrious*. The main armament of the *Majestics* consisted of two turrets each mounting a pair of 12-inch guns. Owing to modifications to the loading arrangements, the turrets on the *Illustrious* were circular. As these already old ships aged even more, some of their guns were donated to the new *Lord Clive*-class monitors, but those of the *Illustrious* were bound elsewhere. In 1917, work began to construct two new batteries: Roberts Battery at Hartley, to the north of the Tyne; and Kitchener Battery at Marsden, to the south. Massive excavations to a depth of 40 feet (12 metres) were needed to hold the reinforced concrete four-storey boxes on which would be mounted a gun turret, one at each site. With the turret set at ground level, but at a height above sea level of 116 feet (36 metres) at Hartley and 252 feet (77 metres) at Marsden, these Tyne Turrets (as they were known) were virtually invisible from the sea. Each battery had a nearby defensible compound containing fire-control and living quarters. The fire of the two batteries was co-ordinated from a six-storey tower behind Tynemouth's Grand Hotel, from whose rooftop control room both sites were visible. Given the sheer volume of material to be excavated and the complexity of the whole operation, the batteries were only completed in 1921. Each of the guns successfully fired twelve rounds in September 1921, to the alarm of neighbours over a wide area. Five years later, they were scrapped. The Tyne Garrison consisted of the reserve battalions of local regiments and extended from Blyth down to Sunderland on the coast, and inland to Morpeth. The Northern Cyclist Battalion and the 5th (Cyclist) Battalion of the East Riding Regiment provided some mobility, and four 15-pounder field guns were available for quick response to reports of a raid. Up to a further dozen, mainly third-line TF battalions were stationed in the area throughout the war.

The Channel Islands, Jersey, Guernsey, and Alderney, lying so close to the coast of Brittany, had been heavily fortified since medieval times. The Channel Islands militia consisted of three battalions of infantry on Jersey and two on Guernsey, with artillery units on the three main islands. From early on in the war, Guernsey's Reserve Battalion and Jersey's Garrison Battalion formed the infantry garrison of their respective islands, relieving regular battalions for service in France. The three Militia Artillery Units served alongside two regular RGA Companies on Alderney and Jersey, and a company of Fortress Engineers across the three islands. These units manned those batteries of modern guns with which selected fortifications on the islands had been rearmed in the early years of the twentieth century. On Jersey, two 6-inch guns were mounted on South Hill, adjacent to Fort Regent and overlooking the harbour at St Helier. Two long 4.7-inch Armstrong (1886 pattern) BL guns were installed in Elizabeth Castle. They were still there in 1935, but were scrapped by the Germans in 1940. They had been mounted on specially adapted barbette emplacements, which remain in the Upper Ward of the castle. Guernsey's two 6-inch guns were mounted in Fort Irwin, the square redoubt next to Fort George, and a pair of 12-pounder QF guns was added to Castle Cornet in St Peter Port Harbour, mounted in the South or Water Battery with attendant DELs. On Alderney, two 6-inch guns were mounted at Fort Albert in 1899, below which, on Roselle Point, opposite the end of the breakwater, was sited a battery of two 12-pounder QF guns to cover the harbour mouth. Two DELs, their directing post and an octagonal pillbox or OP, remain from this period. In addition to these fixed guns, the 1908 Defence Plan included the Militia Artillery's mobile element, consisting of four 5-inch howitzers and six 15-pounder BL guns. By 1914, they had also trained on wheeled 4.7-inch guns, so these might also have been deployed in mobile roles.

Defended Ports in Ireland

Belfast was rated only as a Category 'C' commercial port by the Owen Committee. Two batteries at Grey Point and Kilroot were opened in 1907, each with two 6-inch BL Mk VII guns and three Maxim machine guns (mounted on field carriages and designed for mobility). The standard arrangement of gun pits, underground magazines, BOP, and gun store, all contained within an enclosure with an unclimbable fence, can still be observed at Grey Point. At the mouth of Belfast Lough, the PWSS was established at Orlock. Nearer to the port itself, a breastwork armed with machine guns was constructed on West Twin Island. In the absence of a TF establishment in Ireland, the batteries were manned by gunners of No. 15 Company, RGA, and the Antrim RGA (Special Reserve). Lough Foyle, containing the commercial port and naval base of Londonderry, had long been strongly fortified, but it was Lough Swilly (awarded Class 'B' status), which the Royal Navy chose as a harbour of refuge. Here the fixed defences were accordingly strengthened before the First World War. Two 9.2-inch Mk X BL guns were mounted at Lenan Head, giving a wide arc of fire extending a good distance beyond the mouth of the Lough, while 6-pounder QF guns and machine guns would counter a landing by enemy troops. At Dunree Fort, the coast battery had already migrated up the hill above the old fort, and its armament was upgraded to two 6-inch Mk VII BL guns in 1911. Ned's Point and Inch Forts were reduced to being armed only with machine guns. A boom and A/S net was stretched between Ned's Point and Macamish in late 1914 to replace an improvised affair of hawsers suspended from anchored boats. The PWSS stood on Fanad Head, on the 'wrong' side of the Lough, given that for ease of communication, all the defences had been built on the opposite side.

Cork (Queenstown or Cobh) and Berehaven were also assigned to Class 'B' and appropriately armed. Overlooking the harbour mouth at Cork, Forts Camden and Carlisle each mounted a pair of 9.2-inch Mk X BL guns, those at Camden actually emplaced at the nearby Templebreedy Battery, while Fort Carlisle also mounted four 6-inch guns. In 1913, two further 9.2-inch Mk X BL guns were added to the Spike Island defences in the harbour, where

Fort Westmoreland already mounted five 6-inch guns. Between them, the forts also held a number of 12-pounder QF guns. All this artillery was manned by three companies of the RGA alongside the Cork RGA (Special Reserve). Bere Island's defences were equally strong, with the fire control function split into eastern and western commands and a PWSS at Ardnakinna Point. Four batteries were mounted between them—comprising two 9.2-inch Mk X BL guns, six 6-inch, two 4.7-inch, and at least eight 12-pounders. There were additionally a number of infantry redoubts armed with machine guns.

Defended Ports in Scotland

The new naval base of Rosyth, conceived in 1903, was nestled in the Firth of Forth, upstream from the railway bridge. There was an anxiety that if the bridge became damaged, the effect might be to trap elements of the Fleet inside the Firth; for that reason, Admiral Fisher preferred Cromarty as a base. The Forth defences, assessed as Class 'B' by Owen, had strength in depth, organised into an outer line with Kinghorn controlling its northern sector and Inchkeith Island its southern; a middle line from Braefoot Point through the three islands of Inchcolm, Inchmickery, and Cramond, armed just prior to the war; and an inner line, level with the railway bridge, consisting of Carlingnose and Coastguard Batteries on the north bank, Inchgarvie Island directly under the bridge, and Dalmeny battery on the south bank. Given the need to ensure that any hostile encroachment was kept at bay, coupled with the enhanced ability to achieve this afforded by the new, more powerful guns, the middle and outer lines were strengthened. This happened during the course of the war, and partly at the expense of the inner line, but mainly by a near-fourfold increase in the number of guns deployed. In 1914, the two batteries forming the outer line boasted a total of three 9.2-inch Mk X BL guns, plus a pair of 6-inch Mk VII BL guns at Kinghorn. However, Inchkeith had gained six 6-inch guns by 1918 and additional batteries, each mounting two 6-inch guns had been established at Leith Docks in 1916, and at Pettycur next to Kinghorn. On the middle line in early 1915, Cramond and Inchcolm Island had just two 12-pounders each, and Inchmickery, four more. However, by 1918, the situation had changed. A new battery with two 9.2-inch guns had briefly operated at Braefoot Point, but it had been closed in 1917. Inchcolm's armament had been increased by two 6-inch and four 4.7-inch guns, and Inchmickery had exchanged its 12-pounders for four 4-inch guns—only Cramond remaining unchanged. On the inner line, the 1914 level was reduced drastically when Carlingnose was disarmed, its two 6-inch guns being redeployed, as were the four 4-inch guns from Inchgarvie. Coastguard Battery retained its two 12-pounders and Dalmeny its pair of 4.7-inch guns. An additional pair of batteries was inserted between the inner and middle lines at Downing Point on the north bank, and Hound Point on the south, mounting two 4.7-inch and two 6-inch guns, respectively. By 1918, there were forty-four guns, including six 9.2-inch and fourteen 6-inch, in eleven locations. Anti-submarine nets and booms were stretched across the 8 miles (13 km) between Elie and Fidra, and serviced by boom-defence vessels based at Granton. Boom defences also linked the islands of the middle line. The Forth Garrison consisted of five third-line battalions of the Royal Scots (TF), amalgamated as the Edinburgh Special Reserve Brigade; third-line TF and Extra Reserve battalions; the regular gunners of No. 21 Company RGA, with its HQ in Leith Fort; the Forth RGA (TF), who moved their HQ from Edinburgh to Queensferry in 1914; and the City of Edinburgh Fortress Engineers RE (TF), with their HQ in Edinburgh's York Place.

In contrast to the Firth of Forth, the Clyde was weakly defended. Despite the rejection of earlier suggestions to provide heavy guns to defend the Firth of Clyde and the approaches to Glasgow, the defences had nevertheless been updated in the years leading up to the war. Portkil Battery was built in 1904 with two 6-inch Mk VII BL and two 4.7-inch Mk V QF guns. Another new battery at Ardhallow mounted a single 9.2-inch gun and a pair of 6-inch

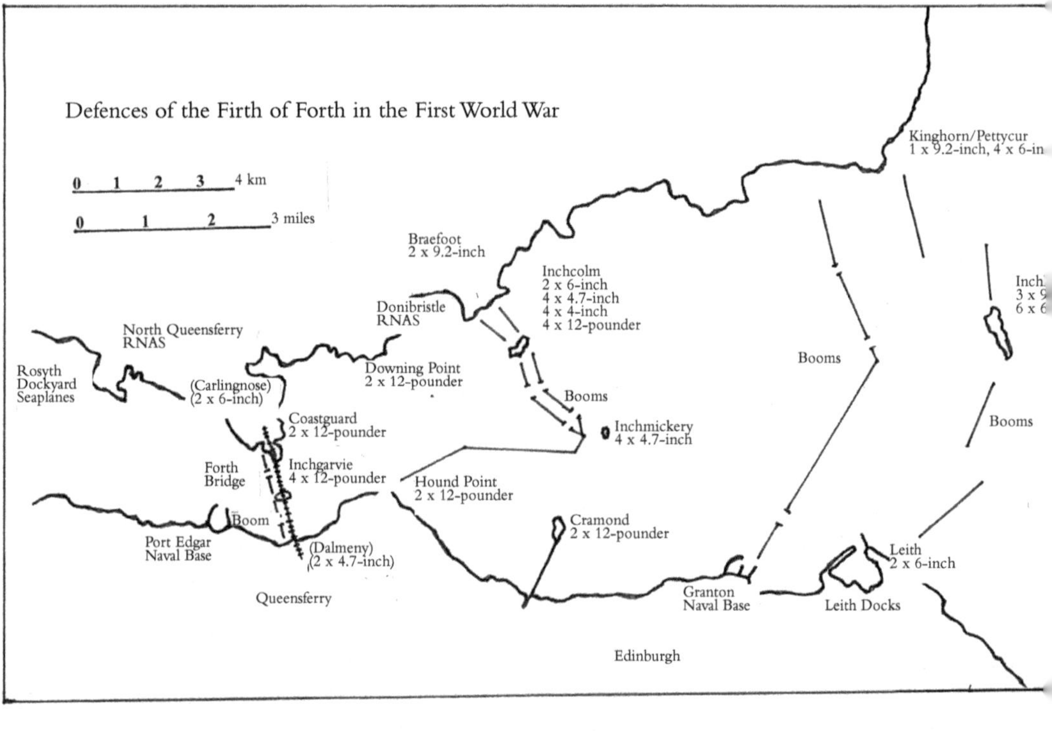

Sketch-map of the Forth defences in the First World War.

Mk VII BL guns by 1905, but the 9.2-inch gun was returned to Woolwich Arsenal in 1911. In 1912, Fort Matilda received two replacement 4.7-inch guns. During the war, a further battery at Cloch Point was constructed, armed with the two 6-inch guns redeployed from Portkil Battery. This was built to cover the boom that extended the 1.8 miles (3 km) across to Dunoon, served by HMS *Barbarian* and illuminated by three DELs, with three further lights emplaced at Dunoon. Clear protocols governed the opening of the gate in the boom while waiting vessels lay under the guns of the battery. Fort Matilda lost its guns to armed merchant ships in 1917, but remained the HQ of the Clyde defences throughout the war. The permanent element of the Clyde Garrison consisted of a reserve battalion of the Royal Scots Fusiliers at Greenock, and from spring 1915, a second-line TF battalion of the Black Watch. There were no resident RGA or Fortress REs in the Clyde, so the batteries and searchlights were manned by TF gunners from their bases in Port Glasgow, Dumbarton, and Helensburgh, and the TF REs from Fort Matilda and Paisley.

Cromarty Firth, an inlet off the Moray Firth, included the Invergordon naval base and a sizeable anchorage. The decision of the CID in 1912 to upgrade the base was the spur for the Admiralty to install powerful coast defence batteries. The Senior Naval Officer against Admiralty policy, Captain Munro, erected an anti-submarine boom near to the narrower part of the channel between Cromarty and Nigg, where the submarine-mining station had been. The entrance to the Firth was guarded by the new forts of North and South Sutor, where, high above the entrance, 9.2-inch Mk VIII guns taken from obsolete battleships—two at North Sutor and a third at South Sutor—were emplaced. At sea level were batteries of 4-inch QF guns, four of them being mounted in two pairs at North Sutor and a third pair at South Sutor. The guns were manned by marines and the garrison consisted of reserve battalions at Invergordon and Nigg.

Dundee and the Tay were defended by two batteries at Broughty Castle, the Scottish coast artillery training school and HQ of the North Scottish RGA (TF), serving the Tay and Aberdeen defences. The City of Dundee Fortress Engineers (TF), with their HQ in Taylors Lane, Dundee, worked the lights alongside a detachment of the regular RE Fortress Coast Battalion. There were two 4.7-inch guns mounted in the castle itself, and two 6-inch guns mounted on its seaward side on Castle Green. The battery's BOP was built into the top storey of the castle's fifteenth-century tower house. Victorian additions included an earthen gun platform contained within a retaining wall and it was in converted emplacements on this platform that the 4.7-inch guns were mounted. Below these was a caponier with vertical musketry loops, and a later, horizontal embrasure for a Maxim gun commanding the foreshore. The 2/4th Battalion, Black Watch, formed the garrison at Broughty Ferry prior to a move to Norfolk in 1916, and the Extra Reserve battalion of the Highland Light Infantry was stationed along the coast at Arbroath. Torry Point Battery, on the cliffs to the south of the port of Aberdeen, occupied a Victorian fort (refurbished in 1913), with a granite perimeter musketry wall and two bastions—its landward one containing a pillbox. Here, two 6-inch guns were mounted. The fort's searchlights were manned by the City of Aberdeen Fortress Royal Engineers (TF), based in Hardgate.

At the start of the war—once the immediate measures of establishing examination batteries for incoming shipping, setting up Port War Signal Stations, and putting in control mechanisms such as booms—there was one absolute priority with regard to coast defence: the fleet anchorage at Scapa Flow, had to be secured. The Orkney RGA (TF) was descended from the Orkney Artillery Volunteers, and they comprised seven companies scattered across the archipelago, with their HQ in the drill hall in Kirkwall. They trained on wheeled 4.7-inch QF guns, but had nowhere to emplace them. The Navy resorted to dismounting two 12-pounder guns from warships and placed them in temporary positions manned by the TF. It was not until early 1915 that two 4-inch and two 6-inch guns were mounted in open emplacements on Hoxa Head. Anti-submarine netting was also installed and some of the narrower entrances into the anchorage sealed by sinking block ships across them. By the end of the war, there were thirteen batteries, mounting altogether eight 6-inch, two 5-inch, two 4.7-inch, thirteen 4-inch, and ten 12-pounder guns. The defences formed a complete ring around the anchorage with only two entry points—Stromness and Stanger Head on Flotta, their fortifications effectively limiting access. All the other channels were blocked, and a guard ship was permanently anchored in Clestrain Sound. The battleship HMS *Hannibal* and, later, the cruiser HMS *Crescent* guarded the Clestrain Hurdles, a formidable anti-submarine obstacle, completed in 1917, and made of framed steel hurdles embedded in concrete, with only a few gaps for controlled access. The other guard ship, acting as a further floating battery at the southern entrance to the Flow, was HMS *Magnificent*, succeeded by HMS *Royal Arthur*. On the outside of the ring, Carness Battery monitored Kirkwall Bay and a flotilla of yachts and trawlers, based on Stromness, undertook minesweeping duties. By 1917, all the guns had been taken over by the Royal Marines, but with some experienced officers seconded to them from the RGA (TF).

The Shetland Isles were defended to a far lesser extent than Scapa. There were two single 6-inch guns on Bressay, defending the approaches to Lerwick, and a further battery on The Knab—a site later refortified. Swarbacks Minn on Vementry, an inlet off St Magnus Bay, was used as a base for ships operating the Northern Patrol to protect North Sea convoys and as an advanced base for the Grand Fleet at Scapa. The cruiser HMS *Gibraltar* was stationed as guard ship, but it was decided to mount two of her 6-inch guns permanently in open concrete emplacements on land. Using logs, the guns were rolled up the hill overlooking the entrance to the anchorage to a position enjoying better visibility than that of the *Gibraltar* at sea-level.

Later in the war, a number of ports were allocated to the US Navy in connection with the laying of the northern minefield. Batteries were established at Corran Point and on the Skye side of the Kyle of Lochalsh, manned by Royal Marines. A single 4-inch gun was also mounted on St Kilda late in 1918 in response to a raid by a U-boat.

Defended Ports in Wales

Around Britain, steps had been taken in the years leading up to the war to modernise coast defences or to abandon them. Milford Haven, containing the Pembroke naval dockyard, had been heavily fortified by the Royal Commission in the 1860s and confirmed as Class 'A' by Owen. Few improvements generally had been made, but the guardians of the entrance, East and West Blockhouse Batteries, were upgraded by the installation of two 9.2-inch guns into the former by 1900 and of four 6-inch guns into the latter in 1904. Searchlights were mounted at water level while the guns were above them on the cliffs. South Hook Fort mounted a 9.2-inch gun and two 12-pounders while Chapel Bay Battery, directly opposite, received a single 9.2-inch, a pair of 6-inch, and two 12-pounder guns. The garrison consisted of four third-line TF battalions of the Welsh Regiment and a battalion of the Kings Shropshire Light Infantry, all based at Llanion Barracks, opened in 1904 at Pembroke Dock. The guns were manned by two RGA companies and the Pembroke RGA (TF). A company of Fortress Engineers worked the searchlights. Cardiff (with four 6-inch guns), Barry (with two more), and Swansea (with a pair of 4.7-inch guns), all manned by the Glamorgan RGA (TF), formerly part of the dissolved Severn defences, were the only other Welsh ports to be defended.

Other Elements of the Coast Defences

The Defended Ports and Fleet Anchorages were only part of the story. While the enemy might have hoped to subdue these concentrations of force, it was likely that their attempts would be made to land where the defences were less well developed. Given the length of coastline surrounding the British Isles, any defences would be spread thinly.

Artillery in Beach Defence

In the early days of the war, the first defences at Scapa Flow were reported by King-Hall as 12- and 18-pounder field guns manned by local TF artillery units on either side of Hoxa Sound and, later, some 4-inch guns taken off naval vessels These were just standing in for what would evolve over time as an effective system of permanent coast artillery batteries, armed with the whole range of available weaponry. Away from the defended ports and fleet anchorages, however, it was necessary throughout the war to provide temporary beach defence batteries to counter either hit-and-run raiders or more serious amphibious landings aimed at outflanking the main defences. The guns seen most often in this beach defence role were the 15-pounder Breech-Loading Converted (BLC) field gun, 4.7-inch, and 60-pounders.

During the South African wars, the Boers had made effective use of QF field guns supplied to them from the German Krupp company. Needing to update the British Army's own weaponry, Gen. Sir Henry Brackenbury, Director General of Ordnance, discreetly purchased 108 Erhardt 15-pounder QF field guns from the Düsseldorf works. These went into service as a stop-gap while the new 18-pounder QF guns were being perfected prior to their introduction in 1904. The 15-pounder Erhardt gun was used by TF artillery units until well into the First World War, when it was eventually replaced by the 18-pounder. Meanwhile, the 15-pounder BLC field gun had been developed from a 12-pounder 7-cwt BL gun of 1885. The conversion involved modifications to the breech mechanism and the addition to the carriage of a spade, which dug into the ground on firing, so absorbing the recoil. Coupled with the introduction of cordite as an improved propellant, the new gun could fire a 14-pound shrapnel shell, but this cheap shortcut to a new QF field gun was only a temporary solution. Once the new 18-pounder guns had been produced and issued to the regular RFA, and their companion 13-pounders to the RHA, then those 536 BLC guns that had been produced could be passed on to TF artillery units. At least seventy-five were mounted at vulnerable points on the coasts of East Anglia and Kent or issued to garrisons between Northumberland and the Isle of Wight for use by quick response mobile columns, reacting to invasion alerts. Both types of 15-pounder field gun used the same shells, but the Erhardt's charge was contained in a brass cartridge case, while those for the BLC were bagged.

The demands of the Western Front limited the number of guns available for the defences at home. The TF RGA (Defended Ports) units were assigned to their war stations and the majority of first-line TF RFA units had found their way to France as divisional artillery by 1915–16, alongside the newly raised artillery units of the New Armies. This left only the second-line TF units, many of which joined their local divisions in Central Force. Where a second-line TF division was assigned to coast defence duties, then its artillery might become established in a beach defence role.

In Norfolk, two 4.7-inch guns were mounted at Cromer and 15-pounders at Eccles, Salthouse, Hemsby, and Caister. Weybourne and Mundesley, still perceived as the most likely invasion beaches, were defended by mobile heavy batteries of the RGA, armed with 60-pounder howitzers, capable of bringing plunging fire on to those exposed beaches. The most vulnerable beaches in Suffolk and Essex, from Dunwich to Clacton, received a number of 15-pounder guns. From the time of the Royal Commission, there had been plans to seal the eastern end of the Portsdown defences with a sea-level redoubt to cover Langstone Harbour. This was finally achieved early in the war and equipped with a pair of 15-pounders, with a further pair placed in Freshwater Redoubt on the Isle of Wight. Older batteries were also given a new lease of life. Parts of Padstow Battery dated from the eighteenth century, but a 60-pounder howitzer was installed after 1914. It has been suggested that Shoreham Redoubt in Sussex, remaining in military occupation until 1921, retained its 64- and 80-pounder RMLs in working order throughout the war. Ammunition supply, let alone the problems of manning and training, must make this implausible. However, it was very often the lighter guns on their field carriages, albeit more vulnerable, less effective, harder to lay accurately on moving targets, and certainly neither deterrent nor effective defence against sea-borne attacks, which were the only weapons available for deployment on the vulnerable coast.

The Defence of Vulnerable Points

Some specific targets were given a greater degree of protection. The Nobel explosives works at Ardeer, Ayrshire, was built on a roughly triangular spit of land between the sea and the River Garnock and was surrounded by a 6-mile-long (9.6-km-long) defended perimeter with fourteen concrete guard posts. Barbed-wire entanglements stretched along the three sides, which bounded the seashore, the river mouth, and the landward access. Initial plans were for a 9.2-inch railway gun to be located on a spur off the line serving the factory. As a stop-gap, an armoured train mounting two 12-pounders stood in until more permanent arrangements were made. In the end, the defences along the seashore consisted of an emplacement for a 6-inch gun, making the railway gun unnecessary, and two 12-pounder guns with their magazines and searchlights, and four guard posts. In the western corner were a fire-control post and an engine house. Two gates, one for pedestrians and vehicles and another for the railway, were guarded by adjacent guard posts, while the remaining eight were strung out along the landward fences. Across the river to the north, its bank also strongly fenced, were two further posts labelled 'temporary' on the plan.

Some 156 of the available BLC guns had been passed to the Royal Navy for the Defensively Armed Merchant Ship (DAMS) programme, part of the response to the U-boat onslaught. When the US Navy became involved in laying the Northern Minefield (see Chapter 4) it was decided that, despite their main base being Inverness, they would use the RN port facilities at Balmacara and Corpach on the west coast of Scotland to unload the mines after their trans-Atlantic journey. To protect these deliveries, two of those BLC guns, on 6-pounder Hotchkiss cone pedestals mounted on open concrete platforms, were allocated to each port, along with two 60-cm (24-inch) searchlights, manned by the Royal Marine Artillery. The Corran Point battery, defending Corpach, mounted a 7.5-inch BL howitzer as well. This was a compact weapon developed by the Navy for use in an anti-submarine role, possibly the only instance of this weapon being mounted ashore. The other battery was at Kyleakin on Skye.

The military complex at Fort Matilda contained three separate elements: Admiralty torpedo factory, coast defence battery, and infantry training camp. For the first eight months of the war, troops of the 5th (TF) Battalion, Argyll and Sutherland Highlanders, from Greenock, manned at least two blockhouses and a trench system. After that, troops from the camp took over guard duties.

Close Defence of Coast Batteries

The CID's memorandum of 1911, reiterating the need to defend coast batteries against landward attack, resulted in an eclectic mix of provision. One solution was to add new defensive installations to existing fortifications. A pentagonal blockhouse was built into the Victorian trace of Torry Point Battery at Aberdeen, and a circular machine-gun post was installed on the ramparts of Fort Burgoyne, behind Dover Castle. At Fort Albert, on the heights overlooking Braye Bay in Alderney, three small pillboxes were built over earlier gun positions on the northern rampart in 1914.

Another approach was simply to make defensible some of the component structures of the battery itself. At Ardhallow in the Clyde defences, the engine room that provided power to the searchlights is loopholed; at Blyth (Northumberland), the DELs are loopholed; and at Roberts Battery, Hartley (Northumberland), site of one of the Tyne Turrets, there is a loopholed latrine. On the landward end of the pier, in front of the Victorian casemates at Fort Bovisand in Plymouth, is a blockhouse functioning as both a searchlight position and an infantry defence position with armoured loopholes in all six faces, as well as in a rectangular extension. On Roselle Point, below Fort Albert in Alderney, an octagonal, concrete structure with wide horizontal slits, now glazed and with iron shutters, was built overlooking a pair of contemporaneous DELs. A structure sharing a similar appearance stands on the Isle of Portland overlooking the coast batteries at East Weare. Here, the 'windows' are said to have come from the Gunnery Director of an old cruiser. These may have been director posts of some kind, made defensible as a nod to their exposed positions.

A third alternative was to ring a battery with numbers of carefully positioned, mutually supporting blockhouses. On the Clyde, Ardhallow had seven of these and Portkil had two—one of which survives. Although it would appear that the Orkney batteries had only minimal defences, the majority of Scottish east coast batteries were protected by blockhouses and wire. Hound Point Battery, for instance, had outer and inner rings of blockhouses, the inner ring being connected by trenches and wire. Neighbouring Dalmeny Battery had a much more extensive area behind wire with fewer blockhouses at points along the perimeter. North and South Sutor batteries covering the entrance to the Cromarty Firth were defended by several blockhouses, trenches, and wire. Similar defences were raised at Kinghorn and Pettycur batteries on the Forth. At the other end of the country, some of the batteries defending Plymouth were defended by blockhouses. Completed between 1908 and 1910, Lord Howard's Battery has a detached blockhouse to the rear, covering the approach via the Military Road. Lentney Battery had opened in 1905, but in 1914, it was given an unclimbable fence and a detached blockhouse. Neighbouring Renney Battery (of similar date) was defended by three concrete blockhouses built in 1914. One twelve-sided example survives at the northern end of the line of the former unclimbable fence.

Finally, the entire battery complex might be enclosed inside a defensive perimeter, creating a concentration of structures within a veritable fort. This approach could be seen on the Humber, where Stallingborough Battery was surrounded by deep ditches crossed by a retractable bridge, and it had four concrete blockhouses at points on the irregular trace. At Sunk Island, on the opposite bank, there was a trapezoidal enclosure surrounded by wire and trenches, with blockhouses at three of the angles. This approach was also adopted in 1916 at Dunree and Lenan Head in Ulster. At Dunree Fort, the redoubt on the hill above the original fort could pass for something out of the Middle Ages, with its sheer masonry walls topped by two blockhouses. Below the redoubt, a line of six more polygonal concrete blockhouses controlled the approaches to the battery of two 6-inch guns. At Lenan Head, three blockhouses were inserted at appropriate points to enfilade the existing ditch. Hawkins Battery, on Maker Heights, was operational from 1892, but it was rebuilt in 1913–14 to take two high-angle 9.2-inch Mk VI BL guns. At the same time, the battery was surrounded on the rear and flanks by a concrete loopholed wall and a dry ditch on the front and flanks. Concrete caponiers were built at the forward corners and at the centre of the rear wall, fulfilling the same function as those Palmerstonian ones of an earlier era (found in the Plymouth land defences and elsewhere). The loopholes in both caponiers and walls were reinforced with armoured plates. In 1911, the extensions at each end of Warden Point Battery on the Isle of Wight were surrounded by concrete walls and blockhouses, two of which remain. The landward wall of neighbouring Cliff End Battery was given a defensive wall with a hexagonal flanking blockhouse in 1912 after the footprint of the work had been enlarged. This matched one already standing at the south-east corner. The submarine mining establishment on the South Gare at Teesmouth has a loopholed wall with corner bastions. Although there was no longer mining activity, the fort accommodated the RGA (Defended Ports) and RE (Fortress) detachments who manned the guns and lights on the breakwater. The extensive batteries on Spurn Head are also surrounded by a defensive wall. On the landward side, facing into the anchorage of the estuary, is a wall with at least five surviving blockhouses.

Blockhouse Design

Unlike in the Second World War, when the majority of defence works (particularly pillboxes) were built to a suite of designs issued by the War Office Directorate of Fortifications and Works—often to be reinterpreted by local contractors and RE officers—it would appear that most First World War works (blockhouses more so than pillboxes) were one-off productions tailored to their individual locations and the resources available for their construction. During the Boer War, although there were substantial two-storey blockhouses with garrisons of platoon strength, there were also much larger numbers of a type constructed by filling the space between concentric cylinders of corrugated-iron with sand, rubble, or whatever came to hand. The example of a blockhouse, illustrated in the 1911 edition of the War Office Manual of Field Engineering, is clearly drawing on the temporary version. It has walls made up of a sandwich of timber with broken stone as its filling. It is surrounded by an outer fire trench with a parapet pierced by loopholes, formed from turves resting on angled bags of shingle. Plans and elevations of blockhouses at Dalmeny and Hound Points on the River Forth, for instance, conform very much to this style. They show a timber chamber with a pentice roof of timber and felt, with high loopholes, making it possible to fire over the top of half-height blast walls built of dry stone or sandbags, and much thicker than the main walls. Alternatively, the inner walls might be strengthened with heaped earth up to just below the level of the loopholes, a practice that has clouded the identification of sites ever since. The shape was more-or-less square, often with one or more corners chamfered to produce irregular pentagons or hexagons. The text-book example is octagonal with two longer parallel sides, like a sardine tin.

Many of the blockhouses built in the years immediately preceding the war were substantial structures of masonry or concrete, often reinforced with metal rods or cast-iron I-beams. The blockhouses at Dunree employ blocks of stone for the lower courses with poured concrete or concrete blocks for the upper half and brick to define some of the corners—on porches, for instance. Their roofs are concrete slabs supported by I-beams. Loopholes appear to be of pre-cast concrete holding iron plates fitted with sliding shutters. At Dunree, the blockhouses traced a variety of shapes: a regular octagon, a pentagon, trapeziums with chamfered corners, and elongated hexagons. The single octagon contained eleven loopholes; both pentagons had eighteen, though in different configurations; the square had fifteen plus another in each of two chamfered corners; and the two trapezoidal ones had eighteen and twenty. On the redoubt, the two hexagonal blockhouses had thirteen loopholes distributed over five faces. One of the blockhouses has a superstructure, and this one has three doorways in the lower level of the rear wall. At Lenan Head, there is one rectangular blockhouse with nine loopholes and a further one in each of the chamfered forward corners. The other two blockhouses are spearhead-shaped, with three regular loopholes in each of the four faces and three more narrow ones in the angles. Many blockhouses at this time were not as geometrically ambitious as these Ulster examples. At Portkil and Kinghorn, simple rectangular structures have three loopholes in the long sides and one at each end. The central concrete caponier at Hawkins Battery's has three wide horizontal embrasures in each side and a seventh in the end wall. The rectangular blockhouse at Lord Howard's Battery at Plymouth has one half-hexagonal end wall. Fort Bovisand has a hexagonal blockhouse with a rectangular extension, while Renney Battery's surviving blockhouse is twelve-sided. Its neighbour's bottle-shaped blockhouse at Lentney Battery must boast the strangest shape of all. At Fort Albert on Alderney, the three structures built on the rampart are hexagonal with rounded corners and only large enough for two men. They contain concrete tables that may have been added by the German garrison who used them as machine-gun posts. The blockhouses on the walls of Spurn Fort at the mouth of the Humber take two different forms. The walls are around 25 feet (7.5 m) high and staggered at intervals of about 30 to 50 yards. In at least three of these, re-entrant angles blockhouses were inserted at rampart level. They are rectangular and have wide horizontal embrasures for the Vickers machine guns, which were mounted on integral concrete tables. Embrasures cover the face of the wall, while others overlook the estuary, and pistol loops cover the entrance and the interior of the compound. As well as this type, there were at least two built onto the face of the wall, projecting onto the shore. These are roughly square with chamfered

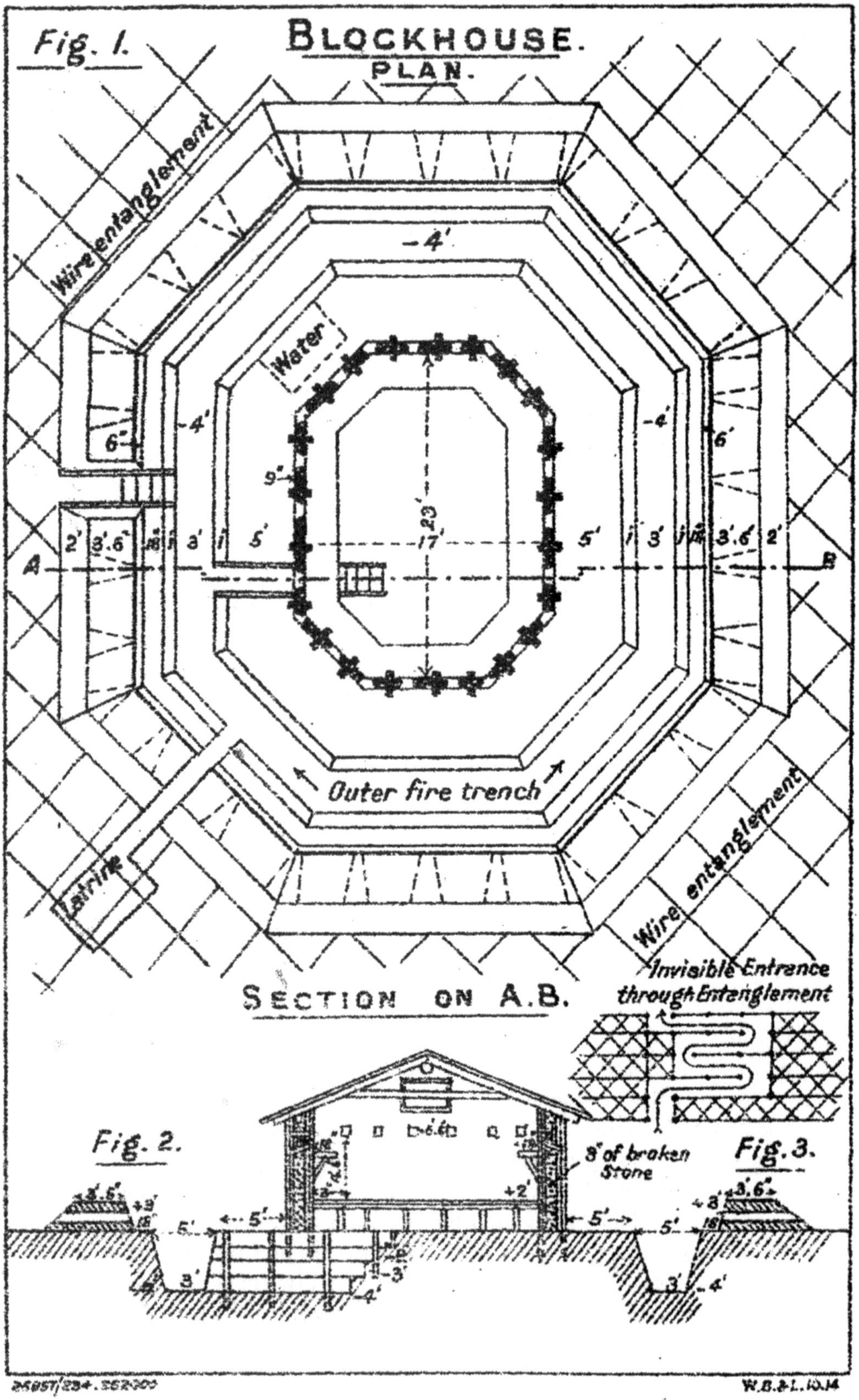

26857/284. 362.300 W.B.&L.10.14

Blockhouses defending (mainly) coast defence batteries

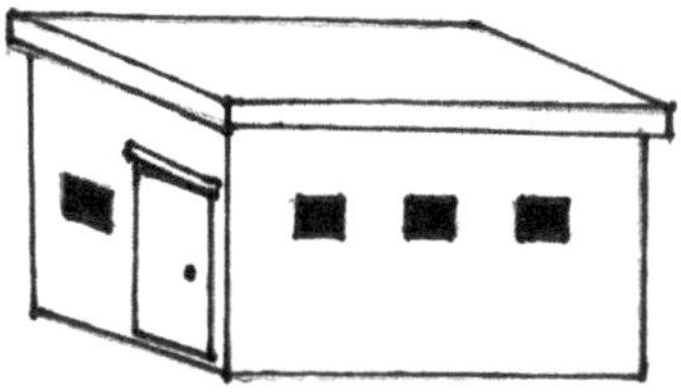

Blockhouse in rendered brick with concrete roof; up to nine or more musketry loopholes and an armoured door.

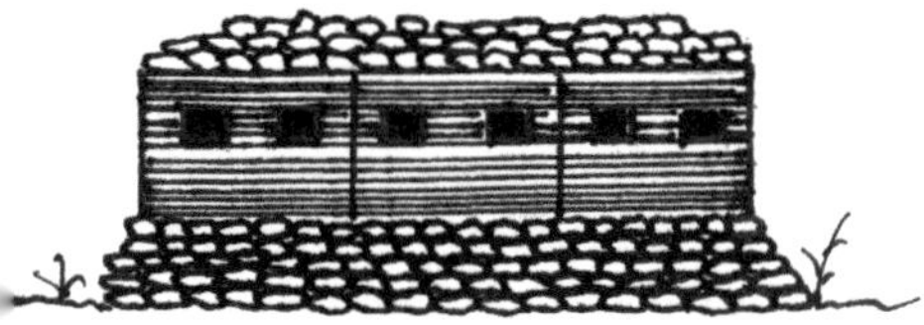

Blockhouse of corrugated-iron sheets and sandbags.

Blockhouse in rendered brick or block-wood for two of more Maxim machine gunes.

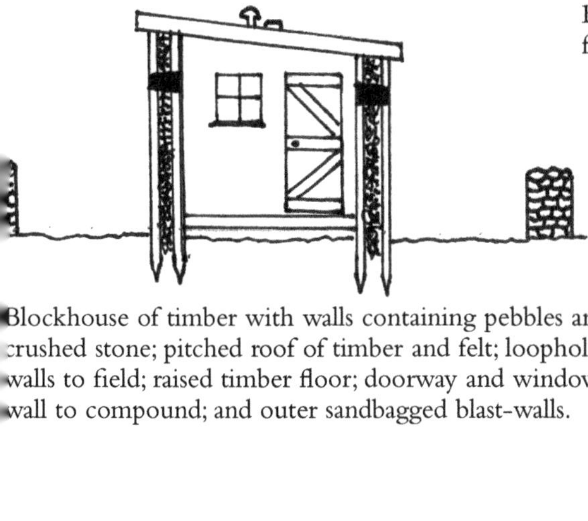

Blockhouse of timber with walls containing pebbles and crushed stone; pitched roof of timber and felt; loopholes in walls to field; raised timber floor; doorway and window in wall to compound; and outer sandbagged blast-walls.

Above: Reconstructed sections and elevations of blockhouses defending (mainly) coast defence batteries.

Opposite: Plan of a blockhouse from the War Office Manual of Field Engineering, 1911.

forward-facing corners, giving three armoured loopholes in each side and one in each chamfer. There were no loops in the front face as the purpose of these blockhouses was to enfilade the fort wall. The Isle of Wight blockhouses are much less generously provided with loopholes, generally having only one in each face. Despite clear similarities between many of these structures scattered across the British Isles, there would appear to have been no official standard design.

Anti-Invasion Defences

So far, this chapter has almost exclusively examined defensive structures built for the protection of coast artillery installations against enemy landings. This next section will explore those defences built to prevent an enemy landing or advancing inland. The outbreak of war in August 1914 prompted a frenzy of trench-digging, especially on the east coast. Preparations to defend London had been in place for a generation and the land defences of Portsmouth, Plymouth, and, particularly, Chatham were well established, if outdated. It soon became obvious that there was much to do and that quite long stretches of the hundreds of miles of Britain's coastline were vulnerable to attack. Where there was a military installation of some kind on the coast, such as the depot of the Royal Marines at Deal, then a formal defence plan would be put in place, but few stretches of coastline enjoyed such provision.

Fieldworks: Trenches, Redoubts, and Gun Positions

By December 1914, trench lines were being dug by TF units and volunteers behind the most vulnerable beaches in East Anglia. At Sheringham, for instance, trenches were dug across the golf links and were being backed up by second and third lines of defence between Hunworth and Briston. Similar defences of trenches and barbed wire protected Sea Palling, Weybourne, Salthouse, and Winterton. More defended the naval base and other military installations at Great Yarmouth and Gorleston. Additionally, some coastal marshland was allowed to flood and to remain under water. Throughout the war, the construction of trenches by reserve and training units made the men fit, helped to defend the coast, and prepared the men for their future on the Western Front. Aerial photography and maps have revealed much more evidence of trench systems than had ever been imagined. A whole network of trenches has been plotted around the mouths of the Forth and Tay, including an extensive line running down the eastern side of Edinburgh. On the Isle of Grain at the mouth of the Medway, trenches with fire bays, revetted with

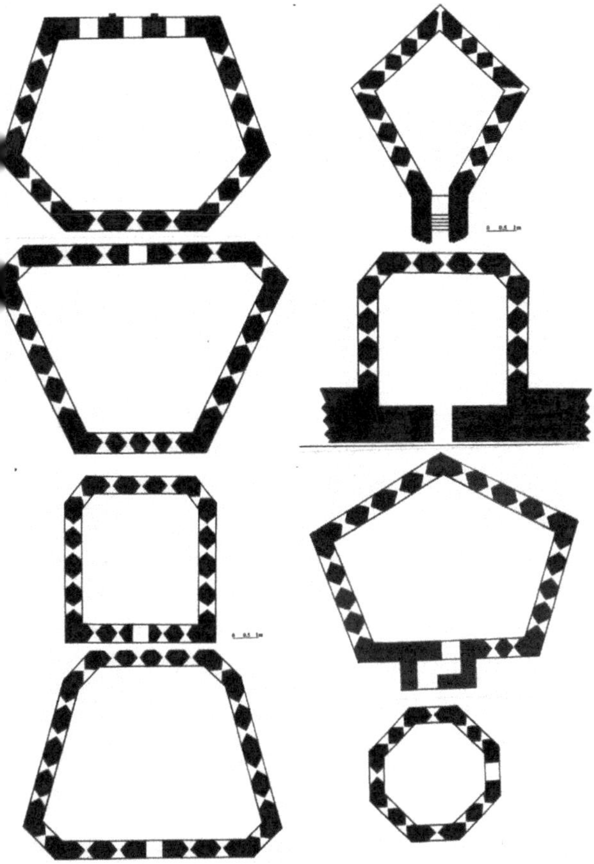

Left: Plans of blockhouses at Dunree and Lenan Head Forts defending Lough Swilly.

Below: Trench designs and layouts as constructed on the Western Front, as anti-invasion defences at home, and as exercises for troops undergoing training.

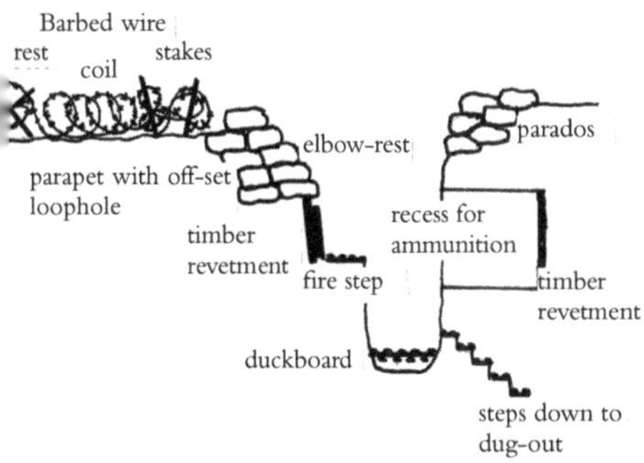

s-section of front-line trench without overhead
r

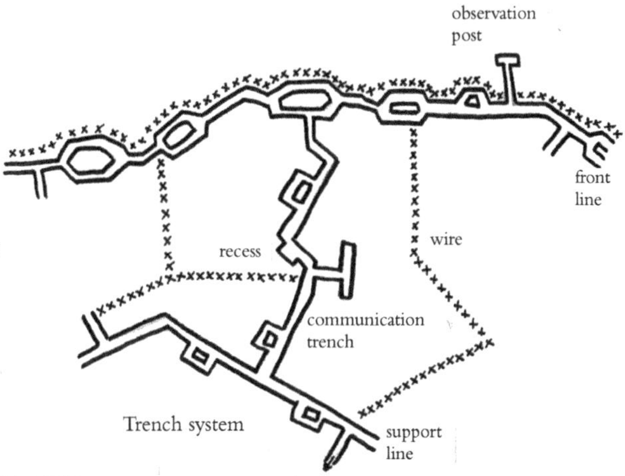

Trench systems in the First World War
Used both as anti-invasion defences and as training in preparation for life on the Western Front

timber boards, were dug to the north—that is, to seaward of Grain Fort, one of a complex of batteries guarding the river and the Medway boom.

The military authorities in Dover were also quick off the mark in commissioning field defences. Within weeks of the beginning of the war, the town's unemployed were mobilised to dig a ring of earthwork redoubts stretching around the back of the town in an arc from Fan Bay to Lydden Spout, over the top of Swingate Hill, round behind Fort Burgoyne, and then over the London road and behind Western Heights. David Burridge lists eleven of these redoubts, which were intended to protect the vital harbour facilities from a landing along the coast and a landward attack from the rear. He describes these redoubts as conforming to the pattern whose component parts are illustrated in the 1911 Manual. Features included the following: wire entanglements and aprons with trip-wire alarms; trenches with fire bays, shelters, and overhead cover; and machine-gun posts. They may not have had telephone lines, but there were certainly signallers, and, with smaller posts in between, inter-visibility would have enabled alarms to be passed on. As well as these redoubts, half a dozen trench systems are listed, with two based on the Duke of York's military school. Dover had been allocated twenty of the 15-pounder BLC field guns and at least thirteen field-gun positions have been identified in the lines around Dover. Burridge cites a locally held photograph which appears to show a concrete field-gun position near Archcliffe Fort. Otherwise, these guns would have been emplaced in pits with sandbags or gabions as protection, as shown in the 1911 Manual. As it became apparent that overhead cover was no protection against HE shells, trenches began more to resemble the open Western Front version. A similar effort was made to secure the landward approaches to Falmouth. A line of trenches, reinforced with wire obstacles, was dug from Swan Pool in an arc around the northern side of The Beacon to the riverbank, protecting the base from a force landing above the castle and attacking from the rear. Natural features, such as the marshy ground west of the town, were incorporated, as well as the railway line to Penryn.

Owing to the German possession of the Belgian ports, Kent was seen as a prime target for invasion, and a large share of the available weaponry was deployed there. As well as Dover, other Kent coastal towns were allocated 15-pounder guns: four to Deal, ten to Margate, and six to Herne Bay. While the home defence formations of the Central Force sought to retain mobility by avoiding being tied down to fixed defences, it was nevertheless necessary for some permanent positions to be installed. As part of a defensive line—north of Maidstone, stretching from Boxley to Upchurch, and shielding the eastern approaches to the Medway towns—eight 6-inch howitzers were emplaced in pairs. The 67th (2nd Home Counties) Division remained in the Southern Army throughout the war so these guns might have been manned by 2/4th Home

:mplacement for a 15-pounder BLC gun on he Isle of Sheppey, camouflaged as a beach halet, and based on photographs in the RE ibrary at Brompton

Emplacement for a 15- pounder BLC gun built into a ruined farm building.

Emplacements for field artillery

Reconstructions of field artillery emplacements.

Counties (Howitzer) Brigade, RFA (TF). Traces of these emplacements remain at Gore Farm and Matts Hill. In 1916, when Field-Marshal French took up the post of C-in-C Home Forces, he organised lines of trenches the length of the east coast, reinforced with batteries of 6-inch howitzers and 60-pounder guns.

Pillbox Design

One of the innovations on the Western Front was the use, by the German Army, of concrete machine-gun posts. Initially, the structure provided a shelter for the crew during the bombardment phase of an attack, and then an elevated platform for the weapon in the mowing down advancing infantry phase. These shelters gradually evolved into protected firing points, particularly, but not exclusively, for machine guns. As Peter Oldham relates, the various British Armies developed their own designs and began to prefabricate parts that were shipped out from Richborough military port for assembly in France and Flanders. On the Home Front, there appears to have been a rather more *laissez faire* approach.

There were a number of designs specifically for use as machine-gun posts. The most common was a hexagonal pillbox for three Vickers guns. There were wide embrasures, splayed to the outside, in the three forward-facing sides, two blank sides, and a longer rear wall with an entrance. Fixed concrete tables were provided for the guns. Examples stood in Kent, on Sheppey and at Sheerness, and on the Lincolnshire coast. Around Stockbury on the defence line that ran from the Swale down to Maidstone, there were several oval pillboxes with two forward-facing loopholes and tables for two Vickers guns. At Redcar on the Cleveland coast, three pillboxes were built into the seawall at 200-yard intervals. With three internally splayed loopholes, they were furnished with tables for Vickers guns. A report by a witness describes them as measuring about 10 feet (3 metres) square, but a recent reconstruction drawing renders them rectangular with two of their three loopholes in chamfered angles, giving them enfilading fields of fire. A trapezoidal pillbox on a Lincolnshire beach has loopholes in only two sides in order to provide such enfilading fire.

Infantry pillboxes came in a number of different designs. The simplest was a square pillbox with loopholes in three sides and a door in the fourth. Examples stood on the beach at Bawdsey (Suffolk); at Newington, near Maidstone (Kent); at Minster, on the Isle of Sheppey; and at Auburn Farm, on the East Riding coast near Bridlington. A second design found on the east coast is a circular pillbox with four or five, often armoured, loopholes, sometimes set at different heights, and a low entrance. This was usually constructed of cast concrete blocks and had a pair of steel doors. There was often an overhanging lip on the cast concrete roof. At least nine of these circular pillboxes have survived in Norfolk, but Bird lists ten in the immediate environs of Weybourne alone and has identified the locations of a further forty across the county. The half dozen or so surviving examples in Suffolk suggest that there were once many more there as well, and they were also built in Lincolnshire. A third design was a regular hexagon in shape with loopholes in five faces and a low entrance with steel doors in the sixth. A number of these survive in East Anglia: two straddle the A47 on the landward approach to Great Yarmouth; there are two more at Rushmere; one in a boatyard at St Olave's; and another at Kessingland. The twelve-sided examples at Chattenden magazine are more guard posts than pillboxes; they are only large enough for two occupants at most, with five loopholes and a low-down, hinged concrete door. Other examples in the Chattenden complex had different configurations of loopholes.

There exist several other examples of one-off structures. At Lodge Hill, near Chatham, Britain's first dedicated AA site (built to protect the Army's magazines), a close-defence blockhouse was included with the gun positions, magazine, and accommodation. It is a symmetrical, but irregular hexagon with three loopholes in each of its two longer sides and a single one in each of two of the shorter sides. The blockhouse is entered from the enclosed compound and its steel door, somewhat surprisingly, is flanked by windows rather than loopholes. On high ground behind Godwin Battery, one of the Humber's counter-bombardment batteries, is Murray's Post. This is an infantry redoubt, built of concrete blocks and sunk into the ground. It has a central crew-room that is surrounded by musketry galleries with machine-gun positions at three corners. It could hold a garrison of about thirty riflemen, plus the three machine-gun crews, signallers, and an officer, and is unique as a survivor of what was, in any case, a fairly rare structure in itself. On a corner of the Purfleet rifle ranges is a circular two-storey tower about 15 feet (4.5 metres) high and 20 feet (6 metres) in diameter. It has a doorway and five large embrasures fitted with iron plates, each of which have a central loophole closed by a moveable shutter. The tower was built as a submarine spotting tower, but it also mounted an anti-aircraft 1-pounder Pom-pom gun. Manned by the Essex and Suffolk RGA, it shared in the destruction of a Zeppelin (see Chapter 6).

Anti-Invasion Defence Systems

The Chatham land defences, recommended by the Royal Commission, were not completed until 1899. The intention was not only to protect the landward approach to the dockyard and naval base, but also to pose a threat to a force invading from the Kent coast and making for London. If an invader chose to bypass the Chatham defences, diverting via Maidstone as far as the Medway crossing, his right flank would be exposed to harassment from the garrison. The first element of the Chatham defences to be built were four polygonal artillery forts stretching from Fort Borstal overlooking the Medway, round to Fort Luton at the other end of the ridge. Next came Fort Darland, based on similar design principles, but designed for infantry, with provision for housing the field guns of a mobile column, and incorporating, in its forward rampart, eleven emplacements for machine guns. The space between Darland and the river at Twydall, to the east of Gillingham, had been filled by two infantry redoubts—Forts Woodlands and Grange—known together as the Twydall Redoubts. These, only designed after work on the rest of the system was underway, employed the new Twydall Profile. Recognition of the increased firepower of magazine rifles and machine guns permitted a no-less robust, but much less massive construction. These redoubts were low profile, hence less visible, and used earth ramparts topped by a rifle parapet, from which the glacis sloped down to a ditch extending around the entire work and containing an unclimbable fence. Within the fort was a block of concrete casemates in which the garrison might shelter during a bombardment. The act of construction itself was an experiment, seeing one redoubt completed by a non-convict workforce of 150 men in thirty-one days at a much reduced cost over the conventional forts. Just as Fort Darland's mobile guns could be emplaced in an adjacent battery, another concealed battery between the redoubts could be furnished with field artillery. During an exercise to simulate siege operations in 1907, it was realised that the accelerating increase in the range of heavy artillery meant that the Chatham forts were too close to the installations they were protecting. However, during the First World War, they could be supplemented by connecting trenches and redoubts, with fortifications extending onto the Hoo Peninsula, where the magazines of Lodge Hill and Chattenden needed to be protected. These defences would probably have withstood raids in force, but not an invading army with heavy siege artillery. Nevertheless, a dug-out (large enough to hold 3,000 men) was excavated in the old eighteenth-century Chatham Lines; this would have accommodated the force that would man the trench lines in the event of an invasion from 1914.

In the years before the outbreak of war, plans were laid down to link up the various defended areas around London into a cohesive defence system. This meant that the London Defence Position (see below) would be extended to join up with the Chatham defences at Halling, on the Medway, via a redoubt at Wrotham Hill. The existing Queenborough Lines, sealing off Sheerness, would also be strengthened with extra redoubts, trenches, and wire. Similar defences would be continued around the coast of Sheppey to Minster (with its 15-pounder guns and redoubts), past the new Fletcher Battery (see above), on to Warden Point (with two more 15-pounders), and Leysdown. Parallel to the Queenborough Lines, a series of redoubts would link Minster to the bridge over the Swale. From there, a defence line continued south to Maidstone through Newington, Stockbury, and Detling, blocking off the old Dover Road and extending down to the Folkestone road at Maidstone. This was the line that would delay an invading force marching on London from the east Kent beaches. Here were trenches incorporating fire bays and semi-circular machine-gun posts, all revetted with stout timber boards or woven hurdles and palings. They were provided with fire-steps, deep-wire entanglements, concrete pillboxes, and earth redoubts. In the Stockbury area were oval machine-gun posts, and around Newington, square pillboxes. Field guns were emplaced along the line itself, while heavy guns, 60-pounder howitzers, 4.7-inch guns, and 6-inch naval guns were stationed behind the line to bring fire down as necessary, guided by spotters well in advance of the gun-positions and possibly even aloft in tethered observation balloons once this had become established practice. Some of these lines consisted of two or more trenches giving defence in depth. Gun positions, initially for 12-pounders and later for 15-pounder guns, were solidly constructed fieldworks, while the positions for the heavier guns, farther back, were solid slabs of concrete. All these works

Cross-section of the Twydell Profile

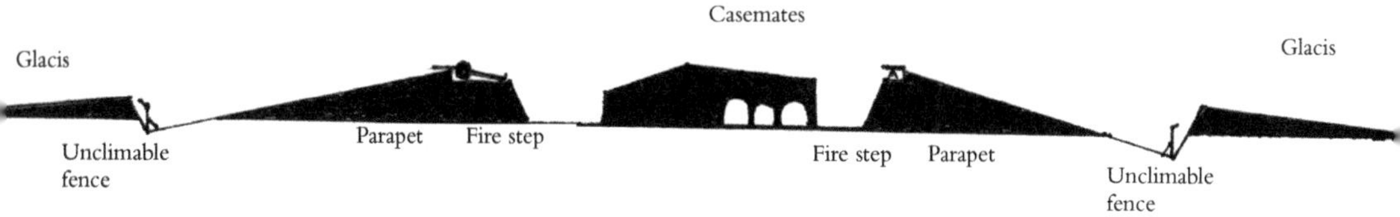

Sketch to show the Twydall Profile as used in early nineteenth-century forts.

were constructed by RE Fortress Companies, with labour from infantry units of 2nd Army—that part of Central Force covering southern England. The 3rd (Reserve) Battalion of the Royal West Kent Regiment was at Leysdown on Sheppey, with the 2/5th Battalion at Tonbridge and Maidstone through 1915–16. Eventually, an impressive array of artillery was mounted on or behind this defence line. As well as the original four pairs of 12-pounders and the eight 6-inch naval guns, there were eight 60-pounders, ten other howitzers, and eighteen positions containing field guns, all emplaced in pairs. For the most part, these would have been manned by second-line TF artillery units of Southern or 2nd Army.

Following on from previous conflicts in which Weybourne Hope in north Norfolk (with its steeply shelving beach) had been seen as the key to England, stop-lines were prepared behind the coastline. The River Ant provided such a defence, ensuring that the crossings were guarded by pillboxes and trench systems. The pillboxes were all circular apart from one at North Walsham, which was bow-shaped, with four loopholes and an entrance in the curved face and a blank, straight back wall. All were built of concrete blocks and most had armoured ports and steel doors.

The London Defence Position

During the French wars, a series of trenches had been dug covering the road from Ipswich through Chelmsford to London, and an entrenched camp for 15,000 troops was built at Widford, south of Chelmsford. In 1860, proposals to fortify London with a ring of thirty forts around a perimeter of 30 miles (48 km), with a further nine forts to defend the arsenal, artillery barracks,

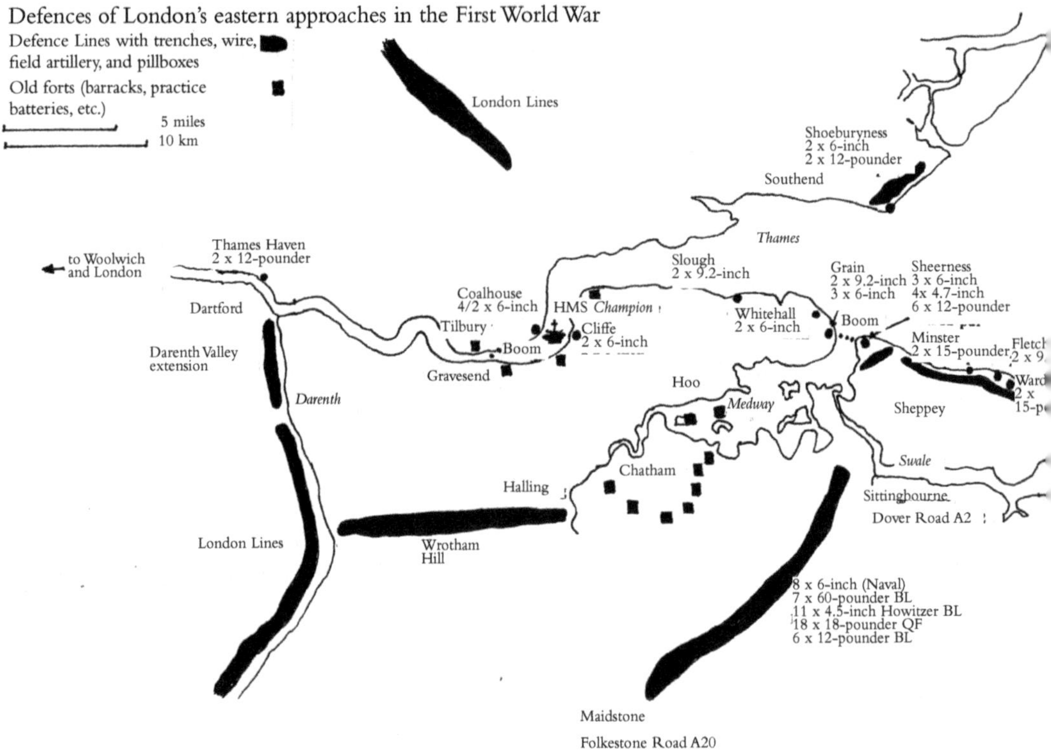

Above: Sketch-map showing the defences of London's eastern approaches.

Below: Sketch-map showing the anti-invasion defences of Norfolk.

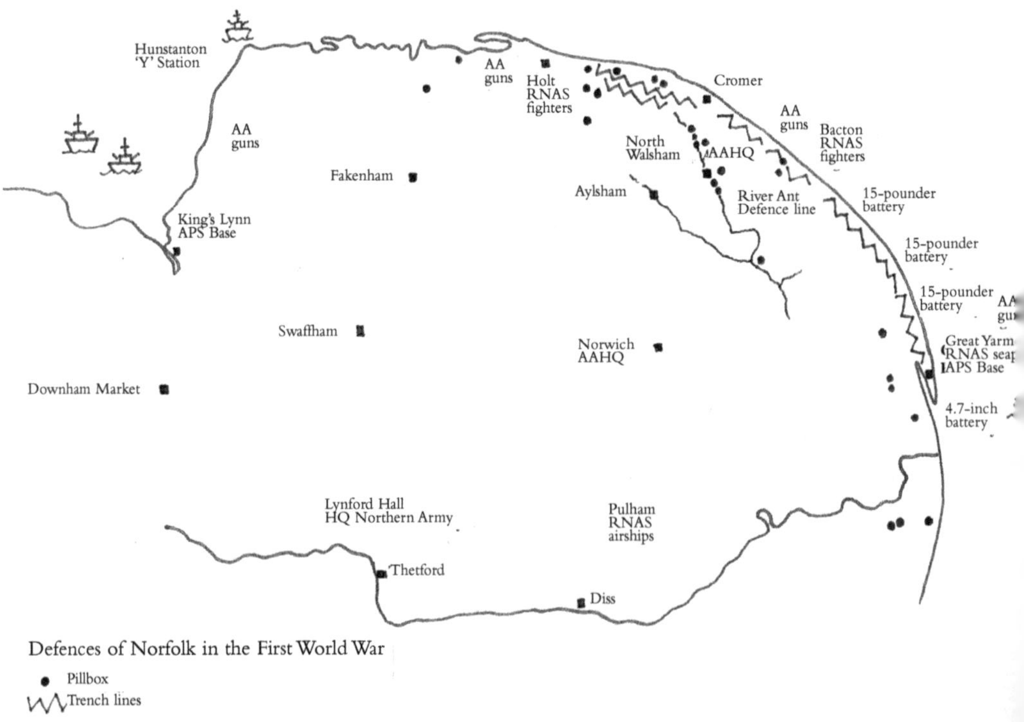

and dockyard at Woolwich, were rejected by the Royal Commission. Nearly thirty years on, the subject came up once more in Parliament. This time it was decided to proceed with a modest scheme, which would provide only the infrastructure of a defensive position as an emergency measure for implementation in the event of imminent invasion. Construction of a line of defensive works, 72 miles (115 km) in length, commenced in 1889. North of the Thames, it consisted of a strong-point at North Weald, from which a line of fieldworks could extend to the Thames near Canvey Island. South of the Thames, a further dozen similar strong-points were spaced at intervals between the Thames near Dartford, down the Darenth Valley, then along the crest of the North Downs from Westerham to Guildford, and anchored on the primary military base at Aldershot. There were two types of strongpoint included in these lines. Four of them were expected to fulfil a role as artillery forts with gun mountings and magazines. Of the remaining nine, eight were classed as defensible infantry redoubts, while Woldingham was unfortified. Although defensible, with ramparts and ditches, unclimbable fences, concrete casemates and caponiers, loopholed guardrooms and steel gates, their primary purpose was to serve as storehouses. Weapons, supplies, and tools would be issued to the volunteers who would extend and man the defences of London in time of war. This role as tool stores, armouries, and magazines was reflected in their designation as the London Mobilisation Centres. A typical artillery redoubt, such as Reigate, located in a commanding position, was bow-shaped with a curved rampart equipped with two casemated gun positions, underground magazines, a barrack building, and a straight gorge wall containing a loopholed armoured gate accessed by a bridge over the moat. Infantry redoubts like Henley Grove or Farningham were similar in shape with casemates and a parapet, but also had brick-built armouries and magazines within the shelter of the rampart. Outside the defended area stood a gabled tool store, and as they were otherwise unmanned, a cottage for the resident caretaker. North Weald was bigger than most of the other centres, provided with emplacements for six guns, accessed by ramps from the courtyard. It was surrounded by ditches and Dacoit Fencing and entered across the roof of a caponier. Its shell stores held 7,200 rounds of 4.7-inch ammunition, but also 2,320 rounds for the obsolete 20-pounder gun. An inventory of 1906 assessed the total stock of 15-pounder ammunition stored in the mobilisation centres as 300 rounds per gun based on a figure of seventy available batteries. By 1914, only TF units were equipped with either type of 15-pounder gun, but whether there were caches of 18-pounder shells stored for the regular artillery units of the field army is not known.

By 1903, when the War Office issued a handbook to the volunteer force, the infrastructure was, apparently, largely in place, but the forward line of mobilisation centres was only part of the scheme. There were base depots

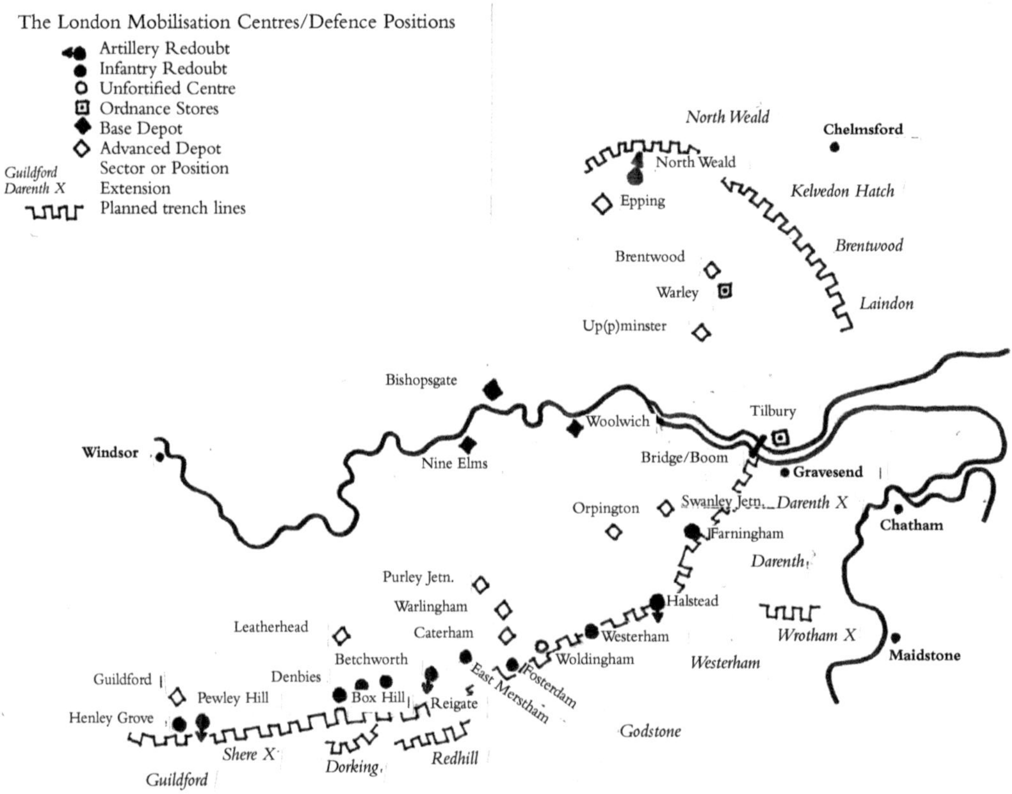

Map of the London Defence Positions showing the Mobilisation Centres and their supporting depots.

nearer the centre of London—at Nine Elms, Bishopsgate, and Woolwich Arsenal—with further weaponry held in Hownslow Barracks and at The Tower. Tilbury Fort and Warley Barracks both operated as ordnance depots and back-up mobilisation centres. North of the river, there were advanced depots at Upminster and at Epping, which had originally been intended as a second mobilisation centre alongside North Weald. South of the river, there were advanced depots at Leatherhead, Swanley, Purley, Warlingham, and Caterham—this last, like Warley, was an important Foot Guards depot.

In the southern line, centres at Box Hill or Farningham, for example, were located in the gaps in the Downs (which might seem attractive to an invading force threatening London) and were supported by forces based at strategic points to intercept enemy landings or else behind the lines of fieldworks, blocking potential lines of enemy advance. On the outbreak of war, those units of the volunteers—or after 1908, the Territorial Force—stationed in the environs of London would mobilise, draw their tools from the centres, and join up all the dots with trenches, gun positions, and redoubts. The appendices of the report of the Royal Commission in 1860 had included estimates of the population's military potential, and this now came into play once more, updated by the 1901 Census. It was reckoned that the line would be manned at the level of 2,000 troops to the mile (1,250 per km) and that the majority of these 144,000 troops would come from volunteer artillery and infantry units, with a stiffening of regulars. Once war had broken out, a great deal of instant digging was required, using civilian labour; it was estimated as achievable (with seven days' notice) with 35,000–40,000 labourers in just four days. Given the speed with which Grange Redoubt at Twydall had been constructed, this was not as unreasonable as it might initially sound, providing that detailed blueprints had been produced and issued to the RE officers who would be supervising the operation.

In 1914, a number of extensions to the London Defence Position were planned. To the north of the river, the line would be taken westwards from Epping to meet the River Lea at Broxbourne, and in the south-west, to Buckland Hills beyond Reigate Fort. The most vital extension, however, lay in the south-east. It was important to ensure that the Chatham land defences might effectively channel an invading force into a position where it could be destroyed by the field army backed by the London Defence Position. Such success would be dependent on joining the two defence lines together, and this would be effected by the construction of a trench line along the North Downs escarpment from the Darenth Valley, via existing defence works on Wrotham Hill to Halling on the Medway.

In the event, there seemed little political will or urgency to safeguard the capital from invasion. Perhaps any invasion was expected on the beaches of East Anglia rather than of east Kent, and it was felt that it would be possible to complete the defences in time. A certain amount of work was carried out under the direction of Major-General Ruck, CRE of the Central Force, who was nominally in charge of London's defences, and his successor, Col. Horniblow, who ensured that adequate accommodation for the troops, in encampments of timber hutting, was provided. For example, in May and June 1915, the 2/1st Battalion, Herefordshire Regiment, were working on the northern London defences at Billericay and the 2/1st Battalion, Cambridgeshire Regiment, was similarly employed at Rayleigh. In spring 1916, General Sir Francis Lloyd, GOC London District since the beginning of the war, assumed responsibility for the defence lines around London as it was considered that insufficient progress had been made throughout the preceding year. Originating in the Volunteer Training Corps (see Chapter 5), the London Volunteer Regiment was formed under the command of General Lloyd. In Essex, 14,000 members were soon digging trenches under the supervision of RE officers, with up to 10,000 of them turning out some weekends. Eventually, a trench system ran from north of Chelmsford by Maldon and Danbury Hill, with another by Ongar and Epping taking in North Weald Redoubt. The acute manpower shortages made any wartime activity difficult to keep on track and the construction of defences round London was not everyone's priority. Despite all these efforts and attempts at motivation, such as the meeting of local commanders in May 1916, when they were told that the continuing threat of invasion made the need to complete the defences more urgent, the London trenches were only finally completed on 27 October 1918, just a fortnight before the end of the war.

Armoured Trains and Railway Guns

The British Army had used armoured trains to good effect in the South African wars, and this experience of both heavy and light armoured trains was renewed in Belgium in autumn 1914. Trains manned by the Naval Brigade (mounting 4.7-inch guns and Maxim machine guns) operated up to the fall of Antwerp in October, when they were destroyed, deactivated, or withdrawn into France to be cannibalised for other purposes. In Britain, a range of railway companies supplied locomotives, infantry wagons, and gun trucks, which were assembled into trains at Crewe. The 0-6-2 N1 Great Northern Railway locomotive was protected virtually all over by 9/16-inch (14-mm) steel plate, with observation apertures to front and side, closed by sliding steel shutters. Each infantry wagon was a converted Great Western Railway coal wagon whose basic frame was covered in ½-inch-thick (12.5-mm) steel panels, pierced by fifty-six rifle ports, similarly provided with sliding steel shutters. Caledonian Railway boiler trolleys were used as the basis for the gun trucks. Each one had a 12-pounder QF gun with its integral shield mounted at one end, and an armoured compartment for two Maxim guns projecting slightly sideways in order to increase their fields of fire. The first completed train—consisting of a locomotive in the centre, an infantry wagon either side, and a gun truck front and rear—was deployed in Norfolk, stabled at North Walsham from December 1914 and maintained at the railway workshops at Melton Constable. Following the first bombardment in November 1914, the citizens of Great Yarmouth had been promised that the train would protect them, but when the town was again bombarded in April 1916, the train, currently thought to have been 'Alice', was nowhere to be seen. Its apparent value lay in its ability to reach otherwise inaccessible parts of a vulnerable coastline. It thus had a tactical value, with its guns enjoying relatively generous arcs of traverse. However, the impact that 12-pounders (designed as anti-torpedo-boat guns) would have had against armoured cruisers would have been negligible. A second armoured train, 'Norna', made up in much the same way as the first, was completed in April 1915 and deployed in Scotland, stabled at the St Margaret's depot in Edinburgh. This fulfilled a more strategic role, tasked with safeguarding the rail links between the key naval bases of Rosyth and Invergordon, particularly recognising the importance of the Forth Bridge and its possible vulnerability to a hit-and-run raid. Although a number of armoured trains were improvised in Ireland, one of them being operated in the defence of the Queenstown naval base, no other such trains operated on the mainland. Some of the hundreds of narrow-gauge petrol and petrol-electric tractors were armoured, but apart from some used for training, mainly at Longmoor (the Army's training base for railway operations), the rest were only ever run in France.

The obvious candidate for use as railway artillery was the 9.2-inch Mk X coast defence gun. This was initially mounted on extemporised flat-bed wagons. By the end of the war, production settled on the Mk XIII on a flat-bed wagon with a central turntable supported by out-riggers for stability. The two 13.5-inch guns produced at Elswick in 1917 were used exclusively in France. Some of the 9.2-inch guns, as we have seen, were stationed in Britain on anti-invasion duties, usually as stop-gaps while more permanent arrangements were made.

Coast-Watching

Up to the First World War, coastguards were administered by the Admiralty as an integral part of the Royal Naval Reserve, attending regular training sessions on static drill ships until 1911 when these were phased out. After then, reservists spent more time at sea, so that as soon as they were mobilised in August 1914, they could join their assigned ships. The resultant gap in the coast defences was often filled by their wives who continued to carry out their observation and reporting duties, sometimes aided by Sea Scouts equipped with rockets, whose less-spectacular semaphore skills also came in handy. Customs officers and fishermen were also briefed to look out for signs of enemy activity, such as minelaying. Numbers of volunteer coast watchers were recruited, particularly to patrol stretches of the east coast. Observation posts were established in even the remotest corners of the British Isles. St Kilda, 100 miles off mainland Scotland, was the site of an Admiralty War Signal Station with a wireless station and three Ops—the highest on Conachair some 1,400 feet (430 metres) above sea-level—reporting on ship movements in the north Atlantic. Regular communication was achieved with Aultbea on Loch Ewe and provisioning by the depot ships *Manco* from Stornoway and *Cyclops* from Scapa. This post was a mixed blessing for the tiny population of St Kilda, causing the bombardment by U-boat in May 1918, but also bringing four years of external contacts and prosperity.

The 'Y' Service

In 1907, the Post Office had built wireless stations at Hunstanton and Skegness with 122-foot-high (37.5-metre-high) wooden masts. The Admiralty also had a wireless station at Waltham, south of Grimsby. It was soon discovered that radio-receivers were able to pick up wireless traffic up to at least 300 miles (480 km) away. Coastguard stations and amateur radio hams all reported picking up German naval traffic from the Wilhelmshaven base and elsewhere. At Hunstanton, Lt-Cdr Hippisley set up a dedicated listening station that reported to Room 40 in the Old Admiralty Building in Whitehall. The primary aim of the three sites in Hunstanton, using aerials mounted on the lighthouse, was to eavesdrop on messages being sent to and from airships and hence have a chance of intercepting them on their bombing missions as they crossed the Norfolk coast. Along with the first naval W/T station at Stockton-on-Tees, this was among the earliest of such sites to gather such useful information. While the Hunstanton operations were housed in the lighthouse, supplemented by timber huts, the Stockton-on-Tees operation was carried out from a substantial two-storey building. This building, along with its accompanying powerhouse and a security post, occupied a compound surrounded by iron railings, 7 feet (2.1 metres) in height, with barbed-wire entanglement and an internal patrol track. Aerials were mounted on solid concrete foundations and feeds into the operations room were specially insulated. The Stockton station picked up signals from Zeppelins, U-boats, and surface vessels. By the end of the war, a network of some twenty Royal Naval Wireless Stations, such as Cullercoats on the coast of Northumberland, covered the entire east and south coasts of the British Isles from the Shetland Isles to the Lizard, with a further eight sited around the Irish coast, and a couple, including that on St Kilda, covering the Western Isles and Anglesey and the approaches to the Mersey. Intelligence was collated at the Admiralty and passed out to those naval units that might benefit from advance knowledge of the enemy's specific intentions.

Strategy and Tactics

Throughout the war, there was very little real change in the strategy involved in defending against invasion. Initially, light forces watching the coast would have harassed the enemy and attempted to delay his establishment of a bridgehead, while awaiting naval forces that would arrive to prevent reinforcement and resupply. The garrisons in the defended ports, along with fortified lines, provided anchor points for the defending forces. Some 10–20 miles behind the coastal screen were stronger formations that would have counterattacked any advance the enemy might have attempted. Backing up those forward divisions were the larger elements of Central Force. The key lay in retaining armies at home that were large enough to overwhelm an invading force. The significant change made by French when he became GOC Home Forces in 1916 was to push his forward lines as close as possible to the coast—onto the very seashore even—while maintaining the ability to move large bodies of troops to pressure points at short notice. By the final few months of the war, many home defence troops had been sent to France to counter the German army's final throw; however, fortunately, the enemy's strength was sapped. The remaining defence forces were then moved inland to operate as mobile columns to respond to incursions as needed.

4

Defending the Homeland: The Role of the Navy

While the dreadnoughts of the Grand Fleet, gathered in Scapa Flow, remained poised to attack the German fleet if it sallied forth into the North Sea—whether in support of an invasion or not—other important naval dispositions were being made around the coasts of the British Isles.

Guard Ships and Floating Batteries

Rendered redundant by the new super-battleships, the old pre-dreadnoughts were nevertheless useful as coast defence ships. Good examples of such vessels were the nine battleships of the *Majestic*-class, launched in the 1890s, whose firepower made them into formidable floating coast defence batteries. The 9th Battle Squadron—consisting of *Mars*, *Hannibal*, *Magnificent*, and *Victorious* (base for the senior naval officer in 1914)—had mobilised in the Humber, and on the day war broke out, they were on station, with *Mars* in the role of port guard ship. One reason for their presence in the Humber was to provide protection prior to the completion of the new 6-inch batteries at Sunk Island and Stallingborough. Late in 1914, as *Hannibal* and *Magnificent* were deployed to Scapa Flow as guard ships while the coast defences there were being organised, the remaining pair were joined by *Majestic* and *Jupiter*. Within a short while, *Jupiter* was moved on as guard ship in the Tyne.

Admiral Fisher had created a system where reserve vessels, named the Third Fleet, were held ready for mobilisation, when their nucleus crews would be completed from the pool of seamen held in naval barracks, and members of the RNR being recalled to duty. In 1914, this Third Fleet consisted of four battle squadrons, each comprising four pre-dreadnoughts. The 7th and 8th, supported by five cruiser squadrons, were stationed at Devonport, and the

5th and 6th at Portland, all protecting the western approaches to the English Channel. In 1915, the 6th Battle Squadron was redeployed to Nore Command at Sheerness, detaching HMS *Grenville* to Dover. The 5th Battle Squadron, meanwhile, remained at Portland.

Following service with the Channel Fleet at Portland and with the Dover Patrol in operations off the Belgian coast, all the individual *Majestics* were consigned to support roles. *Illustrious* (which had begun the war as the trawler depot ship at Loch Ewe), *Mars*, and *Victorious*, for instance, were all partly disarmed, many of their guns going to the new *Lord Clive*-class monitors. Most were then despatched to the Dardanelles (where *Majestic* was sunk) as troopships, but, apart from *Caesar* (which was sent to Gibraltar as guard ship), the others returned home, employed as harbour guard ships or depot ships: *Hannibal*, *Magnificent*, and *Victorious* at Scapa; *Illustrious* in the Tyne; *Mars* at Invergordon; *Prince George* at Chatham; and *Jupiter* at Devonport. Late in the war, *Illustrious* would give up her four 12-inch guns to arm the Kitchener and Roberts coast batteries, straddling the mouth of the Tyne (see Chapter 3). Other pre-dreadnoughts serving in similar roles were the *Canopus*-class battleships *Albion* (built in 1901) and *Goliath* (1898). *Albion* returned safely from the Dardanelles and was moored in the Humber between Killinghome and Sunk Island, but *Goliath*, following service as guard ship at Loch Ewe in 1914, was sunk in the Dardanelles campaign. These battleships were armed with four 12-inch guns in barbettes, twelve 6-inch guns in sponsons along the sides of the ship, ten 12-pounders, and six 3-pounders, a match or better for any raider that might be trying its luck raiding coastal ports. HMS *Benbow* (built in 1885), one of an even older generation of battleships of the *Admiral*-class, had been guard ship at Greenock in the Clyde until 1909 when she was retired. Even some of the newer ships were pressed into port service. HMS *Hercules*, a *Colossus*-class dreadnought of 1910 that had survived an accident in 1913, became the floating HQ of the Senior Naval Officer at Harwich for a time before returning to the Grand Fleet.

King Edward VII had requested that the pre-dreadnought battleship, launched in 1904 and bearing his name, should always carry an admiral's flag. The 3rd Battle Squadron comprised the eight ships of the class, but following a long period at Scapa Flow in support of the Grand Fleet and the Northern Patrol, *King Edward VII* struck a mine and sank in January 1916, and two of the squadron, *Africa* and *Britannia*, were detached for tours of duty in the Mediterranean. In April 1916, a second bombardment of Great Yarmouth and Lowestoft was once more widely regarded as a prelude to invasion. As a quick response, the five remaining vessels of the 3rd Battle Squadron—*Commonwealth*, *Dominion*, *Hibernia*, *Hindustan*, and *Zealandia*, now joined for a while by HMS *Dreadnought* herself as leader—were moved to Sheerness to threaten any invasion fleet approaching the east coast. They were given the added support of three armoured cruisers and eight destroyers. The *King Edward VII*-class ships were heavily armed with four 12-inch guns in twin turrets fore and aft; four 9.2-inch guns mounted singly in turrets; ten 6-inch guns in an armoured casemate amidships; twelve 12- and fourteen 3-pounders along the sides; and two Maxims. It was exactly that unsatisfactory mix of weapons that had made the all-big-gun dreadnoughts so attractive, but in the roles of floating coast defence batteries or interdicting an invasion force of transports escorted by destroyers, the firepower of these obsolete battleships would have been overpowering. After a refit, following her ramming of a U-boat in 1915, and the spell at Sheerness and in the English Channel, *Dreadnought* spent the last two years of the war as a guard ship in the Thames Estuary.

It was not only old battleships that found themselves becalmed. At Chatham, HMS *Wallaroo*, a cruiser of 1890, was rearmed as harbour guard ship in 1914. In order to meet the same temporary, but immediate need for cover that we have seen in the Humber, the 1892 cruiser *Crescent* was moored in Scapa Flow from early-1915 until the new 6-inch, 12-pounder, or 4-inch QF batteries had been completed in Hoy Sound. While her tender remained on station in Scapa, *Crescent* was redeployed to Rosyth. The 1893-vintage cruiser *Hermione* spent the war from 1915 onwards on station at Yarmouth and Cowes on the Isle of Wight and at Southampton. In the Tyne, *Illustrious* was replaced as guard ship by the cruiser *St George*.

With the ability to punch way above their weight, monitors were particularly useful as floating batteries. At the outbreak of war, three new river monitors, being built for the Brazilian navy in British yards, were immediately requisitioned by the Admiralty. HMS *Humber*, *Mersey*, and *Severn*, each mounting two 6-inch guns in forward turrets, were stationed in the Wash for a short while in November 1914; this was in response to an invasion scare precipitated by the shelling of Great Yarmouth earlier in the month. These shallow-draught vessels were ideal for the location, but soon after the immediate danger was judged to have passed, they were posted off to Africa. The German attack on Great Yarmouth had highlighted the impotence of the single ship stationed for its defence. HMS *Halcyon* was a *Dryad*-class Torpedo Gunboat of 1,070 tons, armed with two 4.7-inch, four 6-pounder guns, and five 18-inch torpedo tubes. She was one of five in the class built in 1894, and converted in 1908 as minesweeping gunboats. In the attack, she had only been saved by a smokescreen hastily put up by one of the resident six destroyers unable to take any more effective action in time. Clearly, ships with heavier guns were needed. The *Abercrombie*-class monitors had an armament of two 14-inch guns and two 12-pounders, plus one 3-pounder and an AA pom-pom. HMS *Havelock* and *Roberts* were both completed in 1915 and despatched to the Dardanelles. They then returned home early in 1916 and served as

Eastbourne: Martello Tower 73, the 'Wish Tower', dates from the first decade of the eighteenth century, when an invasion by Napoleon's armies was anticipated.

Portsmouth Dockyard: HMS *Warrior* represents the first in a new breed of armoured steam warship.

Fort Paull on the Humber Estuary: a 7-inch Armstrong RML gun of *c*. 1880; it weighed 7 tons and fired a shell of 114 lb (60 kg) a maximum distance of 4,600 yards (4.25 km).

Plymouth, Fort Bovisand: the granite casemates of one of 'Palmerston's Follies'.

Forth defences: the Battery Observation Post of Carlingnose Battery, part of the inner defences, on the line of the Forth Railway Bridge.

Falmouth: a 12-pounder QF battery at Pendennis Castle.

Newhaven Fort: a 6-inch Mk VII BL gun installed in an original emplacement.

Isle of Sheppey: the BOP of Fletcher Battery, added to the Medway defences in 1918 with two 9.2-inch guns.

St Mawes Castle: a 12-pounder QF gun emplacement, one of six above the castle on the opposite side of Falmouth Roads from Pendennis Castle.

Dunree Fort, Lough Swilly: one of several rehomed 4.7-inch guns.

Dunree Fort, Lough Swilly: a 6-inch BL gun with a loopholed concrete screen to protect its crew from snipers on the heights behind and above the fort.

Killingholme Battery: the towers, now demolished, carried 12-pounder QF guns.

Tynemouth Castle: the right-hand 6-inch gun position, looking across to the mouth of the Tyne.

Tynemouth: the upper stages of the six-storey BOP for the Tyne Turrets.

Alderney: the octagonal OP above the 12-pounder battery on Roselle Point.

Lough Swilly: the two 9.2-inch gun pits at Lenan Head Fort looking across to Fanad Head.

Above left: Broughty Castle: the BOP built into the fifteenth-century tower house.

Above right: Broughty Castle: the caponier with loops for musketry and Maxim guns.

Aberdeen: the Victorian gateway of Torry Point Battery.

Hoxa Head, Scapa Flow: emplacements for two of the four 4-inch QF guns mounted here.

Pembroke Dock: Llanion Barracks housing much of the Milford Haven garrison.

Alderney: one of several pillbox/OPs built on earlier emplacements in Fort Albert overlooking Braye Harbour, and converted into machine-gun posts by the German garrison in the Second World War.

Hartley: a loopholed latrine on the defended perimeter of Roberts Battery, the more northerly of the Tyne Turrets. (*NZ342759*)

Plymouth: the blockhouse with embrasures for Maxim guns at Fort Bovisand.

Portland: a pillbox on the heights above the East Weare batteries. (*SY706735*)

Lough Swilly: a blockhouse acting as a caponier in the ditch of Lenan Head Fort.

Plymouth: one of three caponiers added to Hawkins Battery.

Left: Isle of Wight: a blockhouse on the perimeter wall of Cliff End Fort.

Below: Spurn Point: a blockhouse on the perimeter wall at beach level.

Spurn Point: a machine-gun position flanking the perimeter wall.

The hexagonal pillbox for three machine guns on hollow sub-rectangular plinths at Mud Row, Sheppey, Kent. (*TR007719*)

An oval pillbox for two machine guns at Stockbury, Kent. (*TQ838615*)

A square infantry pillbox at Stockbury, Kent. (*TQ852619*)

A circular infantry pillbox with armoured doors and four loopholes at different heights at Alderton, Suffolk, one of a pair covering a beach exit. (*TM345424*)

A hexagonal pillbox with armoured doors and five loopholes, one of a pair covering the main Norwich road, behind Great Yarmouth, Norfolk. (*TG506091*)

Above left: Chattenden, Kent: one of several multi-sided two-man guard posts at the magazine complex. (*TQ757728*)

Above right: Lodge Hill: the blockhouse integrated into the perimeter of the AA battery. (*TQ758741*)

Murray's Post: an infantry redoubt behind Godwin 9.2-inch battery on the Holderness coast, showing musketry loops and a machine-gun mounting.

Above left: Purfleet powder magazines and rifle ranges were protected by this submarine spotting/AA/close defence tower with armoured loopholes. (*TQ793538*)

Above right: A circular pillbox built of concrete blocks at Wayford Bridge (TG350250) on the River Ant Line in north-east Norfolk.

North Weald Redoubt: the caponier providing access across the ditch of this London Mobilisation Centre.

The *M29*-class monitor *M33*: built in 1915, she survived two world wars and is now a museum ship in Portsmouth Dockyard.

Portsmouth Dockyard: Admiralty House, the local RN headquarters.

Right: The Nab Tower, the only one completed of a planned twenty being built as an anti-submarine barrage across the Straits of Dover.

Below: Dorchester: the Officers' Mess of the Dorsetshire Regiment's depot.

Aberdeen: Bridge of Don Barracks where twenty-four battalions of the Gordon Highlanders' were raised during the war.

Lynford Manor, Mundford, Norfolk: HQ of the GHQ's Northern Army from early 1916, covering the beaches and invasion routes of Norfolk and Lincolnshire.

Willesden, north-west London: the Pound Lane drill hall of the HQ and 'A', 'B', 'D', and 'E' Companies, 9th Battalion, Middlesex Regiment (TF).

Arnold, Nottinghamshire: the drill hall of 'F' Company, 8th Battalion, Sherwood Foresters (TF), whose first- and second-line battalions were serving on the Western Front, and whose third-line battalion was in the North Midland Reserve Brigade at Saltfleet on the Lincolnshire coast. It then became home to a company of the 3rd Battalion, Nottinghamshire Volunteer Regiment (VTC).

A Lewis gun mounted on a biplane.

Montrose: flight-sheds dating from just before the First World War.

Tadcaster, North Yorkshire: a GS hangar, dating from 1916, and often referred to as a 'Belfast Truss' hangar because of the construction of its timber, lattice roof.

Hainault Farm: a twin aeroplane shed, reportedly recently demolished.

Stow Maries, Essex: officers' quarters on this remarkably well-preserved First World War fighter aerodrome.

Plymouth, Mount Batten: a pair of side-opening, Admiralty F-type seaplane sheds at this RNAS base.

Hornsea Mere, East Yorkshire: the workshops of the RNAS seaplane base.

Calshot, Hampshire: the GS hangar, one of an important group of surviving RNAS hangars.

Lee-on-Solent, Hampshire: one of three seaplane hangars on the site. Across the road to the left is the slipway into Southampton Water.

East Fortune, Lothian: the MT Section, later adapted as a gymnasium, on the First World War side of the airfield.

Above left: Catfirth, Shetland: a barrack hut at this RNAS seaplane base.

Above right: Kilnsea, East Yorkshire: acoustic or sound mirror representing an attempt at an early warning system. (*TA411167*)

A 13-pounder AA gun mounted on a Peerless lorry. (*Photographed at IWM, Duxford*)

Lodge Hill AA site showing one of the two emplacements for 3-inch, 20-cwt AA guns in the foreground, with crew room and administration block behind. (*TQ758740*)

Monkhams Hill: emplacement for a 3-inch, 20-cwt AA gun on one of two AA sites defending the Waltham Abbey gunpowder mills. The hold-fast dates from the Second World War, but the platform and magazine are from *c.* 1916. (*TL386024*)

Burray Ness, Orkney Mainland: one of the two emplacements for naval 4-inch dual-purpose guns with the magazine behind. (*ND506965*)

SMS *Moltke* a German battlecruiser launched in 1910 armed with ten 28-cm (11-inch), twelve 15-cm (5.9-inch), and twelve 88-mm (3.5-inch) guns. She took part in the bombardment of Great Yarmouth and Hartlepool in 1914, taking a hit from a 6-inch shell in the process.

Hartlepool, the Heugh-Lighthouse Battery: a 6-inch gun-pit and director tower.

Hartlepool, the Heugh-Lighthouse Battery: the director tower that held the depression range finder guard ships at Lowestoft and Great Yarmouth, respectively. The Dover Patrol contained no less than ten monitors, mainly of the newly built *Lord Clive*-class, employed in the bombardment of the German-occupied Belgian ports known to be the lairs of U-boats and suspected of harbouring invasion fleets. Lowestoft also enjoyed the protection of HMS *Glow-worm*, an *Insect*-class river gunboat, designed for service on the China Station and moored in Hamilton Dock from 1916. Another similar vessel, HMS *Cockchafer*, was based at Brightlingsea. These gunboats were armed with two 6-inch guns, two 12-pounders, and Maxims.

General Fleet Dispositions Early in the War

Following mobilisation, the Grand Fleet had sailed for Scapa Flow as a counter to a German invasion. There were elements of the Grand Fleet in Cromarty, and the Battle Cruiser Squadrons were based in Cromarty and Rosyth, poised to sally forth speedily to intercept raiders or to scout ahead of the Grand Fleet's squadrons of dreadnoughts. Some pre-dreadnoughts were retained with the Grand Fleet, leading from the front, and expendable were the fleet to stumble upon a minefield, the fate, as we have seen, which befell *King Edward VII*. Harwich Force was integral to the Grand Fleet, but tasked with operating as a separate unit. Its role was to carry out reconnaissance in the southern North Sea; to ensure the safety of merchant shipping crossing between the Thames to the neutral Netherlands; to support the Dover Patrol (see below) in keeping the eastern approaches to the English Channel secure; and to prevent enemy minelaying operations. It was also meant to support Grand Fleet actions when called upon. It consisted of eight light cruisers and two flotilla leaders with forty-five destroyers. During the course of the war, a number of submarine flotillas also operated from Harwich.

Squadrons of capital ships were based at Sheerness and on the Swin anchorage off the Essex coast, watching the Thames Estuary and the east coast. Portland and Devonport were bases for others covering the English Channel. Portsmouth, traditionally 'home of the fleet', provided the infrastructure for it to function. The dockyard, employing in excess of 25,000 men and later on many women as well, carried out refits on 1,200 vessels, including forty battleships, during the war, as well as constructing two new battleships and new types of submarines. Millions of pounds worth of naval stores was stocked and issued, and vast quantities more were shipped to France. Shells and other munitions were manufactured and stored. Above all, thousands of recruits were enrolled, trained, and posted, and the WRNS became established. Portsmouth was also the centre of operations for ensuring that the constant stream of ships carrying troops and materiel across the Channel—mainly between Southampton and Le Havre—was protected by the escorts available. As well as these major naval bases, a whole network of smaller ones was needed to implement Admiral Fisher's flotilla-based defence initiative.

Complementing the battle squadrons of capital ships, cruisers were allocated areas of operation: the 7th Cruiser Squadron's area was the southern North Sea; the 8th at Portland, supported the two battle squadrons in the western English Channel; the 12th operated further west still into the Atlantic linking up with the French navy; the 11th Cruiser Squadron was responsible for the West of Ireland Patrol; and the 10th constituted the Northern Patrol.

Anti-Invasion Defence and Patrol Flotillas

Carrying out Fisher's established strategy, the fleet mobilisation in August 1914 saw the dispersal of the flotillas of destroyers and torpedo-boats to their war stations. They would patrol the North Sea to ensure that the Grand Fleet might receive the earliest warning of an invasion necessary for a prompt response. The 8th Destroyer Flotilla at Granton, in the Forth, was joined by the cruiser HMS *Sentinel*. Immingham, on the south bank of the Humber, had only opened in 1912, but its modern facilities, compared to the overcrowded docks of Hull across the river, soon attracted use by the Royal Navy. The 9th Destroyer Flotilla, with the cruiser *St George* as depot ship and supported by the cruisers *Patrol* and *Forward*, deployed four vessels in the Humber, plus two in the Tyne and two more at Hartlepool. In July 1914, the destroyers of the 9th Flotilla in the Humber were joined by the 7th Port Defence Flotilla that, renamed the 7th Patrol Flotilla, had been redeployed there from Devonport. Led by the scout cruiser *Skirmisher*, the flotilla of twenty-two destroyers and twelve torpedo boats detached six destroyers at Harwich and six more at Gorleston, Great Yarmouth's naval port, *en route*. The Harwich boats would soon be greatly reinforced to become a significant player in the southern North Sea. By May 1915, as numbers of vessels had been detached for other duties, the 7th and 9th Flotillas were combined, with eighteen destroyers, the cruiser *Patrol*, and the depot ship *St George*. The modern purpose-built depot ships *Woolwich* and *Greenwich* were based with the larger destroyer flotillas at Rosyth, Harwich, and Scapa Flow. Older, converted cruisers or merchant ships served as depot ships at Cromarty and Leith (HMS *Tyne*); Devonport (HMS *Talbot*); and Buncrana, in Lough Swilly, and Chatham (HMS *Hecla*). Servicing the Grand Fleet's multiple destroyer flotillas (more than ninety vessels altogether) at Scapa Flow and the *Greenwich* were the converted cruisers *Blake* and *Leander*.

Initially, two dozen destroyers formed the nucleus of the Dover Patrol, and the Downs Boarding Flotilla carried out the duties of the Examination

Service, monitoring the comings and goings of shipping through the Straits. Local or Port Defence Flotillas comprising old destroyers and torpedo-boats were stationed at Pembroke Dock, Chatham, Devonport, Portsmouth, Queenstown, and the Nore. Their role was to supplement the fixed defences against raids and to patrol the approaches at night. All around the coast, naval forces were allocated particular patrol areas. Based, for instance, on Holyhead and Queenstown, the Irish Sea Hunting Flotilla was tasked with safeguarding merchant shipping approaching Avonmouth or the Mersey. Ports along the south coast, such as Newhaven, became bases for escorts seeing troop ships safely across the Channel to Boulogne. Granton and Port Edgar (HMS *Gunner* and HMS *Columbine* respectively) were both on the south bank of the Forth. Taking the names of their original base ships, they held the torpedo-boats, destroyers, and minesweepers of the Grand Fleet's Southern Force from 1917 to the end of the war.

The second dimension to Fisher's defensive plans to intercept a German invasion fleet was provided by the submarines which he saw fulfilling a key role. As was the case with the destroyers, submarine flotillas (totalling sixty-eight boats of the *A-E*-classes) were quickly deployed to the east coast, based in the Forth, as well as in the Tyne and at Immingham, where the 6th Flotilla was split between the two. The 8th Submarine Flotilla with *Adamant* operated out of Harwich from 1914, extending to Great Yarmouth in 1915. Other flotillas were based at Sheerness, Devonport, and Dover, with another at Ardrossan at the mouth of the Clyde. By 1915, submarine flotillas had been deployed to the Tees, with a single boat at Hartlepool, and to a newly built base at Blyth. Like the destroyers' depot ships, the submarines were serviced by a complete cross-section of naval shipping. In the Tyne was the battleship *Bonaventure*, which also controlled the area's light cruiser patrols, and its tender—the gunboat *Hebe*. Among the others, based at fifteen different ports—including Great Yarmouth, Harwich, Chatham, Portsmouth, Blyth, the Tees, Gosport, and Devonport—were the purpose-built depot ships *Alecto*, *Forth*, *Maidstone*, *Titania*, *Lucia*, and *Pigmy*. Both *Sokoto* at Scapa and *Sobo* at Cromarty were bought in by the Admiralty to serve as floating torpedo dispensers. Built in 1889 as a depot ship for torpedo-boats, *Vulcan* serviced submarines at Leith, Berehaven, and Blyth.

The whole notion of using submarines to defeat an amphibious invasion force was controversial and it was left to Commodore (Submarines) Keyes at the Admiralty to decide that they should not be wasted attacking small craft, instead reserved for preventing capital ships from bombarding the coast defences in the prelude to an invasion and large transports from landing stores in the follow-up. The achievement of reinforcement and resupply would be the major challenges for an invading force, and submarines could be decisive in preventing it. For anything more ambitious than a mere raid, it would be

Naval bases in the British Isles during the First World War

Map to show ports with an anti-invasion role: fleet, flotilla, local defence, patrol, minesweeping, anti-submarine, and blockading force bases.

necessary for an invasion fleet to capture a port with facilities for unloading heavy cargo; this task could be made impossible by the constant harassment by the patrol flotillas, and the judicious sinking of enemy transports by submarines, in order to block access channels. The Royal Navy had started the war with over seventy submarines to the enemy's twenty-two, and would build many more during the conflict. Keyes was one of many who anticipated problems in expecting these vulnerable craft to operate at two levels: as everyday patrols with the consequent wear and tear on boats and crews and, at the same time, as a strategic quick reaction strike force. Submarine crews were to suffer, proportionately, the highest number of casualties of any of the armed services during the First World War.

The Dover Patrol

Under the command of Vice-Admiral Sir Richard Bacon, the Dover Patrol was charged with the protection of the Straits across to the Flanders Coast and the southern North Sea. It formed around a nucleus of the twelve *Tribal-* or *F*-class destroyers built in 1907–09 by a number of yards, all to differing designs, but each displacing 870–970 tons and mounting a mixture of 4-inch and 12-pounder guns.

In addition, the Patrol included everything from tugs to boom-defence vessels and converted fishing boats used as minesweepers, as auxiliary patrol craft, on anti-submarine duties, and, eventually, as convoy escorts. The force was based on the old cruiser HMS *Attentive* (built in 1904), and was supported by an iron foundry, the Dover Engineering Works. A further element of the Patrol was based in Ramsgate. Here, the Downs Boarding Flotilla consisted of twenty or so adapted fishing vessels, joined late in 1915 by a further group of ten drifters and fifteen Thames steam tugs, which were used for rescue or boarding. One of these, *Little Java* (1905), became HMS *Carcass*. The steam yacht *Surprise* was hired as guard ship at Ramsgate, and by 1918, another yacht, *Surf*, was serving as the nominal base for Rear Admiral (Controlled Minefields) at Dover. By 1916, the Dover Patrol consisted of *Attentive*, twenty-five destroyers, three torpedo-boats, and eight patrol boats, with the *Riviera*, a cross-channel steamer, converted to carry four seaplanes. Also based in Dover was the 5th Submarine Flotilla with ten boats and their depot ship *Arrogant*. Ten monitors completed this formidable line-up. The Downs Boarding Flotilla later gained five dedicated armed boarding vessels and retained its ten tugs.

The Northern Patrol

The Tenth Cruiser Squadron was the basis of the Northern Patrol based at Swarbacks Minn, on the west coast of Mainland Shetland. The original squadron consisted of nine *Edgar*-class, protected cruisers of 7,350 tons launched in 1890–1902 and heavily armed with two single 9.2-inch guns fore and aft, ten single 6-inch guns (split port and starboard), and sixteen 3-pounders. Some of them subsequently lost their 9.2-inch guns for a pair of 6-inch guns forward. Of these nine, *Edgar*, *Endymion*, *Grafton*, and *Theseus* all went to the Dardanelles; *Hawke* was torpedoed in the North Sea in 1914; and *St George* served as a depot ship in the Tyne. *Crescent* became guard ship at Hoy, as did *Royal Arthur* at Scapa, and *Gibraltar* became the depot ship for the Northern Patrol. The first official line-up consisted of the surviving eight *Edgars* plus the armed merchant cruisers (AMC) *Teutonic*, *Mantua*, and *Alsatian*. It was decided that the duties of the Northern Patrol, which consisted mainly of maintaining a blockade of sea traffic into the German ports, were beneath the warships of the Grand Fleet, and in July 1915, the strength was recorded as twenty-four AMCs. Over the course of the war, until the force was stood down in December 1917, some sixty liners and other merchant ships were hired and armed for the purpose. The commander was Admiral Sir Dudley de Chair, flying his flag initially in *Crescent*, but then in the AMC *Alsatian*, formerly of the Canadian Pacific Line. She was armed with 4.7-inch guns, soon to be upgraded to eight 6-inch, with two 6-pounder AA guns, the normal complement for most of these liners. Most were based in Lerwick, in the Shetland Isles, but some, like the White Star liner *Teutonic*, often operated out of Liverpool, where the AMCs *Celtic* and *Laconia* were also based.

In 1915, Admiral de Chair wrote a pamphlet describing the work of these AMCs. When a ship was sighted, the cruiser would close, firing two blank shells to draw the attention of the intercepted vessel to the signal instructing her to heave to. An armed party of an officer and five ratings would then go aboard—a risky operation in itself. If the intercepted vessel was a small trawler or tramp steamer then the boarding party's inspection could be brief, and both vessels might quickly proceed on their way. In the case of a large merchant-man or liner, however, it would take some time to ensure that cargo manifests were accurate and that the possibilities of false decks and hidden compartments had been thoroughly explored. Both ships, in that case, would steam in convoy at half-speed until the boarding officer was satisfied that all was in order. This was to avoid both ships becoming sitting-ducks for any passing U-boats that customarily employed a policy best summed up as 'sink first, and if there's anyone left alive to question, find out who they were and where they were going'. Suspect vessels could be escorted to neutral ports or impounded in the UK. Admiral de Chair provides a range of examples of contraband, perhaps the most surprising being the cargo of bouncing onions that turned out to be balls of rubber—definitely on the forbidden list. The patrolling AMCs attempted to maintain intervals of around 20 miles (32 km) in order both to prevent blockade runners slipping through the net and to provide mutual support. Several of the AMCs were torpedoed in the course of their work. Ironically, the *Lusitania* had been among those liners proposed for conversion to an AMC, but her distinctive silhouette and large size had disqualified her from this dangerous role. Though the Patrol's primary role was to enforce the blockade on Germany, the ships acted as picquets, watching out for enemy activity generally, particularly anything pointing to the transit of an invasion fleet.

East Coast Patrols

The intentions of Admiral Fisher regarding the purpose of the anti-invasion flotillas were quite clear. The torpedo boats and coastal destroyers, the very vessels of which patrol flotillas were composed, were deployed specifically to attack hostile forces attempting raids or full-scale invasion. However, from the moment that those very flotillas had become established in their east coast bases, it was clear that they were subject to conflicting demands. The destroyers and torpedo boats of the 7th Patrol and 9th Destroyer Flotillas in the Humber, the Tyne, and Great Yarmouth, positioned to repel an enemy invasion, were also required to carry out wide-ranging patrols. The Immingham boats were instructed to carry out a limited programme of night patrols, in order to ensure that the enemy might be denied the element of surprise. Michael Hanna has shown how *TB1* spent thirty-three successive nights at 'Action Stations', anchored off Spurn Point, or patrolling the entrance to the Humber Estuary. Despite assurances by the German navy that mines would never be used, the war was less than a week old before mines were being laid off the British coast, resulting in the loss of lives and vessels. Such offensive minelaying operations intensified over the next few months, with extensive enemy minefields becoming established off the Tyne, the Humber, and down the East Anglian coast. It was soon realised that providing that the locations of German mines were clearly recorded, it made more sense to attempt to join them up and to use them as a basis for a defensive minefield rather than to undertake the hazardous business of trying to keep on removing them. The British East Coast Minefield effectively stretched from south of Berwick-upon-Tweed to a point just south of Flamborough Head. Consequently, efforts were concentrated on maintaining a swept channel inside the minefields, 10 miles (16 km) wide, running from Dover up the east coast, past Flamborough Head, and on up to the Firth of Forth, permanently available to coastal shipping.

This discontinuous barrier provided opportunities for enemy minelayers to threaten the integrity of the official route up and down the east coast. The Patrol Flotillas were now directed to engage in more aggressive patrolling of this channel in order to counter enemy attempts to lay fresh mines covertly, and thus undermine merchant skippers' confidence. Although merchant ships were held overnight at Great Yarmouth, Black Deep, and the Downs, only being released once the channel had been swept each morning, there was still the possibility that minelaying U-boats or seaplanes might deposit mines unseen. As such activities posed an ever-increasing danger, the Patrol Flotillas were allocated areas in which a continuous stream of vessels, patrolling singly, would maintain the closest possible watch for mines. These patrol areas were allocated to groups of six boats. One group of Immingham boats, for instance, was given the beat from Spurn Point to Flamborough Head, with another group being given the southern beat from Spurn to Cromer. It was intended that half the boats would be at sea at any one time, placing them at intervals of 20 miles (32 km). Additionally, every few days, six destroyers, in company with *Skirmisher*, would carry out sweeps farther afield—beyond the known minefields. However, the torpedo boats were to spend much more time at sea than was originally envisaged, and spells of ten or eleven successive days on patrol were not uncommon.

Before too long, it became apparent to Rear Admiral Ballard—the admiral in charge of patrols—that his patently contradictory orders presented an impossible task. To mount a comprehensive patrol and early warning screen, while at the same time maintaining a viable strike force, was unattainable with his available vessels. Even with the rapidly expanding Auxiliary Patrol Service, Ballard initially had barely 100 vessels, many of which should have long been retired, to patrol the 600 miles (960 km) of the east coast. The dispersal of the available forces by this form of patrolling was eventually recognised as undermining their intended function in the event of an invasion. Admiral Ballard therefore relinquished his coastal destroyers and cruisers, which would revert to constituting a quick-reaction force. This would leave the patrols to be carried out by the smaller craft, under Rear Admiral Charlton, who had been appointed to organise such operations from east coast ports.

The Royal Naval Auxiliary Patrol Service (APS)

The RNR had been established as early as 1859, but in 1910, a new section, the RNR (Trawler Section), was brought on board. The next year saw the phasing out of most of the RNR's static drill ships, leaving only a small number still in operation. This meant that all RNR personnel were required to put in more regular sea service. The trawler men of course spent their lives at sea and were the best qualified of all the reservists to make a contribution to the war at sea. The use of converted fishing vessels as minesweepers had been explored before the war, and 200 trawlers were duly requisitioned on the outbreak of war, while others had been built to Admiralty specifications, essentially for wartime use. As well as these trawlers, all around the coast, many other boats (such as tugs, paddle steamers, and steam yachts) were requisitioned for a multitude of tasks, the main ones being coastal patrols and minesweeping. During the war, over 700 minesweepers were commissioned. Apart from the purpose-built Fleet minesweepers, the rest were all improvised and included converted gunboats; over 500 trawlers and drifters; and five flotillas of civilian paddle-steamers based at Grimsby, Harwich, Portsmouth, Sheerness, and Larne. Lowestoft was the principal port for minesweepers on the east coast, keeping the swept channel clear. It was believed that any increase in enemy minelaying activity signalled the start of an invasion, so it was necessary immediately to clear those mines that might impede units of the Grand Fleet as they sailed to intercept an invasion armada. German minelayers maintained minefields around their own coasts off Heligoland, the Dogger Bank, and off Zeebrugge, but they also regularly laid mines in British coastal waters off Orkney, Stornoway and the Western Isles, Belfast Lough, Lough Swilly, and Liverpool in order to catch unwary shipping, both naval and mercantile, and stretching the minesweepers to the limit.

Minesweepers, however, only formed one part of the APS. In all, as well as 159 hired yachts, there were 627 Admiralty and 1,456 hired trawlers and 323 Admiralty and 1,492 hired drifters. Many of these boats carried out anti-submarine patrols, escorted merchantmen and acted as despatch vessels, tenders, and harbour defence vessels. A number of APS bases were set up around the coast, most with old naval vessels or converted civilian ones as depot ships. These included a paddle-steamer at Ipswich; cruisers at Ardrossan, Granton, Grimsby, and North Shields; and the ancient frigate *Actaeon*, formerly *Ariadne* of 1859, as the Sheerness APS base, and the almost as ancient 1867 corvette *Eclipse* as a mine depot at Plymouth. Trawlers and drifters served as depot ships for minesweepers at Chatham and Great Yarmouth, for the boats of the Northern and Southern Patrols at Kirkcaldy and Falmouth, and for other APS boats at Grimsby, Immingham, Inverness, Oban, and Swansea; requisitioned private steam yachts at Cromarty, Dundee, Great Yarmouth, Holyhead, Milford Haven, Peterhead, and Stornoway; and gunboats at Dover, Lowestoft, and Ramsgate. Scapa Flow hosted a number of APS units: Stromness was the base for a flotilla of yachts and trawlers, known as the Western Patrol, which kept Hoy Sound swept of mines; *Cyclops* and *Venetia* served as the depot for the Northern Flotilla Trawlers, and the pre-dreadnought *Victorious* was depot ship for the armed boarding steamers from

1916. From 1918, Osea Island, off the Essex coast, was set up as a base for coastal motorboats.

Other roles performed by the little boats were the operation and maintenance of boom defences. Belfast Lough, for example, retained a fleet of trawlers servicing the A/S nets obstructing the channel between Northern Ireland and Scotland, while Stranraer was the supply base for the North Channel Patrol, centred on the armed boarding steamer *Tara*, formerly the *Hibernia*. At Poole Harbour, *White Oak*, a drifter launched in 1913, served as depot ship for the drifters that tended the A/S nets from 1914–19. The Whin anchorage (West Swin and Middle Deep) was protected by five booms, serviced by trawlers and drifters based initially at Clacton-on-Sea, and then at Brightlingsea.

The Royal Navy in the Thames

The Nore Force, based at Sheerness, consisted throughout the war of a flotilla of eight destroyers, fourteen torpedo boats, nine patrol boats, a gunboat, and a flotilla of six submarines. While individual vessels came and went, this structure was to remain constant. Additionally, there were seven boarding vessels based at Southend to examine incoming merchant vessels in the Thames Estuary. HMS *Champion* was moored in the Thames between Coalhouse and Cliffe Forts. Launched in 1878 as a sailing corvette, she had served all over the world. She was constructed with an iron frame, covered in steel sheets, with the whole lot sheathed in 2 inches (50 mm) of teak and copper. Reclassified as a third-class cruiser, she was armed with four 6-inch and eight 5-inch guns, with up to eight Nordenfeldt 3- and 6-pounder QF guns and six Maxim machine guns. Her role was to support the examination service by controlling river traffic in and out of London Docks. A new light cruiser of the *Calliope*-class was commissioned in 1916 and named HMS *Champion*. This has led to reports that she was stationed in the Thames as an anti-aircraft ship, when she had in fact spent her time with the Grand Fleet. The old HMS *Champion*'s armament, particularly the QF guns and Maxims, might have been a useful addition to London's AA defences in the early days, but Commander Rawlinson, who ran London's AA defences until 1916, makes no mention of that, despite being a RNVR officer himself.

The Great Northern Mine Barrage

A proposal to lay a minefield stretching the 240 miles (400 km) from the Orkneys to Norway, in order to prevent U-boats from entering the North

Atlantic, was first made in 1916. It would need to be 30 miles (48 km) in depth and would contain 400,000 mines, laid in water up to 900 feet (280 metres) deep. After the USA entered the war and the unrestricted German U-boat campaign had accelerated the devastation of trans-Atlantic commerce, the idea was re-examined. It was particularly attractive to US politicians as it would show that something was being done about the catastrophic shipping losses without serious risk to US personnel and would also provide an outlet for US industry. In September 1917, it was agreed at an Allied Naval Conference to proceed with the plan. The minefield would consist of three sectors. The central Sector 'A' would be 135 miles (215 km) in length and would be the responsibility of the US Navy (USN). A clear passage 10 miles (16 km) wide would be left east of Orkney and the RN would lay the 5 miles (8 km) of this south-westerly Sector 'B'. At the north-eastern end, the RN would also lay the 70 miles (115 km) of Sector 'C 'as far as the Norwegian coast.

As a result of the US Army's refusal to supply sufficient quantities of TNT to the USN, the more efficient Mk 6 'antenna' mine had been developed using alternative explosives, and the number needed could be reduced to 100,000. These mines were effective down to 200 feet (61 metres), reckoned to be the maximum operating depth of submarines, but would still need 80 million feet (24 million metres) of steel cable. The components were made by automotive factories in Detroit and shipped across the Atlantic by a fleet of twenty-four freighters to ports on the west coast of Scotland at Corpach and the Kyle of Lochalsh. From there, they were transported via rail and the Caledonian Canal to the USN's project base at Inverness. A flotilla of ten minelaying vessels was assembled by the USN, consisting of two converted cruisers and eight merchant ships, including four Southern Pacific Line freighters, and two Old Dominion liners, all painted in dazzle camouflage. By October 1918, they had laid around 70,000 mines in rows, ten deep, and at varying depths of 0–240 feet (0–74 metres). The balance of around 30,000 mines in Sectors 'B' and 'C' was laid by RN minelayers, mainly converted cruisers. The minelayers were given close escorts of RN destroyers, with an outer screen of battleships and cruisers from Scapa Flow. A crewmember on USS *Quinnebaug*, formerly the Old Dominion liner SS *Jefferson*, wrote to a friend to report that fourteen minelayers could lay 7,000 mines in one trip. His own ship could carry 610 mines, and he claimed 6,049 mines as the total laid in a single operation. A number of mines were laid at too shallow a depth and had to be lifted and re-laid. Around 5 per cent of mines exploded prematurely during laying, and as many as 12–19 per cent on some particularly bad days, but there appear to have been few casualties. In terms of the result that this $40 million operation sought to achieve, four U-boats were definitely destroyed, plus two probables, and a further two possibles.

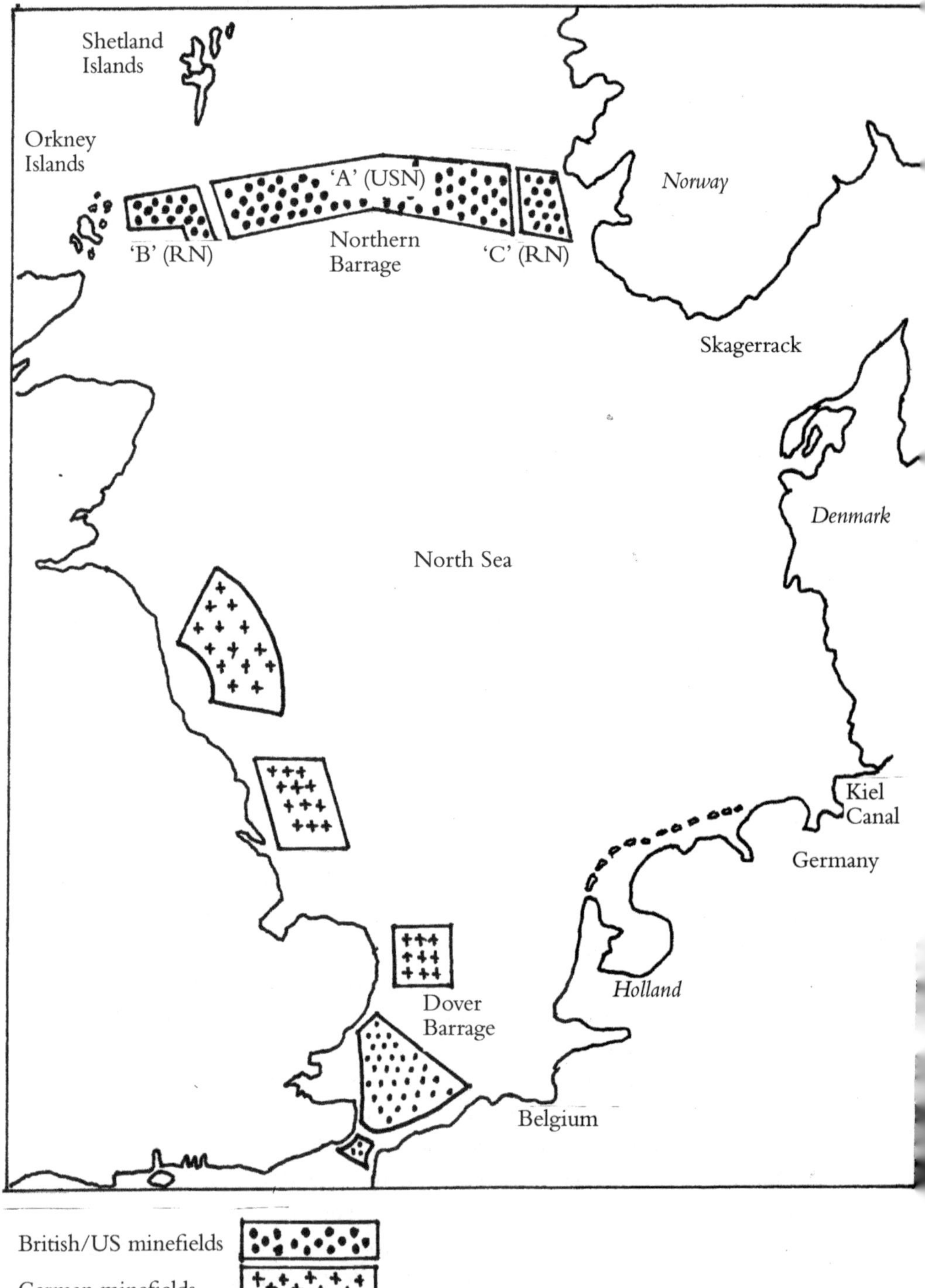

The principal North Sea minefields in the First World War

Map to show the principal defensive minefields around the British Isles.

In April 1919, the clear-up operation commenced. The RN deployed over 400 minesweepers to scour 40,000 square miles (64,000 square km) of ocean. The USN sent out twenty-eight minesweepers and twenty-four sub-chasers, alongside twenty Admiralty trawlers with US crews. All these worked throughout 1919 and reckoned to have swept around 30 per cent of the mines laid. The official opinion was that the remainder had prematurely exploded, been triggered, or had dropped to the seabed. The odd merchant ship was subsequently sunk by floating mines that had shed their cables, and several of the minesweepers were damaged during the lifting operation. As with all preventive measures, there could be no definitive assessment of the effectiveness of the barrage. Any U-boats, deterred from taking the northern route, would have been forced to run the gauntlet of the defences of the Straits of Dover.

The Dover Barrage

Throughout the war, one of the Dover Patrol's tasks was to prevent U-boats slipping through the Straits to attack shipping in the English Channel and in the Western Approaches. There had been a barrage of nets and mines laid from the Goodwin Sands to Dunkirk from early in the war, consisting of nets 1,000 feet (307 metres) in length laid by converted drifters. They were designed to fold up around a U-boat, at the same time signalling its presence by a chemically produced smoke plume. The problem, apart from frequent system malfunctions, was that the nets had to be deep enough to allow surface ships on their normal trips through the Straits to pass safely over them, but this also allowed U-boats to cross on the surface at night. A flotilla of fifteen Barrage Vessels (BVs), each of 275 tons and armed with two 12-pounder guns, patrolled this barrier. They were fitted with powerful searchlights in order to force U-boats to submerge, hopefully then to fall foul of deep-laid mines.

However, by 1917, a more permanent solution to the problem of preventing U-boats from accessing Western Approaches through the English Channel had been proposed as 'Project M-N'. Using the Varne Shoal, a chain of up to sixteen towers would be emplaced roughly a mile apart, linked by booms of steel anti-submarine nets, and backed up by minefields. Each tower would be equipped with guns and searchlights, and manned by around 90 men of the Royal Marines. The idea is credited to Captain Munro of the Royal Marine Engineers, and the design was developed in the office of the Civil Engineer in Chief of the Admiralty, Sir Alexander Gibb, by his assistant, Mr T. G. Menzies, assisted by the future Lord Reith. Each tower comprised three stepped, hexagonal tiers, each 27 feet (8 metres) in height, the base being 200 feet

(60 metres) across. This sub-structure was constructed of reinforced, cellular concrete, allowing it to be flooded and submerged in up to 180 feet (55 metres) of water. The superstructure consisted of a cylinder of steel plates on an external latticework of steel girders, 100 feet (31 metres) high, containing the crew's living quarters, stores, and magazines, with A/S guns mounted on the steel superstructure. A galvanometer-based submarine detection system was also in process of development for installation in the towers. Construction of the towers, each reputed to cost £1 million, commenced at Southwick, at the eastern end of Shoreham Harbour near Brighton. A temporary dam allowed construction in calm waters, also permitting each tower to be floated out on completion, to be towed into position before being dropped onto the seabed. By the end of the war, one tower was more-or-less ready, another had its base and the lower stages of the steel-work in place, while others were still at a much earlier stage. In 1920, that single completed tower was towed to the Nab sandbank, 5 miles (8 km) east of Bembridge on the Isle of Wight, and positioned to act as a Trinity House lighthouse. The Nab Tower remains there, having been converted to automatic working in 1983. The second tower was reduced to scrap in 1924, while all the uncompleted towers had already been used as hardcore. Guy Maunsell was a RE officer involved in the project, and these so-called 'Mystery Towers' were to provide the basic idea for his anti-aircraft towers built in the Thames and Mersey estuaries in the Second World War.

Harbour Defences: A/S Nets, Booms, and Block Ships

Until 1916, capital ships had been fitted with anti-torpedo nets—steel skirts suspended from booms at either deck level or on the waterline. As more powerful torpedoes (fired at greater ranges and arriving more quickly) were developed, it was realised that even if only used at anchor, these nets offered little protection. Nets, however, were still used in attempts to block the passage of submarines into fleet anchorages or to alert the guardians to their presence. Early Indicator Nets, when fouled by a U-boat, sent up a flare, enabling A/S craft to locate the infiltrator and to destroy it. Such a device caused the destruction of *U-8* at Dover in March 1915. A device was also installed at Scapa Flow. Throughout the war, particularly at HMS *Tarlair* (the hydrophone training and experimental base at Aberdour in Fife), one of the goals of the naval scientific researchers was to develop an effective A/S net working through electro-magnetism. Eventually it was the civilian government research station at Parkeston Quay, Harwich, under the direction of Sir Ernest Rutherford, which came up with an effective Indicator Loop. It was this that trapped *U-116* in Hoxa Sound, Scapa, in October 1918, enabling its destruction by remotely detonated mines. Loops were installed in a number of ports, including Berehaven.

It had taken the initiative of the SNO at Cromarty to risk Admiralty disapproval by installing a boom, but this traditional and sensible precaution was subsequently copied in most harbours and anchorages. In 1914, there were converted gunboats or sloops employed as boom defence vessels at Devonport and in the Solent and Spithead. As the war progressed, the need was identified for more of these specialist vessels. Over fifty of these barrage vessels, which we have already seen operating in the Dover Straits, were launched. Mooring vessels of the *Trinculo*-class were employed on boom-defence duties at Granton, Sheerness, Scapa, Portsmouth, and Devonport. Other purpose-built boom-defence vessels, as well as large numbers of lighters and barges, were used in harbours around the British Isles to service a range of obstructions from simple booms as in the Humber or breakwaters at Portland and Plymouth Sound, where gate guards were required to control traffic in and out. Another such obstruction was the pontoon bridge across the Thames, which extended from Tilbury to Gravesend, on the line of the boom that defended against the Spanish Armada in 1588. It was built to facilitate the swift movement of troops between Kent and Essex in the event of an invasion force landing in the Thames Estuary and advancing on London along one or both banks. To enable the essential passage of shipping, the central section was movable, using a flotilla of tenders and boom-defence vessels. This could be a hazardous operation in itself and the tug *Sunbeam* was struck by a merchant ship and sunk in December 1914 while attending the bridge. Portsmouth had been defended by a boom across the entrance to the harbour since medieval times. In 1907, a boom was also laid across the mouth of Southampton Water to defend access to the docks. Located opposite Calshot, it consisted of a row of hulks, secured stem to stern, and anchored to three dolphins—two of them armed with a pair of 12-pounder guns each—to stop torpedo boats smashing through it. This arrangement took up to a week to make secure and had been replaced by 1914 with a far lighter version that could be stored ashore and towed into place. It was serviced by the *Magpie* and *Pike* with half a dozen boom-defence vessels, opening and closing the gate and remaining permanently on station in the Hamble River. It was soon noted that the narrows between Stone Point and Egypt Point on the Isle of Wight also needed defending against submarines. Here, an A/S net was stretched, defended by new batteries and searchlights at each end. The Medway Boom (a simple iron chain installed in 1911) was anchored on Grain Tower (a late Martello) at one end and on Garrison Point Fort, at Sheerness, at the other. The boom at Falmouth is described as an iron network supported at intervals by floating barrels, later replaced by an iron chain. Booms allowed for the passage of shipping, closely controlled by the guns of examination batteries, boats of the examination service, such as the *Champion* in the Thames, and permanently assigned boom-defence vessels.

Where it was more desirable to close a passage permanently, block ships could be used. Access to the fleet anchorage of Scapa Flow was limited to just two channels, covered by shore batteries, guard ships, and patrolling destroyers. The remaining navigable channels were sealed by twenty-one block ships. At Dover, the western entrance to the harbour was blocked by a boom and three sunken ships: the *Livonian*, the *Montrose*, and the *Spanish Prince*, with another boom controlling access through the eastern entrance. At Portland, the old battleship *Hood* was sunk as a block ship.

5

Defending the Homeland: The Role of the Army

The British Army in 1914

Britain's armies in mid-1914, including reserves and Territorials, stood at a little under ¾ million men, including around 250,000 regulars, nearly half of whom were stationed abroad. The Household Cavalry were resident in London or Windsor, and of the twenty-eight cavalry regiments of the line, half were in Britain or Ireland, a third in India, and the rest in South Africa or Egypt. Of the infantry, the four regiments of the Brigade of Guards were home-based, but of the 140 or so battalions comprising the infantry regiments of the line, only fifty were stationed in Britain, with a similar number in India, eighteen in Ireland, and the remainder scattered around the world from Gibraltar to China. On the declaration of war, most home-based battalions had been earmarked for the BEF, and immediately sailed for France; many of those battalions overseas were quickly put on troop ships and sent to join them in France and Belgium. The 2nd Battalion, Queen's Royal West Surrey Regiment, for instance, had sailed from Cape Town, landed at Southampton, and been ferried to Zeebrugge by early October. By the end of 1914, the BEF consisted of three cavalry and ten infantry divisions, including the RN Division. Within a very short time, apart from the Guards Division, the only representatives of the regular infantry remaining on home soil were the reserve or depot battalions.

On the eve of the declaration of war, many TF units were at their various summer camps and troops were sent home to be mobilised at their local drill halls. Once the administrative procedures and medical examinations had been carried out and kit issued, there were often acute accommodation problems. Schools, halls, and cinemas were requisitioned, and many men within walking distance of their mobilisation stations were sent home at night to sleep. In Norwich, men of the 4th Battalion of the Norfolk Regiment (TF) slept in the school in the cathedral precincts, and in Cambridge, the all-Territorial Cambridgeshire Regiment was put up in the Corn Exchange. Each of the fourteen TF divisions was allocated an assembly area where it gathered. The 46th (North Midland) Division converged on Luton Hoo in Bedfordshire, and the 48th (South Midland) Division on Galleywood Common outside Chelmsford. The four battalions of the 4th London Brigade of the 2nd (London) Division (TF) assembled in Hyde Park on 16 August and set off to march to their war stations. Having bivouacked for one night on the way, they arrived in Watford and Luton, and Hemel Hempstead and Hatfield the next day. Their artillery—the 5th, 6th, and 7th Brigades, RFA (TF)—accompanied them to billets in and around Hemel Hempstead, occupying schoolrooms, farms, and church halls. Training commenced immediately.

The War Office was faced with a multiplicity of tasks. To honour its commitment to France, the BEF had to be formed, deployed, supplied, and reinforced. Enormous numbers of new recruits, 1¼ million by Christmas 1914, had to be issued with uniforms, arms, and equipment; however, above all, they had to be trained—most of them from the most basic of start-lines. The Dominions and colonies of the Empire had to be defended against external threats, but, particularly in India and Ireland, there were pre-existing internal security issues that might be expected to grow once the mother country was preoccupied with fighting a global war. However, to many—politicians, generals, and citizens alike—the biggest and most immediate danger was that the long-perceived threat to England from across the North Sea would finally become real as the long-expected German invasion took place. Implementing the plans to defend against this eventuality quickly became a priority.

The TF had been raised in 1908 as the core of a Home Defence Force, but the demands on the Regular Army in autumn 1914 quickly overtook this policy. On 9 September, the four battalions of the London Regiment, which made up the 1st London Brigade (TF), were sent to Malta, while other individual battalions were detached from their parent formations and sent abroad. The 7th Battalion, Middlesex Regiment, went to Gibraltar on 4 September 1914, and the 14th Battalion, London Regiment (London Scottish), landed at Le Havre on 16 September. Also bound for Le Havre, to join an Indian Army brigade in November 1914, was the 1/4th Battalion, Suffolk Regiment. As this dispersal policy took shape, the TF immediately began the process of recruiting second-line divisions. Six weeks into the war, the 42nd (East Lancashire) Division (TF) sailed for Egypt to safeguard the Suez Canal. Early in October, the 43rd (Wessex) Division (TF) and, later that same month, the 44th (Home Counties) Division (TF) both embarked for India. Raised only three months previously, the TF second-line 45th (2nd Wessex) Division also sailed for India in December. Of the TF's remaining twelve infantry divisions, seven were assigned to coast defence duties.

Several possibilities were available for the yeomanry regiments. The Oxfordshire Hussars and the Leicestershire Yeomanry went to France in November 1914 to join the mainly regular 1st and 3rd Cavalry Divisions respectively. The Northumberland Hussars and Surrey Yeomanry were posted to France and their squadrons distributed among different infantry divisions as divisional cavalry with a reconnaissance role. The Warwickshire Yeomanry, the South Nottinghamshire Hussars, and the Sherwood Rangers were just three among many such units that were sent out on the ill-fated Gallipoli expedition. The Cheshire Yeomanry and both Devon's yeomanry regiments were sent to Egypt while others sailed on to India. However, whether they were bound for overseas or not, the first posting for the majority of the TF's cavalry units was to the eastern counties on coast defence duties. Two TF Mounted Divisions had been formed in 1914 for home defence, composed of yeomanry regiments and cyclist battalions. The 1st Mounted Division (TF) (soon to be converted into the 1st Cyclist Division formed in Norfolk and Suffolk) and the 2nd Mounted Division (TF) in Suffolk (soon to be redeployed to Egypt) was replaced by the 2/2nd Mounted Division, which also gave up their horses for bicycles. The major concentration of these cyclist units was in East Anglia, but Kent, the east coast between Newcastle and the Wash, and Scotland (with units centred on Dunbar, Haddington, Cupar, and St Andrews) were protected by cyclist units. The three remaining yeomanry regiments of the South Eastern Mounted Brigade were stationed in the Canterbury area on coast defence duties until mid-1915.

Designated defended ports had permanent garrisons for the duration. The basis of each garrison was the 3rd (Reserve) Battalion of a local infantry regiment that supported the resident Regular and TF RGA and Fortress/Defended Ports RE units. When some regiments formed home service garrison battalions in 1916, these were usually attached to their local port. Thus, in the early years of the war, the Portland Garrison consisted of the reserve battalions of the Dorsetshire and the Wiltshire Regiments, and three companies of the Regular RGA, with the TF Dorsetshire RGA and Fortress RE. When the Dorsetshire Regiment formed a 1st (Home Service) Garrison Battalion in 1917, it came to Weymouth. In all, there were twenty-two designated garrisons stretching from Cromarty to the Thames, along the south coast from Dover, round to Milford Haven, and thence to Liverpool and the Clyde. Jersey and Guernsey were defended by their local militias, after their Regular Army battalions had been withdrawn for overseas service. The Clyde and Cromarty garrisons were both composed of reserve battalions of local regiments, but at Cromarty, they were supplemented, on the insistence of the Admiralty, by Royal Marines manning their new coast batteries. On Orkney, despite spirited resistance on their part, the RGA (TF) companies were gradually absorbed into the Royal Marine units defending the naval base of Scapa Flow. East coast garrisons were strengthened more than elsewhere, as this was where a full-scale invasion, rather than hit-and-run raids, might be expected. The Harwich Garrison, taking in Dovercourt, Harwich, Shotley, Felixstowe, and Parkeston, included nine first- and second-line reserve battalions; two garrison battalions of the Suffolk Regiment; and both Regular and TF units of RGA and Fortress REs. While the line regiments' reserve battalions served as the nuclei of the garrisons, they also had to maintain a firm presence in the regimental depots, inducting recruits into the Army, weeding out the inadequate, and training men for war. During the course of the war, the Gordon Highlanders 3rd (Reserve) Battalion, at their depot by the Don in Aberdeen, processed 800 officers and 20,000 men for active service.

Outside these garrisons, the balance of the TF was deployed, from the very first, to carry out the task for which it was designed, and it was soon to experience its first invasion scare; on the night of 20 November 1914, circumstances appeared to favour a successful German invasion. In December, the German bombardment of north-east coast ports was seen as the softening-up process prior to an invasion. Neither threat materialised, but the pattern was set for large bodies of troops to remain on alert for the entire course of the war. At this time, the TF divisions deployed round the coast were the 52nd (Lowland Division), centred on Edinburgh to man the Firth of Forth defences; the 50th (Northumbrian) Division based around Newcastle and manning the Tyne defences; centred on Hull and the Humber estuary, the 49th (West Riding) Division manned the defences of Yorkshire and Lincolnshire; manning the defences of Norfolk, Suffolk, and Essex, and centred on the north Norfolk coast, Harwich, and Great Yarmouth was the 54th (East Anglian) Division; manning the south coast defences was the 44th (Home Counties) Division centred on Sheerness, Dover, and Newhaven; the 43rd (1st Wessex) Division, soon replaced by the 45th (2nd Wessex) Division, manned the south-west coast defences, centred on Weymouth, Plymouth, and Falmouth; and, centred on Liverpool, the 55th (West Lancashire) Division manned the Mersey defences.

Although individual units—such as the 1st Battalion, Monmouthshire Regiment (TF), landing in France in February 1915—had preceded them, the 46th (North Midland) Division (TF) was the first major formation to be despatched straight to the Western Front in March 1915, closely followed over the next five months by eight more of the first-line TF divisions. By this time, sixteen New Army divisions, a fourth mounted division, and the Guards Division had all gone to France, and before the end of 1915, a further eleven New Army divisions had left Britain. Stripped of experienced and inexperienced troops alike, it was vital that the home commands organised their remaining forces as an effective defence against invasion. The War Book, which governed the optimal deployment of Britain's forces for the duration of hostilities, laid down a coast defence establishment of nine TF divisions, ten mounted brigades, and four cyclist battalions for patrol and reconnaissance. Although the second-line TF divisions began to form in September 1914, and one had even been shipped abroad in the December, it took a while for them to become efficient guardians of the nation's shores, replacing first-line TF divisions (themselves still deemed deficient in training) as they were sent abroad.

The strategy governing coast defence was simple. The garrison troops would defend the ports, also ensuring that the hinterland was denied to an enemy force attempting to outflank the defences by landing along the coast and attacking the rear; the coast itself would be monitored by cyclists, both the cyclist battalions themselves and unhorsed yeomanry; and an outpost line, 10 to 20 miles back from the coast, would be manned by infantry and horsed yeomanry. The reserves would then come into play to support the first line of defence as it was penetrated or forced to fall back.

The Central Force 1914–16

It was partly as a result of the amphibious exercises—which had been conducted in the years leading up to the war—that the planners were acutely aware that coast defence had to be conducted in depth, and that the capability to counterattack in strength, before the enemy could secure an extensive bridge-head, was vital. Therefore, the TF's remaining six first-line divisions were grouped as the Central Force in a quadrant north-east of London stretching from Northampton, where the 53rd (Welsh) Division was stationed, round to Chelmsford, where Galleywood Common was home to 48th (South Midland) Division. Until its despatch to France, the 46th North Midland Division had its HQ in Stockwood Park, Luton. The 51st (Highland) Division was at Bedford, and the 2nd (London) Division's HQ was at the Peahen Hotel in St. Albans. The 1st (London) Division's was in London, near to Horse Guards, where the Central Force HQ was co-located with the HQs of Eastern Command and London District. While this should have eased communication and facilitated co-ordination, it actually appears to have exacerbated problems of demarcation.

By July 1915, all the first-line TF divisions had been posted abroad and their places were taken at home by the thirteen second-line TF divisions, numbered 57th–69th. Nine of these divisions were held centrally and split into three Armies. First Army had its HQ in Bedford. It was composed of the 68th (2nd Welsh) Division—with its HQ at the George Hotel, Northampton—and the

69th (2nd East Anglian) Division—with a HQ at the Great Northern Hotel in Peterborough. In support were the South Wales Mounted Brigade, with its HQ in the University Arms Hotel in Cambridge, and the Highland Mounted Brigade centred on the Godmanchester, Huntingdon, and St Ives area. All these venues were chosen for their rail links to London and Norwich, and the east coast ports of Kings Lynn and Great Yarmouth. Peterborough also had good rail links to Leicester, Lincoln, Grantham, Grimsby, and York, making the speedy transfer of drafts or reinforcements possible. These designated through rail routes, along with others principally linking the area to Salisbury Plain, Southampton, and Scotland, were intended to expedite the movement of an extra seven divisions to reinforce the anti-invasion forces. The 62nd (West Riding of Yorkshire) Division was initially assigned to 1st Army with a HQ in Wellingborough, but it was subsequently redeployed to man the defences of Yorkshire and Lincolnshire, centred on Hull and the Humber estuary. The 2nd Army, with its HQ in Aldershot, operated in Kent and Sussex and comprised the 57th (2nd West Lancashire) and 66th (2nd East Lancashire) Divisions. The 67th (2nd Home Counties) Division had formed at Windsor with brigades in Ascot, Staines, and Sunninghill, but its attachment to the Second Army brought divisional HQ to Sevenoaks, with brigades in Reigate and Tonbridge and its artillery scattered across surrounding villages. Further troops, training at Aldershot or on Salisbury Plain, came under the notional command of the Second Army, which would soon be reduced to a single division as second-line TF divisions were sent abroad. With its HQ at Luton Hoo, the Third Army included the 58th (2/1st London), 59th (2nd North Midland), 60th (2/2nd London)—with its HQ in Bishops Stortford—and 61st (2nd South Midland) Divisions, deployed across Bedfordshire and Hertfordshire. The North Midland Mounted Brigade had its HQ in the George Hotel in Bishops Stortford, and other divisional HQs were in St Albans. This reorganisation saw a reduction in the divisions stationed on the coast itself, from seven down to just four. It is now difficult not to see this constant reshuffling as wasteful of time and effort and counterproductive in terms of the familiarity with the territory that more stability might have provided.

In December 1915, in order to clarify the command structure, Central Force was renamed GHQ Home Forces. The Third Army was disbanded over the winter of 1915–16 as two of its divisions, the 60th and the 61st, had been sent to France during the summer. Consequently, and in view of the anticipated posting of five further divisions to France, it was necessary in March 1916 to reorganise yet again. Sir John French had returned from commanding the BEF to become C-in-C Home Forces in January 1916. He inherited a force that, on paper, was very strong. He had a total of just under 500,000 men organised into two mounted divisions and five mounted brigades, mainly cyclists; nine TF divisions and twenty-three cyclist battalions; the equivalent of up to ten brigades of Provisional battalions (TF men who exercised their pre-war right not to serve abroad); garrison troops; and 440 guns, the majority in second-line TF RFA brigades.

French decided to split the Central Force into two with a Northern Army (HQ at Lynford Hall, Mundford, near Thetford, and subsequently in Norwich), covering the coast from the Humber down to Great Yarmouth, and a Southern Army (HQ at Brentwood), looking after Suffolk, Essex and Kent. The Northern Army comprised the 62nd and 64th Divisions with the 68th Division attached for training. Additional to these second-line TF formations, were the 1st Cyclist Division made up of yeomanry regiments, four cyclist battalions, and thirteen provisional battalions organised into three brigades. The Southern Army was of similar composition, consisting of 65th, 66th, and 67th Divisions and the 2nd Cyclist Division. A mounted division was attached for training, and there were twenty-four provisional battalions in six brigades. Although each of these armies was nominally of reasonable strength (massing, in effect, a combined total of twelve divisions), by early 1917, over half the second-line TF divisions and one yeomanry division had been posted abroad, leaving just three divisions to guard against invasion. Based around Salisbury Plain and Aldershot, two divisions (the 57th and 58th) formed an emergency reserve until their removal to the front at the beginning of 1917. A sixth division acted as a general reserve. Just prior to this, three new Home Service Divisions had been formed from those troops who were either unsuitable or ineligible for foreign service. The 71st Division formed at Farnham, but shortly moved to Colchester when it was assigned to the defence of the coast between Mersea Island and Walton-on-the-Naze. The 72nd Division formed in Somerset with its HQ in Bath, but moved to Bedford and assumed responsibility for the defence of the east coast from the River Deben to Orfordness. The 73rd Division formed in Blackpool, but moved to Chelmsford with its HQ in Boreham House, its brigades being based in Danbury, Southend, and Chelmsford. Of the original second-line TF divisions, only six remained at home for the duration, but they were under continuous pressure to provide drafts for front-line units. Although the regiment was the soldier's traditional service family, it was now common for men to be posted to any unit that needed replacements regardless of cap badge.

Formation deployments were still determined by the need to defend those areas perceived to remain vulnerable to invasion. The 64th Division, raised in Blairgowrie, had been manning the Firth of Tay defences, with its HQ in Forfar, but was moved from Scotland to north Norfolk, centred on Norwich, with brigades in Thetford, Holt, and North Walsham. Similarly, the 65th Division had been manning the Firth of Forth defences, with its HQ in Falkirk prior to its move to Essex. The three new divisions were all based on the most vulnerable stretches of the east coast.

Alongside those two main elements of GHQ Home Forces were what French referred to as local forces. The 69th Division had spent two years in the Peterborough area, but moved its HQ to Doncaster as the core of Northern Command, with three mounted brigades and eight cyclist battalions under command. Scottish Command comprised just two cyclist brigades and four cyclist battalions. Irish Command contained the 59th Division with thirty Irish Special Reserve battalions, and in London, there were the reserve battalions of the Household troops. The Guards Division, including the newly raised Welsh Guards and 2nd and 3rd Battalions of the other four regiments, had been sent to France in August 1915, but all five Guards regiments maintained reserve or depot battalions at Chelsea, Windsor, and Warley, processing new recruits. The Household Cavalry had reserve regiments at Windsor, Hyde Park, and Regents Park, and there were reserve cavalry regiments at Tidworth, Aldershot, and the Curragh (Dublin), serving the TF horsed yeomanry. The garrisons remained in being throughout, and seven ports, such as the Forth Garrison, had Special Reserve Brigades attached. In the summer of 1917, the Home Service Battalions of eighteen line regiments were formed into the Royal Defence Corps. These battalions, formed from supernumerary companies composed mainly of men aged forty-one to sixty, were allocated to garrisons across the country. The remainder of the troops available for home defence were all in training.

Recruiting and Training: The New Armies and the Territorial Force

Alongside the redeployment of the regulars and the mobilisation of the reservists and Territorials, the campaign to recruit what Kitchener called his 'New Armies' was launched from day one. Although the county Territorial Associations had the machinery for raising and maintaining volunteer units, Kitchener nevertheless withheld his confidence in them. There may have been several contributory factors to explain his distrust of the TF. The rationale sometimes attributed to him was based on judgements of the performance of volunteer regiments during the American Civil War. The perception of the TF as 'Saturday-night soldiers' was backed up by the apparent ease with which they could decline to serve abroad or could opt out altogether. Kitchener was a professional soldier, trained as an engineer at Woolwich, and may have had little regard for the amateurs of the minor aristocracy and landed gentry, who officered the yeomanry and the TF battalions of the county regiments. Whatever his reasoning, Kitchener chose to start from scratch with wholly new units, integrated directly into the Regular Army. However, in order to form cadres of officers and NCOs to stiffen and train his new citizen battalions, he had been constrained to transfer Territorials and Regulars into them, as well as recalling veterans (dug-outs) to the colours, if only to train raw recruits. Despite Kitchener's apprehensions, many TF units mustered the required proportion of volunteers to serve overseas and, while they still could, many men opted to enlist in TF units. Their alternative was to choose one of the many different routes into 'New Army' divisions. Battalions were sponsored by mayors, MPs, or local businessmen and offered for adoption by the War Office. Some, particularly the 'Pals' battalions, were recruited from groups of friends or work mates. Other battalions were composed from men who shared an education, a profession, a sporting activity, or, in the case of the bantam battalions, a restricted physique. Some battalions were recruited for either manual labour as pioneers or for garrison duties, specifically at home or abroad. Thus, during the course of the war, an infantry regiment might have elements of a wide variety of such categories. The Middlesex Regiment, for example, had four regular battalions; two reserve battalions; sixteen TF battalions, including (only) one provisional battalion; five New Army battalions; six pioneer battalions, initially recruited from public works employees; three service battalions, recruited from footballers, sportsmen, and public schoolboys; a bantam battalion; three battalions raised by the mayors of Islington and Shoreditch and the local MP; one garrison battalion that served in Hong Kong and another on home service on the Medway; four reserve battalions; and, later, three training battalions, two graduated and one young soldier. This came to a total of forty-nine battalions, taking in 40,000–50,000 men. During the course of the war, infantry battalions were designated under thirty-six different categories.

Once virtually all the regular army and first-line TF divisions, more than half the second-line TF divisions, and many of the yeomanry, had been deployed to overseas battlefronts, the business of training and home defence had become inextricably linked. In the first six months of the war, nearly 2 million men had been recruited into Kitchener's first four New Armies (K1-4) and the TF, roughly in the ratio of 2:1. Direct recruitment into the TF stopped in December 1915, and second-line TF units were capped at 600 men, so that any excess was sent as drafts to first-line units. This had the effect of limiting TF recruitment and, at the same time, removing those NCOs and trained men who might be expected to contribute to the training of recent recruits, with the effect that the training period for second-line TF units was extended to twenty-seven months. This compared unfavourably with that of New Army and first-line TF battalions, respectively just nine and eight months. Although the Territorial Associations had actually recruited a number of New Army units, the War Office was not enthusiastic about such involvement, regarding it as amateur meddling. However, whatever the perceptions of the War Office, the TF contribution to the war effort had been considerable. By the end of the war, there had been a roughly 50:50 split between the TF and the New Armies in terms of numbers of infantry divisions and of infantry battalions. The only major difference in terms of participation was that 72 per cent of New Army personnel in thirty divisions, but only 46 per cent of TF men in twenty-five divisions, had served abroad.

In April 1915, it was realised that the existing machinery for enlisting and training troops was being overwhelmed by the sheer numbers of recruits, even though these numbers were beginning to level out. In order to ensure that drafts were ready to replace losses at the front, the fourth tranche (K4) of the New Armies, was reformed as reserve battalions. By the end of the year, it was clear that insufficient volunteers would come forward as this war of attrition entered its third year, so conscription was brought in through Military Service Acts of Parliament. The implications for training organisations of this new influx of raw recruits meant that a much tighter system would be needed. The reserve units were now organised into first eighteen, and then twenty-six Training Reserve Brigades also taking in K5's Depot Companies. These new training brigades took in new recruits for training and subsequent deployment to battalions in the field. The 13th and 14th Training Reserve Brigades at Kinmel Park near Rhyl, for instance, served the South Wales Borderers, the Welsh Regiment, the Cheshire Regiment, the Royal Welsh Fusiliers, and the Manchester Regiment. From September 1916, the reserve battalions of the TF, still affiliated to their individual regiments, were also grouped into Training Reserve Brigades corresponding to their fourteen TF Divisions, with an extra brigade for London and a sixteenth brigade serving Irish regiments. The West Riding Reserve Brigade at Clipstone, for example, served those regiments that contributed TF battalions to the 49th and the 62nd Divisions: the Princess of Wales's West Yorkshire Regiment, the King's Own Yorkshire Light Infantry, the Duke of Wellington's West Riding Regiment, and the York and Lancaster Regiment. These forty-two training brigades were scattered around the country, making them available, if needed, for home defence. Their camps were roughly aligned with the six Army Commands, the densest concentrations being on Salisbury Plain, the Dukeries of Nottinghamshire, Shropshire, Cannock Chase, and Ripon. The final New Army divisions were sent to France in mid-1916, and the last TF ones in early 1917 in a desperate attempt to make up the losses sustained in the battles of the Somme campaign. From then onwards, reinforcements would go out purely as drafts, allocated to units as needed to make up the numbers.

From May 1917 as eighteen-year-old conscripts completed their basic training in one of twenty-three Young Soldier Battalions, usually numbered 53rd, they were then posted to one of forty-six graduated battalions, usually numbered 51st and 52nd, within the Reserve Brigades to receive the balance of their training, much of which involved the construction and manning of anti-invasion defences. As early as April 1916, so many men had been shipped out to France that those remaining in the UK had received fewer than three months' training. At the beginning of 1917, a total of around 400,000 men were nominally active in Home Forces, but the majority were either in the early stages of training or eighteen year olds—under the qualifying age for service overseas. Of that total, there were at this time only 150,000 men meeting the Class 'A' criteria, and those were mainly RGA, RE, yeomanry, or cyclists. Of the 230,000 infantry available for home defence, 180,000 were either in the first months of their training or eighteen year olds. The three new home defence divisions were made up almost entirely of graduated and provisional battalions. Over the course of their brief existence, the 71st and 72nd Divisions each included four provisional, five or more graduated, and three second-line TF battalions, with the balance made up of an assortment of rag-tag units cobbled together from the training camps. Support units, such as artillery, were equally makeshift. In 1915, the 9th Provisional Brigade, forerunner of the 73rd Division (HQ in Margate), initially had a single battery of four French 90-mm guns, only eventually exchanged for 18-pounders and 4.5-inch howitzers.

The threat of invasion, however, refused to go away. In March 1917, reports that the Germans were massing shipping and 500,000 men in Zeebrugge prompted a trial mobilisation that exposed worrying weaknesses in the home defences. The anticipated target was the east coast, from Aldeburgh to Lowestoft, with the Royal Navy promising disruption to enemy fleet activity thirty-two to thirty-six hours from its first sighting. The west coast and the east coast north of The Wash continued to expect only light raiding parties. This latest threat, like earlier ones, never materialised, but speculation continued. Estimates of his strength in mid-December 1917 reckoned the enemy capable of mounting a raid with no more than 30,000 troops, but given the Navy's apparent tardiness and the clear lack of experience of the defending troops, even this diminished threat remained dangerous.

In 1917, the Home Army consisted of a Northern Army in East Anglia with the 64th and 68th Divisions, the 1st and 2nd Cyclist Brigades, three brigades of former provisional battalions, six cyclist battalions, some artillery, and an armoured train. The Southern Army (HQ in Brentwood) covered the Thames Estuary and fielded the 67th Division in Canterbury, the 71st and 73rd Divisions, three brigades of provisional battalions, two cyclist brigades, plus an independent cyclist battalion, and three further cyclist battalions attached for training. The general reserve consisted of the 1st Mounted Division at Bishops Stortford and 72nd Division at Bedford and Ipswich. The 65th Division, based in Chelmsford with brigades at Billericay and Danbury, was attached to the general reserve for training. Alongside these formations, garrisons continued in existence, the 69th Division was in Yorkshire and various cyclist units were stationed on the north-east coast and in Scotland. The Royal Artillery's Signal Training School at Crowborough and its Central Signalling Depot at Swanage, could provide 2,000 personnel; at Seaford, there was the Canadian training division; and the Machine Gun Corps depot at Belton House, Grantham, could provide two mobile units and twenty-four machine-gun companies. At the end of 1917, the 72nd and 73rd Divisions were disbanded with home service battalions going to 68th and 69th Divisions and the rest being made available for drafts to units in France. Contrary to earlier estimates, the Royal Navy was of the opinion that the enemy still retained the capability to land up to 70,000 troops on the shores of East Anglia. There were still 1.4 million troops in Britain, but only 30 per cent of these were specifically earmarked for home defence. Given that 2.5 million men enlisted during 1917–18, the vast majority of those 1.4 million would have had very little training as, once deemed sufficiently trained, they were immediately despatched to the front. A number of mixed brigades were formed from TF home service troops, formerly categorised as provisional battalions. At the beginning of the war, 80 per cent of first-line Territorials had given less than four years' service, and 40,000 of them had been under nineteen. Since many of these men went overseas with the TF divisions in the first three years of the war, then experience became even rarer. Moreover, many of those Territorials, asserting their right to stay at home, were probably among those who had never been judged fit enough or considered as adequately trained, but were now finding themselves in the front-line against a possible invasion. Thus, well into 1918, an amphibious assault, presumably carried out by seasoned, highly trained stormtroopers in the prime of life and at a peak of physical fitness, would have been countered by forces of untrained eighteen year olds, the medically unfit, and the overage.

The German 'Michael' offensive of March 1918 required the deployment to France of every available fit soldier, including depot units and the instructors from training camps, leaving the Home Army hanging on a shoestring. It now consisted of XXIII Corps covering East Anglia with its HQ in Brentwood, whose three divisions were the 64th at Norwich with brigades based in Kelling, Taverham and North Walsham, the 67th at Ipswich and the 68th at Great Yarmouth. It also mustered three brigades of cyclists, six cyclist battalions, four mixed brigades, and six heavy batteries of artillery. South of the Thames was the Independent Force (HQ in Canterbury). This comprised the Cyclist Division, a further cyclist battalion, three mixed brigades, and four batteries of artillery. Northern and Scottish Commands between them deployed just one infantry division, four cyclist brigades, twelve cyclist battalions, and four batteries of artillery. The role of 69th Division within Northern Command changed with a move of its HQ to Retford and a concentration of its activities within the Nottinghamshire training camps at Clipstone, Thoresby, and

Welbeck. It was fortunate that the defeat of the German army and the collapse of its support at home prevented those patently inadequate home defences from ever being tested.

Formation, Development, and Role of the Volunteer Training Corps (VTC)

The enthusiasm for war, which had caused nearly 300,000 men to enlist in the Army by the end of August 1914, also prompted many of those ineligible for military service through age, state of health, or occupation to find active ways of contributing. Against the wishes of Kitchener (the new Minister of War), who preferred to retain total control of all armed forces, freelance private armies of vigilantes were being formed under superannuated officers. Some adopted names such as 'Citizens' Army', 'Town Guards', 'Infantry Training Corps', or the blanket 'Volunteer Force', which had served as a collective title for the rifle volunteers and yeomanry, until the creation of the Territorial Force in 1908. Throughout the war, these groups would struggle for recognition, resources, and respectability.

Therefore, it was against its better judgement that, as early as 4 September 1914, the War Office allowed the London County Council, responding to an idea mooted on the correspondence page of *The Times*, to raise a London Defence Force of volunteers. They would be trained in the rudiments of military practice, drilling, and shooting. Permission was given on the basis that no uniforms would be issued beyond GR armbands. Other towns and cities soon followed suit. Late in 1914, Leicester recruited its citizens into a volunteer organisation to support the war effort. The Leicester Citizens' Volunteer Training Corps (VTC), or Volunteer League, was raised by the mayor to 'defend the hearth and home if need arise'. The St Neots and District Drill Club in Huntingdonshire formed in November 1914, with members who were able-bodied men over thirty-eight years of age. They carried out route marches and underwent inspections. Burton Joyce in Nottinghamshire raised a company of the 'Citizens' Army' early in 1915. Portsmouth's volunteers numbered over 300 from early in the war, with a further 100 across the water in Gosport, and a Chelmsford Company mustered 150 men and boys. In Dover, the Council agreed in November 1914 to set up a company of the VTC, and by early 1915, this had grown into two companies totalling 320 men, with a detail responsible for manning the obsolete, but exposed, Archciffe Fort. In 1915, the Belfast VTC patrolled the docks every night. Some of these units functioned as clubs, the London National Guard collecting subscriptions from its members to purchase arms and equipment and to hire premises for drill. The common aim of all these organisations was to mobilise those in reserved occupations or otherwise exempt from military service, to undertake activities which would release troops for more important duties, and to engage those at home psychologically with the war. They also complemented the many organisations, such as the Junior and Senior OTCs, TF cadet battalions, and the paramilitary Church Lads' Brigade, in preparing young men prior to their enlistment in the forces.

Even if the War Office was less than appreciative of such efforts, local authorities were soon encouraged by their communities to put an official stamp on these bodies. Their enquiries following the inauguration of the London Defence Force led the chair of its controlling committee, Lord Desborough, to extend its remit, becoming the Central Association of Volunteer Training Corps. This, in turn, encouraged a countrywide expansion. In December 1914, the inaugural meeting of the Norfolk VTC was held at the Assembly Rooms in Norwich's Agricultural Hall. Similar initiatives across the county saw Hunstanton's Lounge Pavilion hosting a VTC recruitment meeting on 21 May 1915. In London, membership was aimed at those who were too old to serve in the regular forces or who were in reserved occupations, particularly aiming at shopkeepers who were invited to drill and use the facilities of the local TF drill hall. In Bow, the miniature range was made available on Thursday afternoons, possibly the local early closing day. They also attracted schoolboys, too young to enlist, but anxious to take part in some military activities prior to enlistment, ready to hit the ground marching. At a meeting in Hemel Hempstead Town Hall on 6 January 1915 to recruit a local VTC, a committee was formed and a fund started. Members would be self-funding, buying arms, ammunition, and appropriate clothing, and, in the first two weeks, over 100 men were enrolled, the first of over 400 who would serve during the course of the war. As more local units, such as Cambridgeshire's three companies, were formed, the numbers soon began to grow. In Birkenhead, a company was raised of men over military age. The subscription was fixed at £5, and some £1,200 was raised locally to subsidise those of the 250 members who could not afford the cost of rifles and equipment.

Despite their reservations and Kitchener's fear that the VTC would divert men who would otherwise have been available for his New Armies, the War Office could not afford not to be involved. Once the ground rules had been laid down, there was an evident role for the Corps and a defined membership which the Army Council could accept. By May 1917, a year after the introduction of conscription, concerns arose that out of a total of almost 300,000 men in the VTC, around 200,000, though of military age, were nevertheless unavailable for conscription since membership of the VTC had been a condition of their exemption. There were others who had volunteered to join the VTC in order to pre-empt their call-up. Additionally, within these two groups totalling about 80,000 men, there was little evidence that military drills were being taken seriously. This all undermined the notion of the VTC as an essential component of the home army that would, in effect, be a shortfall of 100,000 on its designated establishment. An added concern was the suspicion that the General Reserve, which by this time included the VTC, had become a dumping ground for units for which the War Office could find no real use and had thus become an unnecessary drag on Government spending. However, genuine enthusiasm and endeavour could not be wasted, and even if the War Office remained lukewarm, others were more pragmatic. In Huntingdon, a range had been set up in premises in the High Street and volunteers drilled regularly in the grammar school's new assembly hall. Their efforts were recognised in 1918, when Field Marshal Sir John French, C-in-C Home Forces, inspected over 700 of them at Hinchingbrooke. In contrast to the War Office's lukewarm reception of the VTC in 1914, French was consistent in showing his appreciation of the volunteers' efforts, and had previously reviewed 10,000 members in Hyde Park in 1916. Newspaper reports also praised Sir Francis Lloyd, GOC London District, for his almost daily inspection of units of the London Volunteer Regiment.

The Organisation of the VTC

Although the Central Association afforded the VTC official recognition of a sort, local units still tended to operate on a largely *ad hoc* basis, continuing either to be raised by local authorities and employers (generally in urban contexts) or through membership of occupational, educational, or social groups. It was not until September 1916 that responsibility for administering the VTC devolved onto the County Territorial Associations, who by now were less instrumental in recruiting into the Army. The Government had finally got around to legalising the VTC by making them subject to the provisions of the Volunteer Act of 1863 and then by updating that legislation. Members of the VTC would henceforth be bound to serve for the duration of the war, would be given khaki service dress and a cash grant, and would commit themselves to mandatory training. This sudden interest was largely a result of the introduction of conscription, since there would henceforth exist a means of putting conditions on exemption by channelling men into the VTC. This legislation could be regarded as being retrospective as the processes described were, in many places, already well under way.

The underlying purpose of many of those VTC units comprising older men was to involve workers in the war, so they could claim to have done their bit. This often involved night work, carried out after a long day's work. Occasionally, volunteers guarded their own place of work: mine, factory, or railway depot, for instance—so at least they were on familiar territory.

When conscription was enforced in 1916, those men who were exempted from military service by virtue of the vital nature of their work to the war effort could join the VTC. There were other groups, however, whose claim to exemption the Tribunal may have considered tenuous, and these men were directed to the VTC and ordered to attend mandatory training sessions. By 1918, some 35 per cent of VTC members, 101,000 out of 285,000, had been directed to join by tribunals. Their often-negative attitude tended to colour the public perception of the whole organisation. By early 1918, the recruitment of younger exempted men into the VTC was seen as a way of avoiding the compulsory enlistment of fifty to fifty-five year olds. However, it must be remembered that both the Provisional and National Defence Corps battalions were taking men in the forty-one to sixty age group.

In a not wholly enthusiastic, but nevertheless fairly realistic comment on its new responsibilities, the County of London Territorial Association described the VTC as having 'no history, no continuity and consists of those too old or too young for active service, or of exempted men who, for the most part, at any rate, are not the keenest fighting men'. From early 1915, there had been suggestions that County Volunteer Regiments, based on the Army's existing organisation, should be formed, and a number of individual initiatives went ahead, absorbing existing VTC companies. In May 1915, the Hertfordshire Volunteer Regiment was formed and the Hemel Hempstead men formed 'D' Company of the 2nd Battalion whose HQ was Watford. Encouraged by the Central Association, counties began to consolidate their disparate groups. In Cheshire, volunteer companies had been raised by former officers of the local battalion of the TF. In February 1915, these were gathered together as the Cheshire Volunteer Regiment, part of the national movement. Chaired by the Duke of Rutland, a meeting in Leicester in January 1915 brought all the two counties' groups together under the banner of the County Regiment of the Citizens Training Corps—later, the Leicestershire Volunteer Regiment—combining 3,500 men from nineteen discrete units. The Nottinghamshire Volunteer Regiment established a RHQ and the HQ of its 1st Battalion in Thurland Street, Nottingham, whilst the 2nd and 3rd Battalions were located in the Bingham area, and around Hucknall and Arnold, respectively. The 4th Battalion had companies in Retford, Worksop, and Mansfield. Buckinghamshire formed four battalions totalling 2,751 volunteers by November 1915. The Kent Volunteer Fencibles mustered forty-eight companies, including the Cinque Ports Fencibles and some mounted ones, mainly in the east of the county. By June 1915, nationally, there were 1,100 Corps with 390,000 members, affiliated to the Central Association, plus around a further 900 unaffiliated Corps with about 200,000 members. For a wide variety of reasons, the membership would fluctuate throughout the war, and in 1917, the official size of the VTC was given as 288,000.

While the War Office was ambivalent about recognising a role in home defence for the VTC, this official reticence was sometimes overridden by local arrangements. An example of this was the 1st Battalion of the Kent Volunteer Regiment's attachment to 202 Brigade, part of 67th Division, based in Tonbridge in 1916. In 1918, some 13,000 VTC personnel were mobilised for three-month tours of coast defence duty in Special Service Companies, thus releasing troops needed in France. This specific allocation of VTC units for anti-invasion duties in Home Defence formations was most unusual. A more normal practice was to lump them together in each Army Command for deployment as and when necessary, but some VTC units had already forged close working relationships with local army units early in the war. As the VTC gained greater legitimacy after 1915, then these connections became more institutionalised. Permanent staff would be seconded from regular army units to stiffen up the VTC battalions, many of which began to be affiliated to line regiments. As the war raged on, there was enormous competition for the available manpower. Large numbers of special constables needed to be sworn in to ensure that blackout regulations were enforced, and to supervise an evacuation of the civilian population in the event of invasion. Lincolnshire's Chief Constable was one of several who complained that the VTC made it difficult to recruit specials.

It will be remembered that the condition of the War Office's acquiescence to the formation of VTC units was no uniforms and no arms, a policy that only began to change late in 1915. In the meantime, local organisers were faced with the problem of motivating a quasi-military force denied all major defining features. Some such as Leicester ignored the rules and gave the members of the Defence Corps uniforms: grey/green Norfolk jackets, brown leggings, and a peaked cap. Prior to the War Office prescribing service dress in 1916, grey uniforms became more common, and the City of London Volunteer Corps even designed and issued its own cap badge, organising access to rifle ranges for the unit's 1,500 members. After autumn 1915, things generally began to change, but the issue of weapons was still down to local initiative. Rifles could be obtained for VTC use, but they could not be service pattern, and yet they still had to be capable of firing standard service ammunition. Although the War Office specified the sum of £2 10*s* (£2.50) as the ceiling price for a rifle, London boroughs such as Stepney charged their members £3. East Yorkshire placed an order for 3,000 specially manufactured Martini rifles in 1916, while local worthies, including the Rothschild and Astor families in Buckinghamshire, donated 2,000 Snider and Martini rifles in 1916. One of the Nottinghamshire battalions had amassed seventy carbines and sixty shotguns by 1916. In Hertfordshire, volunteer units were provided with uniform and a system of ranks was allowed in 1916, and one company was even issued with a Hotchkiss machine-gun. In Colchester, the VTC were armed with carbines and old Japanese rifles, and units would later man AA Lewis guns and searchlights. Later, in 1917, the supply of standard SMLE 0.303-inch rifles and Hotchkiss machine guns to the VTC improved.

The Role and Training of the VTC

A large element of the War Office's objections to the VTC was based on the fact that it did not form part of HM Forces, and any military role would therefore be illegal. In the event of an invasion, VTC members bearing arms would be treated by the enemy as *franc tireurs* and summarily executed—a fate seen to befall even unarmed civilians in Belgium. However, there remained plenty of other tasks for the VTC to fulfil in non-combatant roles. Guided by schedules of vulnerable points drawn up by the local military, the VTC could stand sentry, carry out night patrols, guard munitions factories, police railway stations, and make random spot checks on sensitive locations. Vulnerable points might include bridges over road, rail, or river; wireless stations; railway lines, tunnels, and sidings; telephone exchanges, reservoirs, power stations, and gasworks; and munitions factories. Specific areas had particular needs. In north Norfolk, for instance, the 'Y' stations required twenty-four-hour surveillance. Some VTC members, ultimately being absorbed into the RAF in 1918, also served as ground crew at RFC and RNAS stations, such as Bacton and Pulham, and at the numerous landing grounds. All such guards were stood down between June and November 1917. Such aid to the military, along with the provision of technical assistance to the Navy, was accepted as legitimate civilian activity. Suggested action of a less overtly military nature included helping with the evacuation of people or livestock in an emergency, working alongside the Red Cross, and clearing up after air raids. Other acceptable activities included providing motor transport and doing weekend shifts in factories. Greatly encouraged was the excavation of defensive trench lines, enjoyed by many VTC units either on the coast or nearer to London on the Essex lines around Chelmsford and Danbury or along the North Downs. Some, such as the Hertfordshire volunteer units, simply practised digging trenches on Shrub Hill Common because that is what soldiers did. In London, in 1917, the VTC formed specialist signal companies.

Automobiles were still a relative rarity in 1914, so offers by owners to make their vehicles available for war-related purposes were gratefully received. Across the country, motor corps were recruited, many of them under the VTC umbrella. The Sussex Volunteer Motor Mobilisation Corps and the County of London Motor Volunteer Corps were typical of these groups, which provided privately owned vehicles with their drivers to operate as staff cars or ambulances. The 1,200 members of the Civilians' Emergency Corps in Norwich operated vehicles, requisitioned by local Emergency Committees or offered up voluntarily, which, in the event of invasion, would transport troops, supplies, or casualties. The Leicester Motor Corps was formed to ferry wounded soldiers from railway station to hospitals in cars, motorcycles and sidecars, and ambulances. Vehicles were made available in towns as part of ARP, either as ambulances or to ferry emergency personnel to incidents.

Even before arms were officially issued to the VTC, shooting on military ranges had become an established training activity for many units. Uniformed volunteers were trained by old soldiers to shoot their obsolete Martini rifles on dedicated ranges, such as that at Mountergate in Norwich. At the Wortham Ling butts, built by the Diss Volunteer Corps, members of the Suffolk VTC were coached by the 'patient instructors' of the Suffolk Regiment. In Norwich, 600 men, in six companies—plus signals, transport, and medical sections (with their HQ in Howard House in King Street)—had enrolled in the VTC by Christmas 1914, were attending drills on Earlham Road Recreation Ground, and holding anti-invasion rehearsals. In Bourne (Lincolnshire), VTC members used an indoor miniature rifle range in the basement of the Institute in West Street and drilled on the nearby open spaces of the castle meadows. Many areas maintained groups that specialised in first aid or motor transport, and there were also cyclist and mounted sections. With a bit of imagination, some physical activities could be made more fun. In Leicestershire, in 1915, a walking contest was held between the Mountsorrel and Quorn companies, along a local circuit. Ten men from each company plus one from a Leicester company took part. In Leicester, at least 3,000 men turned out for regular daily training sessions at the magazine, the County Cricket Ground, and the Empress skating rink; this involved drill, physical jerks, and shooting. In Hertfordshire, training started early on in the war when, as soon as the London TF units arrived, the local VTC requested help with training activities. In Hemel Hempstead, the first drill, led by a sergeant-major from one of the RFA units billeted close by, was at Lockers Park School where there was a miniature rifle range. Indoor drills were held in the Town Hall, Two Waters School, and, later, in the Bury Road TF drill hall. At Frenchay in Bristol, the VTC contingent drilled in the village hall on Tuesday evenings. Some employers or occupational groups set out to provide recruits with specific skills to be targeted at particular units. The GPO, for example, prepared recruits for service in the REs, responsible for the Army's signalling.

Many youngsters were given the opportunity to acquire military skills and habits prior to joining up, and some VTC units were raised for this express purpose. Price's Candles Company in Battersea raised a whole company, which then volunteered *en masse* for the 3rd (City of London) Battalion, Royal Fusiliers. Some units organised parades, inspections, and competitions to heighten the younger members' motivation to improve their turn-out and skills, giving opportunities for lads to acquire military skills and habits prior to joining up. Younger members in the Hertfordshire VTC graduated with proficiency badges and joined those regiments to which they were directed, at least one local lad being taken into the Inns of Court Battalion for officer training. In Leicester, a Junior Training Corps was formed to prepare sixteen to nineteen year olds for the Army. From October 1914, they met at the City Rugby Club for drill and sports activities, attracting a rolling membership of up to 400. The next year, a Cadet Battalion of the Leicestershire Regiment was started with drill stations across the county, involving up to 850 boys.

6

Military Aviation and Home Defence

Public awareness of warnings that London could be obliterated by concerted and determined aerial bombing was raised by H. G. Wells in novels such as *The War of the Worlds* (1898) and *The War in the Skies* (1908). The spectre of the sinister Zeppelins only exacerbated the fears, which ranged from landings by legions of airborne troops to the wholesale destruction of Britain's cities by bombing. Noting the public concern engendered by this literature, Churchill promised in a speech in March 1914 that no German airships or aircraft could penetrate British airspace without being shot down. At a time when Britain had no aircraft capable of getting anywhere near a Zeppelin in daytime, let alone at night when the raids would more probably be carried out, this statement displayed outrageous economy with the truth. Stoking the fears were reported sightings of Zeppelins over British towns, such as those spotted over Whitby in February 1913. Implicit in Von Clausewitz's promotion of the concept of Total War were aerial attacks on civilian populations. From 1902, the German General Staff reinforced such notions, and by 1914, it was reported as not unusual for German schoolchildren to begin their daily assemblies with a cry of 'Gott Strafe England!'

The Development and Military Application of Powered Aircraft

Despite people's fears, the threat from the skies in 1914 was less serious than they had been encouraged to imagine. It was only fourteen years since the first flight of the Zeppelin, which travelled just 35 miles (56 km), had taken place and only ten since the first powered flight by the Wright brothers' aeroplane. Admittedly, the pace of development had accelerated since then. Zeppelins, capable of carrying twelve crewmembers, could travel up to 700 miles (1,120 km) at a speed of 35 mph (56 km per hour) and at a height of 6,000 feet (1,850 metres). Nevertheless, the whole process of flight was still wholly unpredictable. For many years, the British effort had been run by the Royal Engineers at the Balloon Factory and School in Farnborough and had been applied to balloons and airships. Tethered balloons were used for general observation and for artillery spotting during many campaigns including the South African Wars, but the difficulty of transporting them on the ground, their inability to operate in winds over 20 mph (32 km per hour), and problems in producing, storing, and transporting hydrogen gas meant that they were regarded by many senior officers as more trouble than they were worth. The dirigibles, powered airships capable of being steered, developed by the RE for the Army, and named *Nulli Secundus*, *Beta*, *Gamma*, and *Delta*, enjoyed chequered careers. In January 1914, they were handed over to the RN, which assumed responsibility for all lighter-than-air machines. Stacks of tethered kites provided an observer with a platform, but their instability denied them a prolonged career with either army or navy. Meanwhile, experiments with flying machines had proceeded until, in 1910, aircraft were given a place in the annual military war game on Salisbury Plain. At the same time, Colonel Repington's reports in *The Times*, of the participation in the French manoeuvres of fourteen aircraft and four dirigibles, highlighted not only the usefulness of aviation, but also discrepancies in applying these principles on opposite sides of the Channel. These experiences, pressure from the press, notably Lord Northcliffe, and a rethink by Lord Esher's CID all led to the establishment, in 1911, of the first unit of the British Army dedicated wholly to military flight. This was the RE Air Battalion equipped with a mixture of French machines and Bristol Boxkites, and based at Farnborough. At the same time, the Navy was in process of setting up an independent aviation branch at a flying field at Eastchurch on Sheppey. This had started as the Royal Aero Club in 1910, and then become home to Messrs. Short's balloon and aircraft factory, but was presented to the RN in 1911, providing the RNAS with a flying start.

In May 1912, the Royal Flying Corps (RFC) was formed with naval and military wings, a central Flying School at Upavon in Wiltshire, and a Reserve of qualified pilots who could be called upon in time of war. Much of the activity remained centred on the Royal Balloon Factory at Farnborough, and this reflected an official intention to centralise all development, flight-testing, and production through a single channel. By the end of 1912, the RFC had one airship, twelve manned kite balloons, and thirty-six unarmed biplane aircraft. While experiments had been carried out at Montrose in 1913, to mount a Lewis gun on an aircraft, there was no expectation that pilots would need to defend themselves in the air, let alone attack anyone. Although nominally committed to being an integrated service, the Admiralty preferred independence, and despite the Central Flying School being provided to cater for both services, insisted on retaining Eastchurch as a purely naval flying-training school. This set the pattern whereby the RFC and the RNAS went their separate ways with consequent and predictable performance failures.

Hitherto, despite demonstrations of the possibilities and developments in the technology, there had been only minimal notice taken of the potential of the military application of powered flight in Britain. A display of bomb-dropping by Claude Grahame-White at his Hendon Airshow in 1911, elicited a passing show of interest from the War Office, but even the successful use of reconnaissance aircraft during the annual military manoeuvres of 1912 failed to bring anything but ridicule and stronger assertions that cavalry were better than aircraft in this role. On the outbreak of war, Britain had 113 aircraft, including those privately owned, requisitioned, or donated; France had 160; and Germany had 246. In Britain, just over 600 men had qualified as pilots in the previous two years, mainly through the Royal Aero Club, many of whom were available for service via the RFC Reserve. In August 1914, the BEF in France and Flanders included four out of the five existing RFC squadrons, a total of sixty-three aircraft with 900 personnel.

The expectation was that they would be flying reconnaissance missions in support of a war of mobility, but nothing could have prepared them for what developed as a static war of attrition with its unimaginable casualty figures. Furthermore, 40 per cent of trainee pilots were killed in flying accidents before they ever hit the front, and those pilots who survived what passed for training had an even shorter life expectancy than the infantry subaltern's six weeks. The air war over the trenches developed into a seesaw of tactics, technology, training, and experience. First one side, then the other, would have the upper hand. Inventions such as Fokker's synchronised machine guns, a response itself to the deflection plates on the French Spads' propellers, would give German aircraft an advantage. Only in late 1917, a full two years later, did Constantinesco's synchronised machine guns become standard in all British aircraft. The Sopwith Triplanes delivered, in February 1917, to the RNAS, proved superior to the German Albatros, but by April, German superiority had been restored with the Albatros D. III. To complicate matters, the War Office and the Admiralty were in competition, not only in matters of procurement, but also in the distribution of responsibility, and both these factors had grave consequences for home defence. An example from each will demonstrate the problems. In August 1916, Sopwith Pups were delivered to the RNAS, but meeting the RFC order was delayed until early 1917, by which time the Pups were obsolete. The RFC under War Office control was classed as an offensive instrument and thus prevented from becoming involved in home defence. The RNAS was responsible for home defence, but started the war with only six airships and ninety-three aircraft, many of which were floatplanes incapable of intercepting Zeppelins. Many of the RNAS aircraft, furthermore, were operating over France and Belgium, and were clearly unavailable for home defence duties anyway.

Defences Against the Zeppelins and Bombers

Despite Churchill's spurious reassurances, in 1915 there was no effective defence against air raids. There were few telephones either to signal warnings of an approaching raid, or to alert the populace to take cover. The Zeppelins could by now fly at 15,000 feet (4,615 metres) and it took a single-seater Scout aircraft twenty minutes to reach just 8,000 feet (2,460 metres). The Gotha bombers could reach 21,000 feet (6,460 metres) flying at 87 mph (139 km per hour). At the time of the first raids, none of the aircraft that was sent up to intercept a raider was even armed beyond the pilot's sidearm and some grenades. Even had there been any effective way of reporting incoming hostile aircraft, there was little communication, let alone co-operation or co-ordination, between the RFC and the RNAS as the services appeared not to talk to each other on principle.

Initially, the RNAS was wholly responsible for home defence, operating what few AA guns existed and flying anti-Zeppelin patrols with the few suitable aircraft available, generally Avro 504's. RNAS air stations, such as Redcar and West Ayton (Yorkshire), East Fortune (Lothian), and Great Yarmouth (Norfolk), maintained a desultory watch, sometimes sending aircraft up to investigate sightings, but invariably arriving too late. One night in 1915, a RNAS pilot took off from Gosport to intercept a Zeppelin. He was accompanied by a marine armed with a rifle and four rounds—no contact was made. RNAS seaplanes from Grain and Westgate in Kent carried out regular patrols across the Thames and Medway estuaries, but much of the other activity was less intensive. Neither service had a single operational aerodrome within range of London, so the flying field at Grahame-White's Hendon factory had been taken over by the RNAS as a training centre, doubling as a home defence airfield until more could be opened. Joyce Green and Hounslow had been in existence for some time before the war and both were requisitioned as RFC training airfields, later to be joined by London Colney and Croydon. Only in March 1915, did Northolt open as a home defence landing ground with rudimentary facilities and housing a reserve squadron preparing to go to France. Chingford held a RNAS squadron, which was the only unit charged with the defence of the capital. In June, two of Northolt's BE2cs sortied after a Zeppelin, but failed to make contact. In August 1915, a new aerodrome opened at North Weald Bassett with a flight from 39 (HD) Squadron whose

HQ was at Woodford. That October saw the arrival of two aircraft at Suttons Farm, and Hainault Farm opened early the next year. There were just the two aircraft based at each of these three landing grounds until May 1917, when the three detachments joined together at North Weald to combat the Gothas. Outside London, in the early days, there were no more machines available for home defence, than in London.

Early in the war, there was only limited success for any of these fighters. In March 1916, the Zeppelin *L15* was brought down by the combined efforts of a fighter aircraft and ground fire, but only in September was the Zeppelin *SL11* the first to be shot down solely by the action of a fighter aircraft—one from Sutton's Farm. In November 1916, an aircraft from Seaton Carew in County Durham shot down *L34* over the sea off Hartlepool, and in April 1917, two Zeppelins, *L32* and *L33*, were destroyed by aircraft from Hainault Farm. Northolt was a training station, but in June 1917, it sent up an aircraft to intercept a daylight raid by Gothas. It was the only contact in the whole war from Northolt, and resulted in the death of the observer.

Part of the problem was the performance of the aircraft, as each new model went straight to France for the aerial duelling that apparently dominated RFC operations. By July 1917, there were several squadrons of Bristol Fighters (F2As) available to defend London, but although they were fine machines, their underpowered engines prevented optimal performance. This was a result of the situation in which the War Office and the Admiralty competed over procurement. Engine-manufacturing capacity was squandered on ill-considered and untested models ordered by the Admiralty with no underpinning research or operational rationale, which then limited the scope for the development of better models for specific purposes.

The RFC and Home Defence

In February 1916, grudging agreement was reached between the War Office and the Admiralty that necessitated a complete rethink by both services—as neither was in a strong position to implement it. The RNAS undertook to prevent Zeppelins reaching home skies and the RFC assumed the responsibility for destroying those that did. This resulted in the organisation of home defence squadrons of the RFC based on new locations. Formed at Castle Bromwich in the summer of 1916, by the autumn, a new HQ at Melton Mowbray (Leicestershire) for 38 Squadron had been established, nearer to the action, with flights at Leadenham, Stamford, and Buckminster (Lincolnshire). In Dover, 50 Squadron formed and deployed to Class I landing grounds in Kent. In the north-east, 36 Squadron was based at Ashington, Cramlington, Seaton Carew, and Usworth, with its HQ at Jesmond.

Civilian anger at the absence of any meaningful defence against the bombing raids of spring 1917, particularly in London, which had borne the brunt of the attacks, soon pressured the Cabinet into exploring possible solutions. Their deliberations came up with the obvious recommendation that fighter aircraft should be deployed to defend London. Haig and Trenchard steadfastly refused to entertain this suggestion, arguing that every single aircraft was vital to imminent planned operations over the Western Front and implying, incidentally, that a few hundred east-enders would not be missed. The Cabinet finally ordered them to release one squadron to be stationed for a limited period at Bekesbourne, Kent, and another to be based in Calais to patrol the Channel. Although a major raid had taken place on East Anglia while 56 Squadron was at Bekesbourne, they had not fired a shot the whole time they had been on home soil. The day they returned to France, a daylight raid was launched, suggesting that the German fliers enjoyed effective intelligence sources. A particularly damaging daylight raid then forced the Government to insist on 46 Squadron moving into Suttons Farm in Hornchurch. The German aircraft immediately refocused their attacks to the east coast.

By early 1917, eleven HD Squadrons had been formed by the RFC, with four of them committed to the defence of London. Based at Stow Maries, Rochford (Southend), and Goldhanger was 37 Squadron; North Weald, Fairlop, and Hornchurch retained 39 Squadron; Bekesbourne, Detling, and Throwley remained bases for 50 Squadron; and, after a Zeppelin attack on Portsmouth, 78 Squadron was deployed at Chiddingstone Causeway near Tonbridge, Telscombe Cliffs near Newhaven, and even further west at Gosport. Gainsborough was the new HQ for 33 Squadron, with flights of eight aircraft at Elsham, Kirton in Lindsey, and Scampton. Sadly, none of this was as good as it at first appeared. Many of their aircraft were underperforming; these were training squadrons, which meant that only inexperienced student pilots opposed seasoned enemy fliers, and, moreover, their instructors were burnt-out or suffering from either shellshock (neurasthenia in officers, cowardice in other ranks) or the withdrawal symptoms, which went with being taken away from front-line combat. There was also present in fliers a gung-ho fatalism, which was said partly to be a product of the withholding of parachutes by the War Office, also underpinned by the shocking and apparently unquestioned death rate among trainee pilots. In July, 44 Squadron formed at Hainault Farm, and in May 1918, 75 Squadron arrived at North Weald prior to 39 Squadron's autumn posting to France. Formed at Northolt, with flights at London Colney and Goldhanger, was the new 74 Squadron. Biggin Hill, hitherto a RFC signals school, joined the patrol network in February 1918, when 141 Squadron arrived, flying Bristol Fighters.

Other HD squadrons were based outside the London area, mainly on the east coast. Ripon racecourse was the HQ of 76 Squadron, with flights at Helperby, Catterick, and Copmanthorpe (York); Beverley racecourse was home to 33 Squadron, with flights at Tadcaster and Brancroft, near Doncaster; and 77 Squadron was based in Scotland at Turnhouse, Stirling, and Berwick. All the home defence squadrons had the use of a widely dispersed network of landing grounds, both readymade, such as the racecourses at Hull, Thirsk, Pontefract, and York, and others newly selected for their suitability—many of which would later become full-fledged airfields. All these landing grounds enabled aircraft to stay aloft much longer, avoiding constant returns to home bases and extending the cover they provided. Even with an effective home defence organisation in operation, it was still a case of all hands to the pump. Aircraft from the experimental station at Orford Ness, along with its satellites at Butley and Martlesham Heath, were expected to intercept Zeppelins, as they did in June 1917, contributing to the destruction of *L48*.

The majority of operational RFC aerodromes started as little more than a grass field designated as a landing ground (LG). Depending on its location and facilities, it would be assessed in Classes I–III. Some LGs were used only in daytime, while others, equipped with fires in braziers, enjoyed night-time use as well. Some of the Class I LGs grew into quite extensive aerodromes with brick-built hangars with Belfast-truss roofs creating large, open spaces under cover for housing or maintaining aircraft. Canvas *Bessoneau* hangars were common at fighter airfields on both sides of the Channel. The early tents were gradually replaced by timber or brick hutting for accommodating messes, offices, workshops, and living quarters. Stow Maries, Essex, is a unique survival of such an aerodrome, retaining many of the structures associated with a home defence base. Many examples of more elaborate buildings survive from the First World War period, but most other examples appear mainly on training stations, such as Duxford in Cambridgeshire, or on Aircraft Acceptance Parks, such as Bracebridge Heath outside Lincoln.

Royal Naval Air Service Defensive Operations

Parallel to the notion fully enshrined in national defence policy—that the Royal Navy would take care of any threatened invasion, while the Army fought its wars on foreign soil—were assumptions concerning the role of the RNAS. After July 1914, no longer the naval wing of the RFC, the RNAS had become an independent service, taking on the responsibility for air defence and leaving the RFC to support military operations on the Western Front, where most of its strength would be deployed in August 1914. The RNAS quickly developed its own systems for recruitment, training, and administration. The Crystal Palace became the depot for new recruits to the RNVR, the RND, and the RNAS. Basic training covered disciplinary and technical matters and was followed, for RNAS fliers, by a posting to Lake Windermere for flying training. In April 1916, a dedicated RNAS Central Training Establishment opened at Cranwell in Lincolnshire. Preliminary flight training for those destined to fly seaplanes took place at Calshot, Felixstowe, Chingford, or Redcar, followed by advanced training at Cranwell and then on to nearby Freiston for gunnery and bomb-dropping practice over the Wash. For those with futures in kite balloons and airships, preliminary flight training was carried out first at Wormwood Scrubs, then at Cranwell. RNAS Calshot had opened for the RFC in 1913, but became an experimental and training station for seaplanes and flying-boats, with personnel billeted at Warsash, crossing Southampton Water daily by ferry. A RNAS squadron of fighters at Gosport provided fighter cover for the Solent and the Portsmouth naval base, while seaplanes from Calshot patrolled Southampton Water, watching over the constant stream of troop ships ferrying munitions and personnel across to Le Havre. The Isle of Grain seaplane base opened in April 1916, with billets in the Yacht Club. Pilots undertook regular patrols of the Thames Estuary as part of their training. Port Victoria, next door to Grain, became the RN aircraft repair depot and then the Experimental Constructive Department. Fighters from Eastchurch flew sorties to protect the naval complexes of Sheerness and Chatham. As we have seen, the RNAS maintained further fighter squadrons at aerodromes around the coast of the British Isles, with a token presence in London. A typical RNAS landing ground was Killingholme on the south bank of the Humber estuary. Here, four aircraft were stationed from August 1914 to defend the Admiralty oil depot, the wireless station at Waltham, and the Immingham naval base.

The RNAS was faced with a multiplicity of tasks. While undertaking the defence of the homeland, it was also expected to carry out what many sailors saw as its prime tasks: to fly wide-ranging reconnaissance missions acting as the eyes of the Fleet; to provide an aerial strike force against enemy vessels; and to put up a protective screen for the Fleet by identifying enemy vessels, especially submarines, and to aid in their destruction. Each of these tasks generated different development needs. Working in conjunction with designers at Vickers Ltd, the RNAS had been given the challenge of producing its own version of a rigid airship that could compete with the Zeppelin, but in 1911, the *Mayfly* broke her back after only a few flights and was scrapped. Rigid British airships would not fly again for another six years, and the RNAS turned its full attention to a wide range of other possibilities—kite balloons and non-rigid dirigibles or 'Blimps'; fixed-wing aircraft both seaplanes and land-based; and folding-wing ship-based seaplanes.

The SS (Submarine Scout), SS *Zero*, *Coastal*, and *North Sea*-class dirigible airships were all developed primarily to operate A/S patrols around the coasts of the British Isles. Kite balloons performed the same function but were towed by destroyers. At Scapa Flow, HMS *Canning* served as a Kite Balloon Depot Ship from 1915. In 1912, experiments had commenced with fixed-wing aircraft taking off from ships, in order to extend the range of Fleet reconnaissance. Techniques for dropping torpedoes as well as bombs were perfected to strengthen the offensive dimension. Improvements in airship performance had an immediate effect. The *SS* airships, which had operated from RNAS Polegate since July 1915, were replaced the next year by *SS Zero* airships, six of which were stationed there in 1917, and their greatly increased endurance gave them up to seventeen hours in the air. Another year on, *SS Zeroes* from Llangefni on Anglesey were staying aloft for twenty-four hours on patrols over the Irish Sea. The coast was ringed by a dozen airship stations, including the depot at Cranwell and the experimental station at Pulham (Norfolk), with a further sixteen sub-stations—including four on the north and east coasts of Ireland.

Seaplanes were operated by the RNAS to patrol the sea lanes, looking out for mines and submarines and protecting merchant ships. In the west, seaplanes flew from RNAS Fishguard. A seaplane base was established on the relatively sheltered Hornsea Mere in 1916, and Sopwith Babies, two-seaters carrying a Lewis gun capable of firing incendiary bullets at enemy airships and a 60-lb (27-kg) bomb for dropping on submarines, were based at Killingholme. In 1915, Admiral Ballard, in charge of the east coast naval defences, requisitioned two paddle-steamers—the *Killingholme* and the *Brocklesby*—to carry seaplanes out to the Dogger Bank for opportunist launchings against passing Zeppelins. A structured 'spider's web' over the southern North Sea was patrolled from Felixstowe, Killingholme, and Great Yarmouth by F2a Felixstowe flying-boats. After the arrival of the US Navy, Curtiss H12 and H16 flying-boats were flown from Killingholme. Centred on the North Hinder light-ship, the web covered some 3,000 square miles (4,800 square km) of sea, and six of its twenty-four sectors could be overflown in under five hours. Seaplane bases stretched from Stenness, on Orkney Mainland, down the east coast past Cromarty, Peterhead, Dundee, and South Shields to Great Yarmouth, Felixstowe, and Kingsnorth (Kent); from Catfirth in the Shetland Isles and Houton Bay in the Orkney Isles down the west coast to Fishguard and Newlyn (Cornwall); and along the south coast from Torquay to Portland, Lee on Solent, Newhaven, and Dover. Although the convoy system made escorting merchant ships a more straightforward task for the seaplanes, it also had a downside as U-boats were forced into inshore waters for their prey. The RNAS instituted a patrol schedule in the English Channel using land-based aircraft from Telscombe Cliffs and seaplanes from Newhaven to provide a continuous coverage of coastal waters every twenty minutes. While this did not result in the destruction of a single U-boat, it did force them to submerge and scatter.

Naval aerodromes were very different from those of the RFC. The airship stations had vast sheds with windshields ensuring that the airship could not be blown away as it emerged. Such a shed, one of an original pair at Pulham in Norfolk, can still be seen at Cardington in Bedfordshire where it was re-erected after the war to house the *R101*. Alongside these sheds were power-houses and laboratories for producing the gases and chemicals that kept the airships aloft. Balloon stations also had smaller, but by no means insignificant, sheds, a group of which survive at Lee on Solent. Seaplane stations were equipped with a pier or landing-stage, and a large crane to hoist the seaplane out of the water. At Felixstowe, it was a Titan, an example of which stands beside the Clyde in Glasgow. The seaplanes were kept in large wooden sheds or in side-opening Admiralty F-type hangars. Most of the other buildings were either permanent standard designs or temporary utility hutting.

The ultimate goal of the Royal Navy was to launch aircraft from ships and to land them back on-board. Until effective launching ramps had been installed on converted warships or merchant men, seaplanes were brought out of their ship-board hangar, their wings unfolded, and they were lowered into the sea by derricks for take-off on the water. Recovery was by the same method, seas permitting. The development of techniques for taking off and landing on aircraft carriers at sea would greatly extend the ranges of reconnaissance aircraft, and it would also allow aircraft to stay aloft for longer away from land bases. HMS *Furious* was one of several converted cruisers that were equipped with long ramps as flight decks. They could get aircraft away, but it would be almost the end of the war before aircraft were landing consistently and safely on these improvised carriers. On 1 October 1918, a series of take-offs and landings were made on HMS *Argus*. She was the very first carrier with a stem-to-stern flush deck, 527 feet (162 metres) in length. Improvised arrester wires helped the landing aircraft to avoid overshooting. In the meantime, aircraft were forced to ditch, if possible, near to their home ship or to take their chance on being picked up by a passing friendly vessel, with the consequent loss of the aircraft. HMS *Furious* was based at Rosyth and equipped with five Sopwith Pups with conventional landing wheels, and three Short 184 seaplanes. Just winching these aircraft up on deck through narrow hatches was a hazardous operation. Still more risky was swinging the seaplanes out over a rough sea for them to take-off. Even worse was the take-off for a Pup when the slightest hitch could drop the aircraft off the side of the ship with little hope of recovery for pilot or aeroplane. RNAS pilots on the *Furious* were allowed to customise their aircraft with high-visibility paint jobs in order to shorten the odds on survival when forced to ditch. The procedure was to attract the attention of a friendly ship, ditch 500 yards ahead of it, inflate the airbags, and wait to be picked up by ship's boat.

Early Warning of Air Raids

The technology of flight was improving all the time and quantities of new aircraft were beginning to come out of the factories, but there remained problems to be solved relating to operations. Once the firing of weapons from aircraft had been addressed, the major need was for air-to-air and ground-to-air/air-to-ground communications systems. Engineers from Marconi's works in Chelmsford were seconded to the RFC to work on the problem and as radio-communications equipment became more effective, the RFC leadership promoted its use in those aircraft in positions to issue advanced warnings of enemy bombing raids. However, before they could prove their worth, the Admiralty complained that there was a possibility that they might interfere with naval communications, and they were removed from all but four aircraft, which could communicate with the recently established AA operations centre. Very few aircraft carried radios, and only in 1917 was it at all usual for an aircraft, patrolling the sea lanes looking out for submarines or surface vessels, to be equipped with both a transmitter and a receiver.

The most straight-forward system for alerting the fighters of the RNAS and the RFC to raids by either airships or aircraft was the use of a network of spotters on the ground. In early 1915, observers in captive balloons at the RN depot at Crystal Palace watched the skies for Zeppelin attacks on London. A plan was put forward by Major James of MI2 to establish two lines of observers stretching from Dover to Berwick-on-Tweed. The lines would be 10 miles (16 km) apart, and the intervals between observers would be 10–15 miles (16–24km). In the event, this proved too ambitious and patrolling police officers were ordered to report sightings of aerial intruders. However, information thus gained visually, even if urgently telephoned to a central clearing house, would soon be overtaken by events. Even so, in the absence of any better procedure, attempts were made by recruiting special constables—especially in those areas regularly overflown by enemy aircraft—to provide those directing the fighters with information on raiders as they appeared over the land. These first steps in the establishment of what would one day become the (Royal) Observer Corps were initially unsuccessful, but a reorganisation in 1916 led to the setting up of some 200 observation posts linked to local AA commanders and with quick access to telephone trunk lines. In the London Area, sightings could be reported by telephone—initially to the Admiralty and later to Horse Guards. By late 1916, a central Operations Room at Spring Gardens, near the Admiralty, was receiving reports and co-ordinating a response from AA guns, searchlights, and fighter interceptors. Although this brought an immediate improvement in the speediness of reporting, the inevitable time lag continued to prevent the defences successfully destroying intruders. Denied the use of radio, home defence pilots were forced to follow the arrow-shaped strips of white material, laid out on the ground by spotters, invariably bearing only historical significance by the time they could be picked out from the air.

We saw in Chapter 3 how the 'Y' Service provided information regarding the airships' intentions by listening in to their radio messages and inferring estimated times of arrival, direction of travel, and likely target, but this information was still subject to delays in transmission. Eventually, equipment would be provided by Marconi, which enabled direction-finding stations to plot the movements of Zeppelins, enabling RFC fighters to be in good positions to intercept them. In the meantime, the railway authorities realised that it was in their interests to monitor the progress of hostile aircraft, in order, on the one hand, to safeguard their passengers in transit, but on the other, to avoid suspending services until it was absolutely necessary. This wish to avoid unnecessary stoppages extended to industry, where warnings, often with the status of little more than rumour, could bring half the country's factories to a standstill for hours at a time. The Railway Executive Committee (REC) had been set up in 1912, with its HQ in Westminster, to ensure that in the event of war, the privately owned railways would come under Government control. Given the means to operate a national system, the opportunity was taken to establish regional control centres aligned with the GPO's telephone network. Each region was divided into 30-mile (48-km) squares, each representing half-an-hour's over-flying for a Zeppelin travelling at 60 mph (96 km per hour). In the Eastern Region—that most likely to see Zeppelins—a control centre at Liverpool Street Station received the first report of a sighting, probably over the Norfolk coast near the Happisburgh lighthouse, and then plotted its progress; it passed staged warnings to those sectors over which the airship was expected to pass via railway telegraph—a quicker system than the telephones. Rail traffic on those sections of line could then keep running until the airship was actually close enough to warrant a shutdown. All these warning messages and progress reports were communicated to HQ Home Forces at a national level and to AA defence commanders locally. Given that London termini were themselves vulnerable to aerial bombing, a duplicate control centre was set up in cellars adjoining Liverpool Street Station as a back-up—just as well when the station was the target for an intensive raid by sixteen Gotha bombers in June 1917, which dropped seventy-two bombs on it. As enemy activity by air or sea continued to be interpreted as a prelude to invasion, local commanders in camps and barracks were also kept in the loop.

Another attempt to gain early information of hostile aerial activity prompted experiments with sound location. These ranged from the low-tech—coops of pheasants on the cliffs at Cromer—to the sophistication of acoustic mirrors on the north-east coast and around Dover. Pheasants appeared to pick up the vibrations from aero-engines before their human minders.

Unfortunately, although their cooing indicated an awareness of approaching aircraft, the pheasants proved unable to communicate speed or direction. Large versions of ear-trumpets or gramophone horns were also developed, but failed to distinguish specific sounds among the ambient. Sound mirrors, concrete bowls up to 30 feet (9 metres) in diameter, could pick up sounds that an operator could hear on a stethoscope. Mounted on gimbals, the mirror could track the incoming aircraft. Some static mirrors were sculpted into the chalk cliffs at Fan Bay near Dover and elsewhere. Others (at Kilnsea, near Hull, and Fulwell, near Sunderland) were monolithic concrete dishes, angled within vertical poured-concrete slabs. At Denge is a variation in the form of a 200-foot-long (61-metre-long) wall, with a twin still extant in Malta. Some of these structures date to the war years and others to the post-war period, after which they were overtaken by developments leading toward the introduction of radar. The major drawback with the genre was that they could only distinguish sounds up to a maximum of around 15 miles (24 km). One of the tasks of the Butley Acoustic Research Station, a satellite of the RFC Armament Experimental Research Station at Orford Ness, was to find ways of silencing their own aero-engines.

These sound locators were not a complete waste as, even if they had little to offer in long-distance terms, they could still play a useful role at a local level. From the beginning, searchlights, often in pairs, had been set up to search the skies for the Zeppelins. Sound locators were employed in providing guidance to the searchlight operators, often enabling them quickly to pinpoint a target and thus sparing them preliminary aimless wanderings around the night sky. In early 1916, one of the first actions of the War Office on assuming control of anti-aircraft operations was to set up a searchlight belt, stretching from Sussex in the south up to Northumberland and 25 miles (40 km) in from the coast. These were co-ordinated with the home defence squadrons so that aircraft might be aided in their search for intruders.

Anti-Aircraft Artillery

On the outbreak of war, the AA defences were almost negligible. Although an extremely effective AA gun, the 3-inch 20-cwt model, had been developed by Vickers in 1912, only two were actually mounted. These protected the Chattenden–Lodge Hill magazine complex on the Hoo peninsula. Beyond those, about a dozen 1-pounder pom-poms, manufactured by Maxim and mounted on naval Hotchkiss pedestals, were deployed to potential military targets. London's only gun was a pom-pom defending the Admiralty. By September 1914, a dozen 3-inch and forty-odd pom-poms had been assembled, mainly for the defence of London. These would be supplemented by numbers of naval 3- and 6-pounder guns on adapted high-angle mountings. Faced with the impossibility of defending specific targets and the dawning realisation that aerial bombing would only be random and indiscriminate, the decision was taken to build up blanket coverage as guns and searchlights became more plentiful. In London, these were initially deployed around Whitehall and then extended to the City, and thence out to the eastern fringes. A strange anomaly, however, existed in the division of responsibility. Naval targets continued to be defended by the gunners of the RGA, while all other AA guns were manned by the RNAS/RNVR as part of the Navy's home defence responsibilities. Admiral Sir Percy Scott, appointed as AA supremo, soon discovered that, while he had been given to understand that the Admiralty had placed orders for AA guns for the defence of London, no order had actually gone through and no firm would accept orders from Sir Percy without the Admiralty's say-so. In mid-September, twelve static AA guns defended London, and two months on, this number had only doubled, each gun being paired with a searchlight. Guns were emplaced on the most prominent places, such as the top of Tower Bridge or on Admiralty Arch, and one must assume that this was as much to reassure the public as for fulfilling tactical considerations. Experimentation continued, with a dozen 6-inch naval guns on railway trucks being transferred to the RGA in 1915 and 8-inch naval guns installed in 1915 at Woolwich. Cdr Rawlinson, OC the RNVR armoured-car squadron, was charged with organising mobile AA defences for London. Emulating the fire-brigade model, he responded to sightings by driving his guns across London at high speed to intercept the raiders. Keen to up-gun his unit, he actually drove to Paris and brought back a French lorry mounted 75-mm auto-cannon—the first of an order for thirty-five. Rawlinson based his mobile units in Notting Hill and at the Artillery Ground in Moorgate, with a favoured gun position on Hampstead Heath. Grand Duke Michael of Russia made his London residence available to Rawlinson's force, which thankfully moved into HMS *Kenwood*, a much roomier base than their previous quarters in assorted garages had been. Other mobile units, equipped with trucks armed with machine guns on high-angle mountings, were based at Newmarket, Chelmsford, and Caterham at different times. In London, a total of eleven trams were commandeered to be converted into mobile searchlight platforms, each carrying a 24-inch (60-cm) light. This was mounted on the open, upper deck along with a crew shelter, while the generating equipment was housed in the lower covered deck. These trams were manned by REs, including specialists from the two TF Electrical RE units: London's, based in Regency Street, Westminster, and the Tynemouth-based Tyne company. It was probably purely coincidental that the chosen path of the Zeppelins over the Norfolk coast came worryingly close to Sandringham, where Queen Alexandra was often in residence, but a mobile unit was deployed there to ensure the dowager's safety.

As the capital gained more AA guns, Rawlinson had taken the decision to intercept the Zeppelins at source. In the summer of 1916, he had begun to install some of his mobile units, Rolls-Royce cars armed with machine guns and some 3-pounder QF guns on trucks, on the Norfolk coast. In the autumn, having acquired more of the French 75-mm auto-cannon mounted on rotating platforms on Panhard and De Dion Bouton cars, he sent twelve of them, with accompanying searchlights, to a new base in North Walsham in north Norfolk. From there, using information from the 'Y' Service in Hunstanton and in concert with RNAS fighter aircraft from Bacton and Holt, they would be able to fire on the Zeppelins as they crossed the coast. This mobile force later transferred its HQ to Eaton Hall in Norwich.

Outside London, the provision of AA guns was sketchy. In early 1914, a total of just twenty-six assorted AA guns was emplaced or earmarked, mainly at naval bases, government munitions facilities, and the shipyards at Elswick on the Tyne and Barrow in Furness. A year later, these had increased to nearly 150 guns at around twenty-five separate venues, widened out to include new bases such as Rosyth and the other east coast naval bases, and to reflect the growth of the munitions industry with its factories and gunpowder-works. Portsmouth, the Solent, and the Isle of Wight were defended by two dozen weapons ranging from 4-inch to pom-poms mounted in forts, batteries, depots, and magazines. Dover enjoyed the protection, similarly spread out, of weapons including 18-pounder guns on high-angle mountings, newly adapted to fire a 13-pound (6-kg) shell, with an 18-pounder cartridge, to greater heights, and a generous allocation of 3-inch 20-cwt guns. The Army's assumption of home defence responsibilities in February 1916, however, brought an immediate increase all round. Eight of the twelve airship stations of the RNAS each received guns and searchlights; several seaplane bases and landing grounds outside the complexes already receiving protection were now given guns; and eight non-military 'vulnerable areas', such as Leeds, Birmingham, and Sheffield, were designated AA defence commands. By 1917, smaller industrial centres, particularly those like Lincoln and Peterborough, which were busy producing aircraft and tanks, were also given AA protection. While the Army took over most of the AA guns, some must have been retained by the RNAS, with such a position mentioned in Bristol as late as 1918. By 1918, the Northern Air Defences, which included the three Scottish Commands, had amassed a total of 173 guns, 259 searchlights, and 124 height finders, but had only a small proportion of the approved allotment of sound locators.

The majority of those locations outside London mounted single guns with an accompanying searchlight site nearby. While the site of Lincoln's Burton Road 12-pounder 12-cwt gun itself cannot be identified, its companion searchlight site exists in allotments and displays an approximation to the approved layout. Huts from Peterborough's Garton End AA site were auctioned off in 1919, providing useful clues to the layout and appearance of these sites. Although many AA guns were mounted on pre-existing structures, merely requiring the insertion of a holdfast as at Hilsea Lines in Portsea for instance, the surviving battery at Lodge Hill, which mounted two 3-inch 20 cwt guns in separate gun pits, points to the design of purpose-built AA batteries on green-field sites. The gun platform on One Tree Hill, at Honor Oak Park in south London, and the structures at Monkham's Hall, near Waltham Cross, reused in the Second World War, each provides further such information. Two AA sites defending Scapa Flow have survived. At Burray Ness, two 4-inch high-angle guns, manned by Royal Marines, were mounted on free-standing concrete platforms in front of a stone magazine. At Carness, the remains of the emplacement of a 4-inch gun, thought to be one of a pair, possibly in a dual-purpose role, consist of a low stone semi-circular parapet with a ready use locker built into one end, with traces nearby of a magazine.

Prior to the switch from the RNAS/RNVR to the Army, London had been woefully under-gunned, and early 1916 saw an immediate increase in the AA defences, taking the total to sixty-four guns, and by November, to eighty-four in mainly two-gun sites, organised across seven Sections. These guns were, almost exclusively, credible AA weapons: 3-inch and 75-mm auto-cannon, with a few of the less successful 12- and 18-pounders. Not only were the London AA defences gaining in strength, but an increase in the armament of coastal AA sites from Great Yarmouth to Dover, with a particularly strong presence in the Thames and Medway area, meant that raiders might be expected to run a gauntlet of fire, even before they approached the capital's ring of guns and lights. One outcome of this reorganisation was that instead of the Thames being sign-posted by individual guns and lights, making it easy for raiders to follow its course into the city, the increased density of weaponry blanketed the eastern approaches, blending the river into the landscape.

The AA defences were steadily improving in both quantity and quality and, in tandem with other improvements in spotting and reporting systems, and in the performance of the fighter aircraft, especially at night, were approaching the point where they began severely to curtail the freedom to which the Zeppelins had grown accustomed. Despite this, there were still some very real failures of management. A problem exacerbated by the profusion of AA weapons was the proliferation of large chunks of hot metal, especially from those guns firing shrapnel, falling on those being defended, sometimes with fatal consequences. Early in 1917, Sir John French, C-in-C Home Forces, had announced a moratorium on AA batteries firing on any aircraft at all even when clearly identified as hostile. This proscription, albeit temporary, was interpreted in some circles as a prelude to shifting the guns wholesale to France, a reprise of the policy that had kept aircraft away from home defence duties earlier in the war. When the order was countermanded that June, it appeared to British pilots that open season on aircraft generally had been declared, with indiscriminate fire proving more dangerous to the defending aircraft than to the enemy. This was an issue that demanded an early solution, but only the full implementation of LADA after July 1917 would enable it adequately to be addressed.

The London Air Defence Area (LADA)

The London Air Defence Area was the product of both the practical and theoretical. In 1916, the universally hated Noel Pemberton Billing MP published a book entitled *The Air War: How to Wage It.* It included a section on the protection of the homeland against aerial attack, describing a system that used a network of numbered grids to plot enemy raids. The system also employed a chain of visual spotter posts, manned by volunteers; high wooden towers mounting amplified sound locators to pick out approaching aircraft; and a command centre with wall-boards and map table to record sightings and direct intercepting aircraft. This prescient vision came very close to the system that operated throughout the Second World War, with radar substituting for sound-locators. His command centre or operations room would be instantly recognisable to those who worked in Fighter Command's filter rooms or the Group HQs of the Royal Observer Corps. The next year, in his report on 'Home Defence Against Air-raids', Lieutenant-General Smuts recommended that the RFC and the RNAS should be under a single command; that there should be better AA defences for London and a proper air-raid warning system; that three squadrons of fighters should be permanently available to counter air raids; and that the entire air defence system for London and the south-east should be under a single unified command. Practical experience dictated that early warning of approaching raids was vital, the skies should contain an element of segregation to avoid problems of friendly fire, and there should be a degree of protection from air raids for the civilian population. All these influences hastened the adoption of a fresh approach.

Brigadier-General Edward Ashmore, a former commander of both RFC and Royal Artillery formations, was appointed by Lord French to plan and implement the new scheme, which was based on clearly defined areas of operation. The innermost core of central London was protected on its east by a balloon apron, trialled in Richmond Park, and extending from Edmonton to the Thames, then to the south of Woolwich. It consisted of a row of balloons, linked together in a continuous line by cables from which were suspended heavy wires. The balloons were tethered at a height of 8,000 feet (2,460 metres), later raised to 11,000 feet (3,380 metres). German bombers unable to fly through the curtain were forced to fly over it, very near to their own ceilings, and the AA shells were therefore fused to explode at that height. Wrapped around this core, which contained AA guns within the balloon apron, was a horseshoe-shaped fighter patrol area, within which were located the aerodromes of this inner aircraft zone: Biggin Hill, North Weald, Suttons Farm, and Hainault Farm. Their aircraft flew fixed straight line or dog-leg patrol paths. The next layer contained more guns and was followed by a further, outer aircraft zone with patrol lines based on Goldhanger, Stow Maries, Detling, and Rochford. Two further artillery zones crossed Kent, north to south, the more easterly one taking in the Dover area, delineating two more aircraft zones based on the aerodromes at Throwley and Bekesbourne. The in-between areas, now aircraft zones that had previously held guns, were given over to searchlights to illuminate hostile aircraft for the fighters to intercept. Crucially, guns and aircraft were kept apart, and the gunners knew that any aircraft that came within either sight or earshot would be a legitimate target. The hitherto fairly haphazard aircraft spotting system was now organised into the Metropolitan Observation Service.

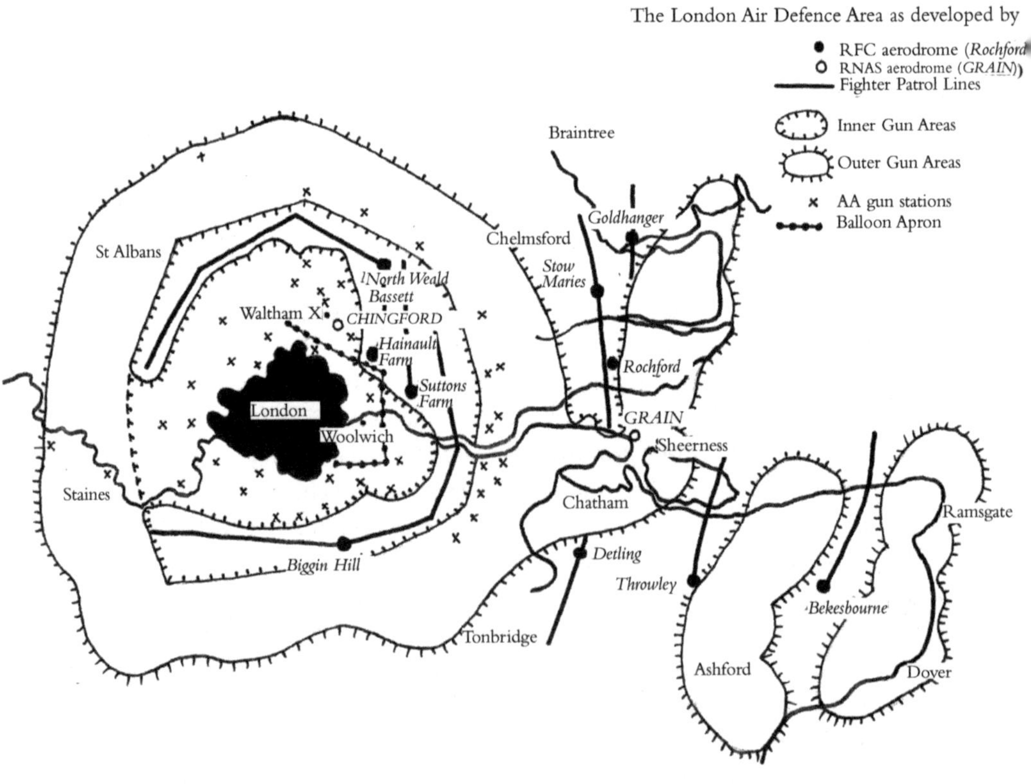

Map to show the operation of the London Air Defence Area.

As is so often the case, the war finished just as these new arrangements approached fruition. By January 1918, there were 250 AA guns defending LADA. These included two mobile brigades with thirty-two 13-pounder 9-cwt guns; the fifty-five guns of the inner London AA defences organised in four sub-Commands; 320 searchlights; and the ninety-four guns of the London Gun Barrier. This last element extended as an outer ring from St Albans through Epping, right round to Staines and on to Redhill, and was designed to provide that chimerical phenomenon, the barrage, which would prove just as illusory in future wars. As Ashmore himself conceded, curtains of fire were unlikely to hit any aircraft, but would frighten and distract whole formations of bombers, many of which, he said, must have been 'fended off', shedding their bombs harmlessly in open countryside. The area defined as LADA finally extended as far as a line drawn between Grantham and Portsmouth, and was further enhanced by a central fighter control centre at Biggin Hill. A Northern Air Defence Area covered the rest of the country.

Ships as AA Batteries

Given the early shortages of AA guns, there were many instances, especially in the Defended Ports, when ships' armament provided a welcome supplement to land-based AA defences. At times, this principle also extended to other locations. We have already met the *Champion*, moored in the Thames, specifically to support the Examination Service, but also mounting a useful AA armament. Other ships may also have contributed, though no overt reference is cited. The *Racecourse*-class minesweeper *Chelmsford* and the paddle-minesweeper *Eglinton* were both based in the Thames in June 1917. Each mounted a pair of 12-pounders and Maxims, while the *Eglinton* carried an additional two 6-pounders. From January 1917, the *Cricket* (an *Insect*-class gunboat with two 6-inch guns and two 12-pounders) was moored off Hunstanton Pier to protect the vital 'Y' Stations, and the *Hearty* (a tug or despatch vessel with four 3-pounders) was also stationed in the Wash from the same date.

Passive Air Defence and Air Raid Precautions

From the time of the earliest air raids in 1915, the authorities were reluctant to issue warnings to the civilian population. Although the Admiralty informed Scotland Yard by telephone when Zeppelins were observed crossing the coast, they refused to issue public warnings even when they knew a raid was imminent. It was felt that time would be lost if work stopped before a raid, especially as a response to false alarms, and casualties would be caused by people going into the streets to seek shelter or to gawp. Despite the disapproval of the police, communities organised their own volunteer street patrols to go on watch and warn people. Legislation to ensure that blackout would be rigorously enforced in the Greater London area came through a provision of the Defence of the Realm Act (DORA), which came into law in October 1915. This reinforced previous regulations governing the cities of London and Birmingham. Other areas, particularly down the east coast, were also subject to light and movement restrictions.

A year later, there were still no public warnings, but the police did undertake to inform hospitals, and people were told to leave telephone lines clear for official business. Only after the Harvest Moon raids of late September 1917 were the hitherto independent ninety fire brigades of the Greater London area brought under central co-ordination under DORA. The Command Centre at County Hall, on the Thames Embankment opposite Westminster, could contact eighty fire-stations triggering their sirens, which would warn of an impending raid. These air-raid warnings were reinforced by police officers, boy scouts, and boys of the Church Lads' Brigade riding around on bicycles waving placards or sounding bugle calls. There were few official shelters, mainly the crypts of churches, the basements of public buildings, caves, and, in London, underground stations. This latter source of shelter was a matter of some controversy as those sheltering unavoidably impeded the operation of the trains. Additionally, most stations had no sanitary facilities, and such overcrowding in inherently dangerous environments inevitably led to accidents and some fatalities. The total capacity of London's underground stations was published as well over 200,000 places, but some stations were occupied at levels well over their highest estimates. Eventually, a new warning system of firing maroons to alert people to an impending air raid, during day or night, was instituted on 7 March 1918. Bugles were used to sound the 'all clear'. This system was in place by the final raid on London. However, there was still no attempt to co-ordinate the use of air-raid shelters. There were the beginnings of a system of inspecting premises, but there was insufficient understanding of what constituted effective protection. People were being killed by blast at street level, even when appearing to be protected inside buildings with concrete frames and floors, and the controversy over the use of underground stations would rumble on into the next war.

Conclusions

The significance of the air war is reflected in the numbers of personnel and quantity of materiel involved by the end of the war. There were 17,500 AA troops on home defence duties. At the time of their amalgamation with the RFC, the RNAS consisted of 55,000 personnel with 3,000 aircraft and 100 airships, a large proportion of which were involved in coastal patrols, A/S duties, and convoy protection. In November 1918, the new RAF had 22,000 aircraft in 133 squadrons with 290,000 personnel, perhaps a quarter of whom were engaged in home defence or were based in the British Isles in maintenance units, training, or working up. The slowly evolving home defence procedures were beginning to bear fruit. By October 1917, a quarter of all enemy bomber aircraft were intercepted and shot down. On 18–20 May 1918, in the final raids on London, six out of fourteen Gothas were shot down. Germany had begun the war with only a dozen Zeppelins and added a further 112 by the end. Of the eighty operational Zeppelins, twenty-three were shot down by guns or fighter aircraft or destroyed by bombs on the ground, with a further thirty-one being destroyed in flying accidents or in bad weather. That level of attrition could not be sustained. Although it could be argued that only small numbers of hostiles, a total of ten Zeppelins and twenty-two aeroplanes, were verified as having been shot down by either guns or fighters during the war, it was generally agreed that the success of any future air defence effort would most likely lie with the fighter. This was conditional on improvements in air-to-air and ground-to-air communication in early warning systems and in fighter-direction. However much Lord Haig and others preferred to sit on the fence when it came to declaring winners and losers, one very important lesson was learnt. General Ashmore's LADA provided a blue-print for Air Defence Great Britain (ADGB) that, with the addition of RDF or radar, would account for much of the RAF's success in the Battle of Britain in the next war.

7

Did the Kaiser Come?

Would the Kaiser Come?

It would appear that expectations on the part of the British that the Germans were planning to invade were to some extent shared by the German people themselves.

Seeing off a German neighbour from Victoria station a few days before war was declared, a Londoner was told not to worry as he and his family would be looked after when 'we come over to England'. Perhaps the best jokes are those enigmatic ones that offer just a hint of the possibilities. Anecdotal evidence from the no-man's-land conversations of Christmas 1914 would suggest that some German troops were under the impression that a successful German invasion had already taken place. One British officer reported being asked how many German troops it had taken to capture London. To some in Britain, an invasion was a certainty that overshadowed everyday life. An American, who flew the Stars and Stripes from the lawn of his country mansion in what he intended as a gesture of solidarity, was warned that he was thought to be advertising his neutrality in the face of an invading German army, and would be wise to lower his flag before his outraged neighbours took incendiary action. One way of dealing with fears of invasion was to plan a pre-emptive strike. Admiral Wilson was not alone in wanting to put a force ashore on Germany's North Sea coast. Churchill, First Lord of the Admiralty, recruited Erskine Childers—fresh from an overt, but largely unpublicised gun-running trip supplying Irish nationalists—to advise on possible invasion routes into Germany. Churchill was desperate to invade somewhere, preferably Germany, but was deflected into the disastrous invasion of Turkey instead.

Rumours Continue into the War

Even after the war had begun, there was no decrease in the wildness of the rumours that circulated, especially along the invasion coasts. In December 1914, three months into the war, the Committee of Imperial Defence had concerns over the 25,000 Germans and Austrians of military age resident in the London area alone. Rumours of buildings with concrete floors, erected by German businesses around London and intended as emplacements from which German siege howitzers would be able to bombard central London, were matched by other buildings with flat concrete roofs, occupying vantage points from which the fire of those guns might be directed. These stories and many more were propagated by the *Daily Express* and the London evening *Globe*, thus encouraging a proliferation of such reports and wild imaginings on the part of the more credulous among the general public. Even a letter to *The Times*, written by the expert commissioned by Scotland Yard to investigate these sites (reporting the whole business as totally spurious and a complete waste of time), did not altogether allay the fears of those who wanted, for whatever reason, to believe them. One particularly fatuous example, from Norfolk in December 1914, demonstrates the problem. A citizen of substance in Sheringham writing to his cousin, a High Court judge in London, describes the local preparations. Having reported soldiers digging trench lines across the golf course and two further lines some way inland between Hunworth and Briston, itself an injudicious, if not treasonous act, he then relates a conversation with the supervising officer. The Germans, he was told, had constructed flat-bottomed boats, each of them capable of accommodating three railway trains, carrying a total of 40,000 men. The plan was to hide these men in secrecy under Sheringham Cliffs until the whole force had disembarked. One must hope that the talkative officer had identified our correspondent as a particularly gullible member of the chattering classes. In September 1915, *The Globe* was shut down because of the paper's false statements about a divided Cabinet and Kitchener's resignation, which 'depressed his Majesty's subjects' giving 'comfort to the enemy'. Copies were seized and the presses removed. Only after a fulsome apology and the removal of the editor from control of the paper's content was *The Globe* allowed to reopen a fortnight later, but it continued to print malicious accusations of treachery, particularly against a number of prominent people—including Margot Asquith (wife of the Prime Minister), Richard Haldane (architect of the Army's transformation), and Admiral Prince Louis of Battenberg (the First Sea Lord), these latter two being pushed into resigning.

Internal Security

Much of the effort of Vernon Kell's MO5(g), later to become MI5, was devoted to assembling a card index of suspected spies, saboteurs, and aliens, which eventually included nearly 40,000 names, cross-referenced on a million cards. Those sharing the obsessions of Le Queux cited the lack of any hard evidence as an indicator not of a virtual absence of enemy activity in Great Britain, but as proof of the enemy's cunning in avoiding detection. Le Queux, accompanied by people who should have known better, went to the lengths of going out at night to set traps for enemy spies who might have been signalling to their compatriots using flashlights. In early August 1914, twenty-one of the spies known to be operating in Britain were arrested, while just one escaped to Germany. There was nevertheless a fear of sabotage by the many Germans living in Britain, and overreaction to anyone acting in a mildly suspicious manner. German waiters were suspected of being members of what a later war would call the Fifth Column. Olympia became an internment camp for German and Austro-Hungarian nationals, guarded by troops from Wellington Barracks.

The National Registration Act came into force in August 1915, requiring everyone between the ages of fifteen and sixty-five to carry an ID card at all times. Those engaged in war work also had to carry a card detailing their occupation and place of work. The security services reckoned that they were able to identify those engaged in espionage, partly through the inept behaviour of the putative spies themselves. A number were tried, convicted, and shot at the Tower of London; others were imprisoned for the duration, deported, or extradited to other allied nations. Discovery, arrest, and preliminary interrogation of suspected spies was the responsibility of Basil Thomson, the complacent head of Scotland Yard's Criminal Investigation Department. In his memoirs, he puts the lack of information from Britain reaching Germany's intelligence services down to the incompetence of their operatives. What is particularly interesting is his observation that, by 1916, the Germans were more eager to gain knowledge of morale and the mood of the country than overt military detail. This deduction was based on eavesdropping on officer POWs at Donington Hall in Leicestershire, captured documents briefing spies, and conversations with captured spies themselves. These sources all revealed a change of emphasis from the fantasies of Le Queux's *Spies of the Kaiser* and the actual reports sent by real spies earlier in the war, enumerating the battleships in Rosyth Dockyard.

Invasion Scares during the War

Just as in the Second World War, when many expected London to be destroyed by bombing on the first day of the war, there were expectations that the

Germans would land on British shores immediately after war was declared. In fact, it would be nearly four months before a plausible and specific fear of an invasion was excited. Study of the tides and the phases of the moon identified the night of 20 November 1914 as presenting all those circumstances that might facilitate a successful invasion by a German army, whisked across the North Sea to the east coast on fast transports. The nation's defences were hurriedly prepared to resist such an attempt. The Grand Fleet prepared to sail from its Scottish bases. Diverted from their scheduled sailing to Africa, the shallow-draught monitors *Humber*, *Mersey*, and *Severn* were anchored in the Wash, and 300,000 troops were held ready to repel the enemy on the beaches. In December, both the bombardment of north-east coast ports by German battlecruisers (see below) and the bombing campaign begun by the Zeppelins in January 1915 were seen as possible preludes to invasion. Once again, such threatening activities coincided with occasions on which the state of the tides in the North Sea and the easterly prevailing wind were cause for alarm, and reinforcements were duly mobilised and despatched. As it happened, none of these threats materialised, but the pattern had been set whereby large bodies of troops would always be maintained against the threat of invasion. On each such occasion, the patrol flotillas would be recalled, their scattered ships returning to their war stations. Resulting from the early scares, plans were made to strengthen the defences, particularly in the Humber Estuary, and to explore the possibilities of flooding the Fens.

The appointment of Field Marshal Sir John French as C-in-C Home Forces in 1916 had instigated a new appraisal of Germany's military capability. It was thought that they could land 160,000 men, but there was not sufficient manpower to carry out an invasion. Nevertheless, *The Times* continued to warn of the possibility. There were more rumours of impending invasion at the time of the Easter Rising in Dublin in 1916. While it was thought that both weapons and German troops might be landed in Ireland in support of the rising, it was also suspected that such operations might constitute a feint for an invasion on the east coast and a march on London. As far inland as Northamptonshire, Special Constables were called out and arrangements made to evacuate civilians along specified routes so as not to interfere with troop movements. It was learned that the German Fleet had left its ports and Lowestoft was shelled on the 25 April. This caused two divisions to be readied for deployment from the Midlands to the coast. French was reluctant to send troops to Ireland as he felt this would play into German hands by weakening the defences in Britain. All these events together may have been contributory factors to Sir Francis Lloyd's push to complete the defences around London, which he considered doubly necessary in view of expected German success at Verdun. He opined that if the French line were to be breached, Paris would fall and the way would be wide open for a German invasion via the south coast.

It appears that Lloyd exploited the rumours to ensure that war weariness was not allowed to erode the invasion readiness of his troops, but he laid himself open to criticism with such cynical manipulation.

While the Battle of the Somme and the struggle for Verdun continued, sucking in every available soldier on both sides, the country was safe from a full-scale invasion. A raid by 20,000 troops near the Wash, however, remained a more likely scenario. In March 1917, rumours that the Germans were massing 500,000 men and large numbers of ships in Zeebrugge caused a 'period of vigilance', followed by further rumours on Sunday 25 March that there had been an actual German landing on the east coast. This news provoked panic stories and men were hurriedly recalled to their units. Views were expressed about the poor state of the country's home defence capability, which would, apparently, be pushed to 'repulse (a force of) about 450 attackers'. It is highly likely that the rumours were actually initiated by French and Lloyd, who were concerned over the poor performance of the Home Defence Army in a recent test mobilisation. The problem was exacerbated by naval concern over the ever-growing U-boat threat, and what was interpreted as a willingness on the part of Hindenburg to hazard the High Seas Fleet in support of an invasion. It might be argued that Lloyd rather gave the game away when, in a speech delivered in south London that summer, he said:

> The theory is that the enemy, realising at length the futility of their plan to starve out this country by indiscriminate destruction of shipping, and realising also that there is no real prospect of achieving decisive military success, will be driven to make a desperate dash to land troops on our shores.

After French was sent to Ireland as Lord Lieutenant, the Chief of the Imperial General Staff General Sir William Robertson assumed full responsibility for home defence. He felt that the forces available could contain a raid of up to 20,000 men, but by the end of the year, estimates of German capabilities had risen to a raid by over 30,000 men and he thought a force now inflated to 170,000 was feasible. Beyond these general concerns, there were also worries over particular vulnerabilities. One such fear was that weaknesses in communications between coastal strong points on the Kent coast could permit a lightning strike by up to 15,000 German troops who could land and go on to take Canterbury and the inland military port of Richborough. Some fears were more specific and localised. Fliers at the experimental air station on Orford Ness were apprehensive about the large number of German POWs retained there to maintain the airfield's drainage arrangements and to construct sea defences, outnumbering their hosts four to one and constituting a serious threat in the event of a German naval raid. In March 1918, casualties caused by the Germans' successful 'Michael' offensive meant a further weakening of the Home Army as large numbers of replacements were required in France. In a command reshuffle, Robertson was replaced as CIGS and appointed C-in-C Home Forces. By September 1918, however, a new CIGS reported to the War Cabinet that there was not 'the remotest prospect' of invasion. The Admiralty watched the demolition of the home defence armies and conceded that the most the Germans could manage would be a raid involving fewer than 5,000 men. Troops were then moved inland from the coast and organised as mobile columns to intercept enemy raids.

The Assault on the Coast: The Bombardment of the East Coast

While the German admirals were wary of engaging the British fleet in full-scale battle, they were content to wage a different type of naval warfare. This consisted of attacks on shipping, both naval and mercantile, by U-boats; the sowing of mines by U-boats, surface vessels, and aircraft; attacks on merchant ships by commerce raiders; and the bombardment of coastal towns. The first coastal raid came on 3 November 1914, when German armoured cruisers fired on Great Yarmouth. Fortunately, it was a misty day and most of the shells landed on the beach at Gorleston. One of the German cruisers, the *Stralsund*, laid some mines, one of which sank the British submarine *D5* as it chased after the raiders. The gunboat *Halcyon* was caught out in the open and was damaged, before being rescued by a smokescreen from one of Gorleston's destroyer flotilla. While it came as a shock to residents all along the east coast that German ships could carry out such an operation without being challenged by the Navy, very little physical damage was done; yet, the next month, some of those same German ships were back.

In December, a large part of the main German High Seas Fleet sailed out into the North Sea in the hope of luring a British battle squadron into a trap. Led by Admiral Hipper in the *Seydlitz*, and including the *Moltke*, *Von der Tann*, *Derflinger*, and the older *Blucher*, the First Scouting Group left the main German fleet and headed through the gap in the minefield off the north Yorkshire coast. The *Von der Tann* and *Derflinger* were despatched to bombard Whitby and Scarborough, while the *Kolberg* was to lay mines off Filey. Meanwhile, the *Seydlitz*, *Blucher*, and *Moltke* sailed on to raid Hartlepool, where British naval vessels were based but unable to match the firepower of the German cruisers. The four destroyers, at sea as the German ships arrived off the port, tackled them but were driven off after taking hits. The two cruisers were caught trying to manoeuvre out of their berths, and one was severely damaged by two direct hits from the *Blucher's* 11-inch guns. The two coast artillery batteries engaged all three German ships, and while her two companions shelled the town, the *Blucher* attempted to silence them and took a direct hit for her pains. Both batteries received hits, killing men and smashing masonry, but other shells either skidded off the glacis to explode elsewhere or failed to explode at all. The RGA scored several hits on the battlecruisers, but many of their shells were seen, by a nearby fishing vessel, to bounce off their armour into the air. Finally, frustrated by misfires, dud shells, and the disappearance of the German ships into the mist, the gunners could cease fire and take stock.

The submarine *C9* managed to get out of harbour but overshot its intended course having had to submerge to avoid the *Blucher*'s shells. The German ships got away and only a combination of bad weather and poor communication prevented the squadron's destruction by a strong naval force sailing out of Rosyth to intercept it. Scarborough had received about thirty hits, which killed nineteen people including women and children. Whitby got off more lightly, being hit by thirty shells out of around 200 fired, which caused three deaths. The ships bombarding Hartlepool were estimated at the time to have fired over 1,000 rounds, killing 112 civilians, almost equal numbers of men, women, and children, and causing widespread damage. Nine soldiers in the batteries were killed and five sailors. The guns of the Heugh and Lighthouse Batteries at Hartlepool were the only ones to engage enemy ships in the war, and though they were bravely fought, many problems arose relating to the technology of the guns and shells themselves, and to their situation in a built-up area with restricted visibility.

In the early hours of 25 April 1916, a further attack was made on Great Yarmouth and Lowestoft, which took most of the hits. Inexplicably, the German ships were firing armour-piercing shells, most of which failed to explode. Nonetheless, four people were killed and some forty houses destroyed with many more damaged. Again, the damage was psychological, as people fled the town each night in fear of a repeat attack. The German fleet had planned a follow-up raid on Sunderland on 31 April, but this was called off by a change of plan. During the preparations for what was envisaged as the showdown of Jutland, a sweep of the North Sea was substituted for the Sunderland raid.

At the end of the year, an armed trawler was sunk patrolling off Great Yarmouth, and early in 1917, the little Suffolk coastal resort of Southwold was shelled by a flotilla of destroyers that pumped over ninety shells into it, but caused minimal casualties and little physical damage. Raids on south coast towns, such as Dover, Ramsgate, and Broadstairs, continued throughout 1917, and Scarborough was shelled by a U-boat on 4 September, when three people were killed. In January 1918, Great Yarmouth was shelled, suffering six deaths, and a U-boat shelled the island of St Kilda in May, firing eighty shells and destroying the naval W/T station. While Henry James, suggesting in 1914 that the prominent chimney pots on his Rye home, Lamb House, had been identified as a target for German warships, may not have been serious, Lord Northcliffe fared differently. Appointed in 1917 as Director of Propaganda in Lloyd George's Government, he was regarded as a legitimate target for assassination. His home, Elmwood House, at Woodnesborough, near Sandwich, was actually shelled by a German warship despatched for that specific purpose, causing the death of the gardener's wife.

The Assault from the Air: German Bombing Raids on Britain

Despite the success of a vote at The Hague Convention of 1899 to outlaw the discharge of explosives from aircraft, the expectation of the German armed forces was that, in the event of a war breaking out between the two countries, Zeppelins would be used to bomb British targets. Given the complete lack of precision involved in dropping bombs from a great height onto a populated landmass, hitting homes and civilians would be inevitable. The German airship, *Z6*, had set out to bomb the Liege forts on the third day of the war, albeit unsuccessfully. Under pressure from his military advisers, the Kaiser—who had previously forbidden bombing forays over British targets and certainly never over London where he had relatives and, moreover, an attachment to its historic buildings—relented. However, he limited the Zeppelins to military targets at night and at weekends, when he decided women and children would be safe at home. In December 1914, two German aircraft dropped bombs onto Dover and Sheerness, and Winston Churchill predicted to a friend an attack on London by a hundred Zeppelins to mark the Kaiser's birthday on 18 January 1915. In the event, it was late the next evening when two Zeppelins attacked targets in Norfolk. Mistaking the Happisburgh lighthouse for the mouth of the Humber Estuary, the airships had proceeded, as they thought, to bomb Hull. Several HE bombs and incendiaries were dropped over centres of population, and in Kings Lynn, these killed two women and injured a further thirteen civilians. In Great Yarmouth, two people were killed by a bomb that fell next to St Peter's Church. In April, the Zeppelins raided Wallsend on the Tyne and targets on Humberside. The first raid on London was mounted in May 1915, killing a dozen people including a child; this was followed by eighteen further raids on London that October. Casualties across the country mounted, and in March 1916, a bomb that fell on a Baptist chapel in Cleethorpes, where soldiers of the Manchester Regiment were billeted, killed thirty-one and injured many more. In January 1916, a number of bombs were dropped on Loughborough from one or more Zeppelins, killing ten people and injuring others. In May, the Zeppelins attacked York. By the end of

1916, many towns and cities, mainly in the eastern half of England, had been bombed, but the Zeppelins had begun to suffer serious losses and raids had to be cut back for lack of trained aircrew.

A change in tactics was made in November 1916, when the first raids on London carried out by aircraft were initiated. Once the success of this form of assault had been evaluated, large scale production of Gotha bombers began in early 1917. May saw the first serious raid on London by twenty-two twin-engined Gotha bombers, each carrying seven 50-kg (110-lb) and six 12.5-kg (27.5-lb) bombs. Although the primary target was obscured by low cloud, the Zeppelins found clearer areas on which to drop their bombs, killing ninety people in the Folkestone area. The next month, raids killed 160 people including eighteen pupils in a primary school in Poplar, East London. In September, London was bombed by four-engined Zeppelin-Staarken biplanes, and a further tactical switch was made to night attacks. An attack on Chatham killed over 100 sailors in the naval barracks. At the very end of September 1917, raids by Gotha and Giant bombers on five nights in succession killed forty-seven and injured 226. The Giant had a wingspan of 138 feet, was powered by up to six engines, and carried a payload of 2 tons of bombs. Altogether, the raids by the airships and, subsequently, by the bomber aircraft, killed over 1,400 people, more than half of those being civilians, and caused severe injuries to more than twice that number. In the year from May 1917 alone, 836 people were killed and 1,965 seriously injured. Through the course of the war, there were fifty-three raids by Zeppelins and a further fifty-seven by bomber aircraft, mainly Gothas and Giants. Using the map produced by the *Daily Mail* in 1919, which plotted the fall of bombs in the London area, it is impossible to escape the conclusion that the majority were either dropped at random or on known built-up residential areas. Although the bombers had initially followed the Thames into London, only a tiny number of bombs were dropped on the Docks and very few on Woolwich Arsenal or Barracks. The vast majority fell on the residential East End, the square mile of the City, and along the lines of the main arterial roads into the centre, with fewer in the West End, and a scattering over the entire LCC area.

The civilian response was a mixture of panic among those working in the docks and armaments factories of London's East End and anger at the apparent lack of concern on the part of the authorities, who did little to alleviate the situation. Funeral parades for the victims of bombing became a vehicle for protest. In mid-1917, the east-enders lost patience after some particularly bad raids. There was little the police could do about strikes, serious rioting, or looting, targeting 'German' businesses across south-east England. There was also a feeling that London's West End, with its more numerous underground stations, was less vulnerable to aerial bombing than the less salubrious east.

The Assault at Sea: The German U-boat Campaign

Both Britain and Germany adopted blockade as central planks of their policy. Both nations were heavily reliant on imports of food and raw materials, and merchant shipping represented a vital lifeline for ensuring their ability to keep fighting. In the case of Britain, there was the additional burden of maintaining cross-Channel routes—those taking reinforcements and munitions to the front and returning the vast numbers of wounded back to Blighty.

Ironically, so much had been invested in building up both Germany's High Seas Fleet and Britain's Grand Fleet that there was great reluctance to commit them to a decisive battle. Fisher's flotillas represented the major presence in the North Sea, and the German navy put a heavy emphasis on its U-boats, which commenced their campaign from August 1914. By Christmas, the Royal Navy had sustained losses of a pre-dreadnought and five cruisers, while half of Germany's original force of thirty-eight submarines had been lost. In February 1915, the assault on merchant shipping began in earnest with the German declaration of unrestricted U-boat war in retaliation for the British blockade of the German North Sea ports. The area around the British Isles, declared a war zone by Germany, became dangerous to all shipping including neutrals. All these indiscriminate attacks on merchant ships, including liners such as the *Lusitania* in May 1915, alienated the neutrals (especially the USA) and resulted in the delivery of ultimata to Germany, who suspended the policy in September 1915. In the seven months of their campaign, the U-boats sank ¾ million tons of British shipping, as well as significant numbers of neutral vessels. The British merchant fleet, at the time totalling some 21 million tons, could afford the losses, but only for a short while. An added hazard to shipping was contributed by German minelaying operations in the North Sea, particularly when carried out by submarines. One double-edged sword was the use by the Navy of 'Q' ships, disguised converted merchantmen that acted as decoys. When a U-boat surfaced to attack using its deck-guns rather than its precious torpedoes, it found itself facing a heavily armed warship. This provided U-boat captains with an excuse for staying submerged and leaving merchant sailors to drown.

On 1 February 1917, the Kaiser—under pressure from his admirals, who realised that unless Britain could be starved into submission first, Germany would succumb to the blockade—approved the resumption of unrestricted submarine warfare, with over 100 U-boats available. The USA declared war on 3 February 1917. Shipping losses soared dramatically from half a million tons per month up to 0.8 million tons through the summer. During March 1917, around 25 per cent of all inward shipping to the British Isles was sunk, resulting in a struggle to build more ships. The highest loss occurred in April 1917, when 880,000 tons were sunk, over half of which comprised British vessels. Such losses escalated, and three-quarters of all sinkings took place in the last two years of the war. Over half of all attacks carried out on merchant shipping were aimed at British ships, with the USA enduring 2.4 per cent. Eventually, on 27 April 1917, the Admiralty reluctantly instituted a convoy system, but only in September was it fully implemented; following this, losses were immediately reduced, stabilising at an average of around 300,000 tons per month. During 1918, 2¾ million tons were sunk at a monthly average of 230,000 tons, for the loss of sixty-nine U-boats. Through the course of the war, Germany had operated a total of 351 U-boats, of which 178 (50 per cent) were lost in combat and a further thirty-nine (11 per cent) accidentally. On the Allied side, around 5,000 ships with a total tonnage of 13 million were sunk.

Lessons for the Future

While it has become fashionable to accuse the military of fighting the previous war, the First World War provided opportunities for experience to influence the conduct of aspects of the next major conflict. The recommendation to defend the coast with a chain of coast artillery batteries—ignored in the First World War—was taken up in the Second with the construction of fifty emergency batteries, in summer 1940. The integrated elements of LADA, taken on to inform ADGB, gave the controllers of Fighter Command an enormous advantage during the Battle of Britain. The crucial significance of what came to be called the Battle of the Atlantic was not lost on the Navy, who ensured that escort vessels, Liberty ships, and aircraft carriers received priority in the shipyards both sides of the Atlantic, and that air cover was extended as far out from the land as might be possible. Most of these measures had been identified by leaders in the First World War, who often lacked the technology to apply them.

The Role of Civilians

In October 1914, leaflets were printed ready for distribution, if necessary, to every household in Dover, informing them that 'under Military Orders they are to evacuate the town IMMEDIATELY'. Included in the leaflet were details of the transport available for the infirm, and instructions regarding what people should take with them in the way of warm clothing and sustenance for twelve hours. Checkpoints were set up on the Deal, Canterbury, and Folkestone roads, to control all movement in and out of the town, and 22,000 special passes were issued, which had to be shown by anyone wishing to pass through them. In October 1915, these passes were replaced by the National Registration ID cards.

In the first two years of the war, recruitment was voluntary, even if social pressure was applied, and recruiting offices and drill halls had been immediately inundated from 4 August 1914. However, it became necessary to maintain levels of recruitment as the initial enthusiasm for the war waned. The Derby Scheme of attestation identified potential recruits, but full conscription was introduced in February 1916.

For those not in uniform, however, there were many ways of contributing to the war effort. Special constables were sworn in to cover for volunteers to the forces and young lads could participate in the work of the military by joining the Boy Scouts, serving as coast watchers, orderlies, and messengers in army camps, and gaining badges for working three hours per day, for twenty-eight days. Scouts also guarded telegraph wires and generally kept their eyes open for anything arousing suspicion. The dozens of hospitals catering for the wounded, the sick, and the convalescent were staffed by volunteers of the Voluntary Aid Detachments. Civilian effort also went into keeping the home fires burning by working in agriculture, the mines and docks, and, especially for women, in public transport and munitions production. The Munitions Inventions Department was set up by David Lloyd George in summer 1915 under the chairmanship of Ernest Moir, a civil engineer, responsible for the Dover defences. Scientists investigated, *inter alia*, defence against Zeppelins and had use of a proving ground at Wembley. Similar groups were working for the Admiralty and the War Office in parallel, but not necessarily communicating. In 1916, the Department of Scientific and Industrial Research was set up with Sir Ernest Rutherford as a member. In 1917, they established a Fuel Research Board and a Food Investigation Board to look at diet and health. This co-ordinating body was the brainchild of Frank Heath, Secretary to the Board of Education, under whose guidance the National Physical Laboratory at Teddington came up with an effective and easily manufactured steel helmet—the 'Brodie', which had become standard issue by the middle of 1916. At Woolwich, the Inventions Branch of the Royal Arsenal's Laboratory developed a Belgian grenade that became the Mills Bomb. A freelance collaboration between a newspaper editor and an engineer at Ransome & Rapier in Ipswich produced the Stokes Mortar, finally accepted by the Ordnance Board in late 1915. However, as in later wars, such private initiatives were often resented by the professionals and a new Trench Warfare Department imposed a monopoly on the manufacture of weapons, often stifling new ideas in the process.

There was a great deal of discussion in Britain's newspapers as to whether there should be resistance from the civilian population if the country were to be invaded. Despite voices calling for resistance as a matter of duty, more cited the experience of the Belgian populace, heavily reported by the papers as atrocities perpetrated by the beastly Huns, to argue the contrary. Although many of the stories were wildly distorted, there were nevertheless many cases of Belgian civilians being summarily executed, suspected (usually wrongly) of being *franc tireurs*. As things turned out, these matters would never be put to the test.

APPENDIX I

'Defended Ports' as Classified by the Owen Committee, 1905

Class 'A'

Chatham/Sheerness/Medway/Nore
Plymouth/Devonport
Portsmouth/Solent
Pembroke Dock/Milford Haven

Class 'B'

Berehaven
Cork/Cobh/Queenstown
Dover
Forth/Rosyth/Granton/Leith
Lough Swilly/Buncrana
Portland/Weymouth

Class 'C'

Aberdeen
Barrow-in-Furness
Barry
Belfast Lough
Cardiff
Clyde/Greenock/Ardrossan
Dublin/Dun Laoghaire/Kingstown
Falmouth
Hartlepool
Harwich/Felixstowe
Humber/Grimsby
Liverpool/Mersey

Lough Foyle/Londonderry
Newhaven
Swansea
Sunderland
Tay/Dundee
Thames
Tyne/North and South Shields

Not included in Owen's Classification

Great Yarmouth/Gorleston (established 1912)
Immingham in the Humber (established 1912)
Invergordon/Cromarty (established 1912)
Scapa Flow (established 1914)
Scilly Isles (disarmed 1905)
Severn Estuary (disarmed 1905)

APPENDIX II

The Royal Navy in Defence of the Seas: Shore Bases and Support Ships

Notes:
i: dates in brackets after ships' names are launch dates
ii: support ships moved around from base to base as required
iii: all vessels are pre-fixed 'HMS' unless designated otherwise

Aberdeen: Auxiliary Patrol base with the yacht *Nairn* (1913) as depot ship.
Ardrossan: *see* Clyde
Barrow-in-Furness: Civilian shipbuilding yards.
Belfast: Civilian dockyard with large graving dock and repair yards; base for minesweeping trawlers and for the 130 drifters servicing the 36-mile-long (57-km-long) Northern Channel anti-submarine nets, as well as APS armed trawlers and the Belfast Armed Yacht Squadron, which patrolled each end of the net barriers.
Berehaven: Naval base used by Royal Navy for Atlantic Patrols and by Division 6 of the US Navy Atlantic Fleet, 1917–18. The depot ship for the 14th Submarine Flotilla was the *Vulcan*, then the converted merchant cruiser *Ambrose* (1903) from 1917.
Blacksod: Auxiliary Patrol base moved to Killybegs in 1915.
Blyth: From 1915–19, a base for the 5th Submarine Flotilla with the *Titania* (1915) as depot ship.
Brightlingsea: Base, from 1915, for the vessels tending the Whin anchorage booms with the rearmed cruiser *Wallaroo* (1890) as guard ship until 1916, succeeded first by the *Wildfire* (1888), and then by the drifter *City of Perth* (1907) as the base for six patrol launches until 1919.
Bristol: HQ of Bristol Division RNR/RNVR at 37 Jamaica Road after the drill ship *Daedalus* was sold in 1911.
Buncrana: *see* Lough Swilly
Campbeltown: Submarine base with the *Platypus* (1916) as depot ship 1917–18, succeeded by the cruiser *Thames* (1885)
Cardiff: Naval base open for the duration, closed 1920.
Chatham: Primarily a dockyard building ships for the RN, and one of the three manning bases, providing the crews for hundreds of ships. A base for destroyers

with the depot ship *Hecla* (1878); for submarines with the depot ship *Maidstone* (1912); and minesweepers with the depot ship *Raymont* (1916); the cruiser *Wallaroo* (1890) was guard ship 1914–15.

Clacton: The original base in 1914 for the boom defences of the Whin anchorage.

Clyde/Ardrossan: Base for Clyde Division RNR/RNVR who crewed the gunboat *Rattler* (1886), and for submarines and the APS with the *Pactolus*, a converted cruiser of 1896, as combined depot ship, 1914–19. The paddle ships *Balmoral* (1900), *Princess Mary* (1892), and *Lorna Doone* (1891) were hired as minesweepers, and also served as base and accommodation ships. By 1918, base for the 12th M/S Flotilla.

Cork/Cobh/Queenstown: HQ C-in-C Western Approaches in the cruiser *Endymion* (1891), and Auxiliary Patrol base in the depot ship *Colleen* with the cruiser *Medusa* (1888) as her tender. Four torpedo boats formed the local defence flotilla with the 8th M/S Flotillla in 1918.

Corpach: US Naval base for delivery of mines for Northern Barrage operation, 1917–18.

Cromarty/Invergordon: Fleet anchorage and flotilla base for the sixteen *M*-class destroyers of the 11th Flotilla with the *Tyne* (1878) as depot ship; for submarines with HMS *Soho* (1899) as depot ship; for APS with the *Evening Star* (1894) as depot ship in 1914, then the yacht *Eileen* (1910), then the armed boarding ship *Stephen Furness* (1910) to 1916. The former troopship *Thalia* (1869) acted as base ship at Cromarty and Peterhead, with the battleship *Mars* (1896) serving as depot ship, 1916–20. The local defence flotilla comprised five destroyers. US Naval base for Northern Barrage operation, 1917–18.

Devonport: An important naval Dockyard and one of three RN manning bases, home to elements of the Second Fleet and a destroyer flotilla with the cruisers *Talbot* (1895) from 1913–14, *Eclipse* (1894) from 1915–17, then *Essex* (1901) as depot and accommodation ships for 2nd and 4th Destroyer Flotillas early in the war. The 3rd Submarine Flotilla had the *Pigmy* as depot ship, 1910–14, the sloop *Onyx* (1892) from 1914–16, and then the new destroyer leader *Stuart* in 1918. The old *Valiant* of 1863 served as a store for the destroyer flotilla and as a kite balloon vessel, and the sloop *Reindeer* (1883) as a boom defence vessel. The local defence flotilla comprised six destroyers and eight torpedo-boats.

Dover: Home of the Dover Patrol with the cruiser *Attentive* (1904) as base ship, and the *Surf* as depot ship for Rear Admiral (Controlled Minefields) in 1918; the gunboat *Hazard* (1894) served as a submarine depot ship 1914–18, and the yacht *Surprise* (1896) was hired for the duration as guard ship.

Dublin: *see* Dun Laoghaire

Dundee: APS base with the yacht *Iolaire* (1902) as depot ship.

Dun Laoghaire (Kingstown from 1821 but 'Dublin' to the Admiralty): Base for APS served by the *Boadicea II*; for motor launches with the cruiser *Patrol* (1904) as depot ship; for the Hydrophone Flotilla patrolling the Irish Sea; for the eleven destroyers of the Irish Sea Hunting Flotilla by 1918; closed in 1919.

Edinburgh: *see* Forth/Granton/Port Edgar

Falmouth (HMS *Vivid*): APS base with the drifter *Dreel Castle* (1908) as depot ship, 1915–19; also base for the *Venerable*, tender to the *Research*, the sometime depot ship for the Southern Patrol; base for 15th M/S Flotilla by 1918.

Felixstowe: *see* Harwich: Base for 20th M/S Flotilla in 1918.

Fleetwood: RN submarine base closed 1919.

Forth/Granton/Port Edgar: Base for Edinburgh Division RNR/RNVR; Granton (HMS *Gunner*) and Port Edgar (HMS *Columbine*) served as bases for the Grand

Fleet's Southern Force torpedo boat destroyers and minesweepers with the *Columbine* (1876) as depot ship until 1917, when it became the land base HMS *Lochinvar*. The light cruiser *Sentinel* had been depot ship for the 8th Destroyer Flotilla at Granton in 1914, followed by another cruiser, the *Leander* (1882) with the 3rd Destroyer Flotilla. The APS base had the trawler *Gunner* (1915) as depot ship in 1916; base for 16th M/S Flotilla by 1918.

Gateshead: Base for Tyne Division RNR/RNVR formed ashore in 1905, then with cruiser *Calliope* as drill ship, 1907–31.

Gosport: Fort Blockhouse, HMS *Dolphin*, was the RN's submarine training and experimental base. The sloop *Ladas* and the War Department vessel *Pigmy* (1905) served as depot ships for the 5th Submarine Flotilla.

Great Yarmouth/Gorleston: Flotilla base for the 7th Patrol Flotilla in 1914, with the destroyers *Violet*, *Vixen*, *Lively*, *Success*, *Earnest*, and *Leopard*, and the 8th Submarine Flotilla with the *Alecto* (1911) as depot ship from 1912; APS base, HMS *Kingfisher*, with the trawlers *Miura* (1911) 1914–15, *Adele* formerly *Kingfisher*, and *Dorothy* (1915) 1915–19 as depot ships. The trawlers *Cairo* (1902) and *White Ear* (1914), and the yacht *Zarefah* (1905), acted as M/S base ships, 1914–15. The HQ of the Flag Admiral Commanding East Coast, 1914–18, was the yacht *Sagitta* (1908), and the monitor *Roberts* (1915) was guard ship from 1916–18.

Greenock/Clyde: The *Admiral*-class battleship *Benbow* (1888) was guard ship from 1909.

Grimsby: *see* Hull/Humber/Immingham: APS base, HMS *Pekin*, with the cruiser *Leander* (1882) as depot ship for trawlers in 1914, and then the trawlers *Pekin* (1907) from 1914–19, and *John Dunkin*, 1915–19; base for 7th M/S Flotilla in 1918.

Hartlepool: *see* Tees

Harwich: Flotilla base for 1st Destroyer Flotilla with the *Woolwich* (1912) as depot ship in 1914 and then the cruiser *Blake* (1889); the 7th and 9th Submarine Flotillas had the *Maidstone* (1912) and the *Pandora* (1902) as depot ships 1914–19, and the cruiser *Forth* (1886), from 1916–18. The SNO had a floating HQ in the dreadnought *Hercules* for a short while. First the *Ganges II* (1863) served as the harbour launch/base ship, and then the yacht *Oriflamme* (1890) formerly *St George* became the base ship in 1915; in 1918, base for the 6th M/S Flotilla.

Holyhead: APS base with the yachts *Vanessa II* (1899) as depot ship 1914–19, *Ilex* (1896) and *Boadicea II* (1882) from 1914–15, and the *Amethyst III* (1877) 1915–17.

Hove: Base for Southern Division RNR/RNVR (forerunner of HMS *King Alfred*)

Hull/Humber/Immingham: Flotilla Base at Immingham Dock with the cruiser *St George* (1892) as depot ship, for destroyers and the APS, 1914–15; the 10th Submarine Flotilla was serviced by the cruiser *Forth* (1886), from 1914–16, replaced by the submarine depot ship *Vulcan* (1889) from 1916–17, then by the gunboat *Hebe* (1892) for the 3rd Submarine Flotilla 1917–19 with the cruiser *Wallaroo* (1890) as her tender in 1918. Handing over boom defence duties to the trawler *Sheraton* (1907), *Wallington* (1911), became the APS base from 1916–18. In 1914, the *Majestic*-class battleships of the 9th Battle Squadron (*Mars*, *Hannibal*, *Victorious*, and *Magnificent*) mobilised in the Humber with *Mars* as port guard ship, and the SNO flying his flag in the *Victorious* (1895). The battleship *Albion*, was moored as guard ship between Sunk Island and Killingholme in 1916. Eight destroyers and six torpedo boats had been added to the twenty destroyers of the 7th Destroyer Flotilla by 1918. The Hull DAMS office closed in 1919.

Invergordon: *see* Cromarty

Inverness: APS base with the drifter *Lavatera* (1913) as depot ship, 1915–19. The port was later used by the USN for minelayers with USS *Blackhawk* as depot ship.

Ipswich: APS base with the *Emperor of India* (1906) hired as base ship in 1916.

Killybegs: APS base moved from Blacksod in 1915.

Kings Lynn: Trues Yard PH, base for RNR Trawler Section from 1910.

Kingstown: *see* Dun Laoghaire

Kirkcaldy: Base for Northern Patrol with the *Venerable* (1899) the tender to the *Research*, and the cruiser *Gibraltar* (1892) as depot ships in 1918.

Larne: M/S and APS base with the drifter *Vigorous* (1913), the yacht *Valiant II* (1893), and the cruiser *Thetis* (1890) as depot ships. Four destroyers formed the North Channel Patrol.

Leith: Flotilla base for 8th Destroyer Flotilla with the former store ship *Tyne* (1878) as depot ship 1917–19; the *Vulcan* (1889) served as depot ship for the 7th Submarine Flotilla and the torpedo boats, 1914–16, replaced by the gunboat *Hebe* (1892) from 1916–17.

Liverpool: *see* Mersey

Loch Ewe/Aultbea: An occasional fleet anchorage and trawler base with the battleships *Goliath* (1898) as guard ship 1914–15 and *Illustrious* (1896) as depot ship, succeeded, 1914–15, by the yacht *Vanessa* (1899).

London: *see* Thames

Lough Foyle/Londonderry: APS base with HMS *Eagle* as depot ship.

Lough Swilly/Buncrana: Temporary fleet anchorage in late 1914; Patrol Area HQ at Buncrana; flotilla base with the *Hecla* as depot ship for 2nd (twenty-five vessels) and 3rd Destroyer Flotillas and APS, succeeded by the *Hecla II* in 1917; the yacht *Beryl* (1898) was hired in 1915 as depot ship for the 2nd Submarine Flotilla, succeeded by the repair ship HMAS *Platypus* (1916) in 1917; base for North Channel Patrol and North Sea Hydrophone Flotilla detachment.

Lowestoft: APS base with the gunboat *Halcyon* (1894) as depot ship, 1914–19. The monitors *Havelock* and *Glow-worm* were moored in Hamilton Dock from October 1916 and January 1917 respectively as guard ships.

Mersey: APS base with the drill ship *Eagle* as parent; base for 11th M/S Flotilla in 1918; the Port Convoy Office, closed 1918.

Methil (Fife): Six destroyers formed the Methil Convoy Flotilla by 1918.

Milford Haven/Pembroke Dock: APS base, HMS *Vivid V*, with the yachts *Portia* (1903) as depot ship in 1914, then *Sabrina II* (1899) in 1915, and *Idaho* (1910) from 1915–19. The cruiser *Venus* (1895) was depot ship for the Third Fleet in 1914. Four torpedo boats and nineteen patrol craft comprised the local defence flotilla.

Newhaven: APS base until 1918, with local defence flotilla of four torpedo boats.

Newport (Gwent): Base for a division of Harwich Force destroyers early in the war.

Nore: *see* Sheerness

Oban: APS base from 1917 for West Coast of Scotland and Hebrides armed yachts, with the trawler *Lord Lansdowne* (1913) serving as depot ship, and then the cruiser *Crescent* (1892) with the drifter *Nesmar II* (1911), as tender. By 1918, base for 13th and 14th M/S Flotillas.

Osea Island (Essex): Base for coastal motor boats from 1918.

Pembroke Dock: *see* Milford Haven

Penzance: APS base closed in 1919.

Peterhead: APS base with the depot ship *Stephen Furness* (1910) in 1914, then the former troopship *Thalia* (1869) in 1916, and the yacht *Nairn* (1913) from 1918–19.

Plymouth: *see* Devonport: Naval Mines and Ordnance depot using the hulk *Eclipse* (1867), formerly the corvette *Sappho*, for mine storage; Port Convoy office.

Poole: The drifter *White Oak*, (1913) was depot ship for A/S net drifters, 1914–19.

Portland/Weymouth: The shore establishment HMS *Victory VII* was replaced by the survey ship *Research* (1888) as the APS depot ship, from 1915–19, along with her tender *Venerable* (1899), from 1918, sometime depot ship for the Southern Patrol. The sloop *Heather* (1916) served as an A/S School and an APS depot ship. The paddle ship *Exwey* (1888) was hired as a minesweeper and used as an accommodation ship at Weymouth. Five torpedo boats formed the local defence flotilla. The drifter *Sarepta* (1906) served as the parent for the experimental Hydrophone Craft and the Listening School.

Portsmouth: Naval Dockyard, Manning Base, and Fleet base, with the *Victory* (1765) as depot ship for the Auxiliary Patrol, 1914–18; the cruiser *Venus* (1895) was depot ship for destroyers and the *Arrogant* (1896) for submarines, 1914–16. The cruiser *Furious* (1896), renamed the *Forte* in 1915, was harbour service ship from 1912. The local defence flotilla consisted of nineteen destroyers and twenty-one torpedo boats.

Queenstown: *see* Cork

Ramsgate/Downs: The torpedo gunboat *Harrier* (1894) was depot ship for the APS from 1914, followed by the yacht *Ceto* (1885) in 1915. The office of the Downs Boarding Flotilla was in the Clock Tower.

Rosyth: A Fleet Anchorage and Dockyard from 1912, only fully operational from 1915, as HMS *Columbine*, the plan to establish a naval barracks as a Manning Base not being implemented. Flotilla base with the cruiser *St George* (1892) as destroyer depot ship, 1913–14, followed by the *Woolwich* (1912) with the *Princess Louise*, the former SS *Princess Royal*, as her auxiliary from 1915–17. The cruiser *Fearless* (1912) and the destroyer *Ithuriel* (1915) were the depot ships for the 12th and 13th Submarine Flotillas respectively, 1917–18.

Scapa Flow: Fleet Anchorage from 1914, occupied by the Grand Fleet throughout the war; also base for Northern Patrol with the battleship *Implacable* (1899) as depot ship, alternating between Kirkwall and Lerwick. The battleship *Hannibal* (1896) was replaced by the repair ship *Cyclops* (1905) as depot ship for the Northern Flotilla Trawlers from 1914, and succeeded by the RFA Store Carrier *Zaria* (1904) in 1915. The *Cyclops* remained at Scapa as a depot ship for APS vessels, with the *Cyclops II* tending the 21st M/S Flotilla at Kirkwall. Stromness was the base for the Western Patrol, a flotilla of yachts and trawlers that kept Hoy Sound swept of mines. The trawlers *Strathderry* (1911), *Strathleven* (1910), and *Margaret Wetherley* (1911), along with the drifter *Violet* (1904), serviced the boom defences and A/S nets, with a further boom defence vessel, the *Cinceria* (1911), off St Margaret's Hope in 1918. The battleship *Victorious* (1895) was depot ship for armed boarding steamers, 1916–19, and the battleship *Imperieuse* (1869) was converted as a trawler repair and depot ship in 1914. The cruisers *Blake* (1889), converted in 1908, and *Leander* (1882) both served as destroyer depot ships, 1914–19, along with the *Greenwich* (1915) from 1916. The *Sokoto* (1899) was the submarine depot ship from 1914–19. From 1915, the *Canning* (1896) was on station as Kite Balloon Depot Ship. The cruisers *Crescent* (1892) and *Royal Arthur* (1891), along with the battleship *Magnificent* (1894), served as guard ships off Flotta.

Sheerness/Nore (HMS *Actaeon*): Fleet base for the 3rd Battle Squadron consisting of the *King Edward VII*-class pre-dreadnought battleships: *Commonwealth*, *Dominion*, *Hibernia*, *Hindustan*, and *Zealandia* in 1914–15. The cruiser *Thames*

(1885) was depot ship for the 5th Submarine Flotilla, 1914–18; the frigate *Actaeon*, formerly the *Ariadne* (1859), was depot ship for boom defence vessels and APS. The local defence flotilla in 1916 comprised nine destroyers and sixteen torpedo boats.

Shetlands/Lerwick: The battleship *Implacable* (1899), depot ship of the Northern Patrol, was based in Lerwick at times. The APS used the cruiser *Brilliant* (1891) as its depot ship, replaced by the drifter *Ambitious* (1907), hired in 1914. Four C-class destroyers formed the Shetland Patrol.

Shetlands/Swarbacks Minn (latterly HMS *Sandringham*): The cruiser *Gibraltar* (1892) was depot ship for the armed trawlers of the APS Northern Patrol, 1915–18. The yacht *Beryl* (1898) was borrowed from Buncrana to cover for, *inter alia*, the *Gibraltar's* refit in 1918.

Southampton: The motorboat depot ship *Resourceful* was relieved by the cruiser *Hermione* (1893), which served as guard ship and APS depot ship, moored in the Hamble River in 1914; the *Magpie* (1889) served the *Pike* (1872) and the other boom defence vessels, 1908–20.

Stornoway: The yacht *Vanessa* (1899) acted as temporary depot ship for the APS in 1914, until relieved by the yachts *Manco* (1908) and *Iolaire* (1902).

Stranraer: Supply base for the North Channel Patrol with the *Tara*, formerly the *Hibernia* (1900), an armed boarding steamer in 1914.

Swansea (HMS *Longset*): Bristol Channel APS base; the yacht *Ombra* (1902) and then the trawler *Shikari* (1914) served as depot ships; base for 19th M/S Flotilla in 1918.

Tees/Hartlepool: Flotilla Base where the 10th Submarine Flotilla's depot ship, the *Lucia* (1907) had been converted from a captured vessel to serve from 1916; the light cruisers *Patrol* and *Forward*, with the four *River 'E'*-class destroyers *Test*, *Moy*, *Doon*, and *Waveney* formed the local patrol force.

Thames: Base for London Division RNR/RNVR in a drill hall in Lambeth, with the sloop *Buzzard* (1887) from 1904, renamed the *President* in 1911, and moored in the Thames at Blackfriars. The screw corvette *Champion* (1878), moored at Coalhouse Fort, supported the examination battery. The APS was serviced by the trawler *Fentonian* (1912), and the trawler *Edward VII* (1906) served as a cable repair ship. In 1917, the *Racecourse*-class minesweeper *Chelmsford* and the paddle-minesweeper *Eglinton* were both based in the Thames. The paddle steamer *Golden Eagle* (1909) was hired as accommodation, possibly, for balloon crews. The *Dreadnought* served as guard ship 1916–18. Port Convoy office.

Torbay: The sloop *Onyx* (1892) was depot ship for the APS from 1917–18.

Troon: Naval base closed in 1919.

Tyne: Civilian shipbuilding and repair yards and Flotilla Base with Northumberland Dock as APS Base, M/S bases at Milldown and South Shields, and A/S vessels based at North Shields. The gunboat *Hebe* (1892) until 1916, and the battleship *Bonaventure* (1892) from 1914–18 served as submarine depot ships for the 7th, 2nd, and 10th Submarine Flotillas in turn. The cruisers *Naiad* (1890) and *St George* (1892) were depot ships for minelayers 1916–20, and the APS respectively. In 1914, the battleship *Illustrious* (1896) was guard ship handing over to *St George* in 1915. The battleship *Victorious* (1895) was a depot ship in 1915. The *Bonaventure* with her tender, the submarine depot ship *Elfin* (1905), was the HQ for patrols from 1914–18. The trawler *Island Prince* (1911) served as depot ship for the A/S vessels. The cruiser *Satellite* (1881) was the depot ship for the APS and minesweepers; then, in 1919, it reverted to being the Tyne RNR Drill Ship at North Shields.

The Wash: The three monitors *Humber*, *Mersey*, and *Severn* were stationed in the Wash in anticipation of an invasion, in November 1914, and the *Hearty* from January 1917.

Yarmouth/Cowes/Isle of Wight: The cruiser *Hermione* (1893) was guard ship in 1914, replaced by the boom defence vessel *Magpie* (1889) in 1915.

APPENDIX III

The British Army in Defence of the Homeland: Garrisons, Home Defence Formations, and Reserve Forces Bases

Garrisons

Notes:

i: This section lists those places designated as 'Garrisons' as well as those with fixed defences and permanent complements of troops.

ii: The RE (regular) Fortress Coast Battalion comprised detachments from Nos 6, 16, 18, 39, and 49 Companies.

iii: RE and RGA units are regular unless specified as TF.

Aberdeen Garrison: North Scottish RGA (TF) (HQ Broughty Ferry) covered Tay and Aberdeen; City of Aberdeen Fortress RE (TF), HQ, Hardgate; 3rd (Reserve) Bn Gordon Highlanders

Alderney: No. 17 Company RGA (regular), Alderney; No. 34 Company Fortress RE, Channel Islands

Barrow-in-Furness Garrison: Lancashire and Cheshire RGA (TF), HQ Liverpool; 3rd (Reserve) Bn South Lancashire Regiment; 12th Bn Royal Defence Corps (5th Home Service Garrison Bn. Royal Welsh Fusiliers)

Belfast Lough: No. 15 Company RGA, Carrickfergus, later No. 34 (Antrim) Fire Command Antrim RGA (Special Reserve) Carrickfergus; 6th (Reserve) Bn Royal Fusiliers, Carrickfergus, 1917–18; 4th (Extra Reserve) Bn Royal Irish Fusiliers, 1914–16; 4th and 5th (Extra Reserve) Bns Royal Irish Rifles, 1914–18

Berehaven and Bere Island: Detachment of No. 33 Company Fortress RE; 4th (Extra Reserve) Bn Connaught Rangers, 1915; 3rd (Reserve) Garrison Bn Royal Irish Fusiliers, 1916–17

Buncrana/Lough Swilly: No. 35 (Donegal) Fire Command, Antrim RGA, Lenan Fort; Detachment of No. 33 Company Fortress RE; 4th (Extra Reserve) Bn Royal Inniskilling Fusiliers, 1914–18; 3rd (Reserve) Bn Royal Irish Fusiliers, 1914–18

Clyde Garrison: Clyde RGA (TF) (HQ Port Glasgow); Detachment of No. 49 Company Fortress RE, Greenock; Renfrewshire Fortress REs (TF), HQ Fort Matilda, Greenock; 3rd (Reserve) Bn Royal Scots Fusiliers, Greenock; 2/5th Bn Black Watch, spring 1915; Ardeer Company, Royal Scots Fusiliers (TF) at Nobels Explosives Factory

Cork/Queenstown: Nos 10 and 43 Companies RGA; Cork RGA (Special Reserve) Fort Westmorland, Spike Island; No. 33 Company Fortress RE, Cork; 3rd (Reserve) Bn Royal Dublin Fusiliers, 1914–17; 1st Garrison Bn Royal Munster Fusiliers (former DLI), 1917

Cromarty Garrison: 3rd (Reserve) Bns. Seaforth Highlanders & Cameronians, Invergordon; 3rd Reserve Bn Black Watch, Nigg until November 1917; 18th Bn Royal Defence Corps (1st Home Service Garrison Bn. Cameron Highlanders), Invergordon

Dover Garrison: Nos 40 and 46 Companies RGA; Kent RGA (TF), HQ initially Sheerness, then Dover in 1914; No. 3 Company Fortress RE; Cinque Ports Fortress RE (TF), HQ, Bench Street, Dover; 3rd Reserve Bns The Buffs & East Surrey Regiments; 5th (Reserve) Bn. Royal Fusiliers, 1914–18; 3rd Reserve and 4th (Extra Reserve) Bns Warwickshire Regiment; 3rd (Reserve) Bn Oxfordshire & Buckinghamshire Light Infantry, 1917–18; 2nd Bn Royal Defence Corps (1st Home Service Bn The Buffs), Dover

Dublin/Kingstown/Dun Laoghaire: No. 15 Company Fortress RE; 2nd (Home Service) Garrison Bn Royal Irish Regiment, 1916–18; 3rd (Reserve) Bn Berkshire Regiment, 1917–18; 2/6th Bn Sherwood Foresters, Dublin and the Curragh, 1916–17; 2/5th Bn South Staffordshire Regiment, Dublin and the Curragh, 1916–17; 1st (Reserve) Garrison Bn Worcestershire Regiment, 1918

Falmouth Garrison: Cornwall RGA (TF), HQ Falmouth; No. 18 Company Fortress RE Cornwall Fortress RE (TF), Pendennis Castle; 25th (Reserve) Garrison Bn Rifle Brigade; 5th Bn Royal Defence Corps (2nd Home Service Garrison Bn Devonshire Regiment)

Forth Garrison: No. 21 Coy RGA, Leith; HQ and No. 21 Company RGA in Leith Fort; Forth RGA (TF) (HQ Edinburgh, moving to Queensferry in 1914); Detachment of No. 49 Company Fortress RE, North Queensferry; City of Edinburgh Fortress REs (TF), HQ York Place, Edinburgh; 3/4th, 3/5th, 3/6th, 3/7th, and 3/8th Bns Royal Scots amalgamated as Edinburgh Special Reserve Brigade via Lowland Reserve Brigade, Catterick; 3/4th and 3/5th Bns Royal Scots Fusiliers, Kinross; Kings Own Scottish Borderers, Dunfermline; 4th (Extra Reserve) Bn Cameronians, Haddington; 3rd (Reserve) Bn Highland Light Infantry, Malleny; 53rd Bn Highland Light Infantry, Kirkcaldy, from 1917; 1st Bn Royal Defence Corps (2nd Home Service Bn. Royal Scots) Leith

Great Yarmouth: No. 4 Depot RGA, Great Yarmouth

Guernsey Garrison: No. 34 Company Fortress RE, Channel Islands; 2nd (Reserve) Bn Royal Guernsey Militia; 17th Bn Royal Defence Corps (2nd Home Service Garrison Bn North Staffordshire Regiment), Guernsey

Harwich Garrison (including Felixstowe): No. 13 Company RGA, Landguard Fort; Essex and Suffolk RGA (TF), HQ, Dovercourt; No. 21 Company Fortress RE, Harwich; Essex Fortress RE (TF), HQ, Market Road, Chelmsford; 3rd (Reserve) Battalions of the Essex, Bedfordshire, Kings Own Royal Lancaster, North Lancashire and Suffolk Regiments; 4th (Extra Reserve) Bn East Surrey Regiment; 2nd (Garrison) Battalion, Suffolk Regiment May 1916; 5th and 6th (Reserve) Bns Worcestershire Regiment; 6th Bn Royal Defence Corps (2nd Home Service Garrison Bn. Suffolk Regiment)

Humber Garrison: East Riding RGA (TF), HQ Hull; Detachment of No. 16 Company Fortress RE, Paull-on-Humber; East Riding of Yorkshire Fortress RE (TF), HQ, Colonial Street, Hull; 3rd (Reserve) Bns Lincolnshire Regiment, Grimsby; Leicestershire Regiment, Hull; 3rd (Reserve) and 3/4th Bns East Yorkshire Regiment, Hornsea, Withernsea, and South Dalton; 3/4th and 3/5th Bns Princess of Wales's Own Yorkshire Regiment, Hornsea; 3rd (Reserve) Bns

Lancashire Fusiliers and KOYLI, Withernsea; 3rd (Reserve) and 4th (Extra Reserve) Bns Manchester Regiment, Cleethorpes & Riby 3/5th–3/9th Bns Durham Light Infantry, Hornsea, Sutton-on-Hull, 1917–18; 3rd (Reserve) Bn Royal Dublin Fusiliers, Waltham and Grimsby, 1918; 2/1st Northern Cyclist Battalion, Skegness then Burton Constable; 2/1st Huntingdonshire Cyclist Battalion, Mablethorpe/Skegness area, 1914–18; 4th and 8th Bns Royal Defence Corps (2nd Home Service Garrison Bns), Lincolnshire Regiment, Grimsby, and East Riding Regiment, Hull

Jersey Garrison: No. 20 Company RGA, Jersey; No. 34 Company Fortress RE, Channel Islands; Royal Jersey (Militia) Garrison Bn from 1916

Londonderry/Lough Foyle: No. 15 Company RGA; 3rd (Reserve) Bn Royal Inniskilling Fusiliers, 1914–18

Mersey Garrison (including Liverpool): Lancashire and Cheshire RGA (TF), Liverpool and Seacombe; Detachment of No. 35 Company Fortress RE; Lancashire Fortress RE (TF), HQ Liverpool; 3rd (Reserve) Bns Cheshire Regiment, Birkenhead, 1914–17; Royal Welsh Fusiliers, Litherland; Border Regiment, Great Crosby; South Wales Borderers, Hightown; 11th Bn Royal Defence Corps (3rd Home Service Garrison Bn. Cheshire Regiment)

Milford Haven Garrison: Nos 44 and 57 Companies RGA, Pembroke Dock; No. 35 Company Fortress RE, Pembroke Dock; 3/4th, 3/5th, 3/6th, and 3/7th (Cyclist) Bns Welsh Regiment; 3/4th Bn Kings Shropshire Light Infantry, Pembroke Dock; 3rd (Reserve) Bn Royal Dublin Fusiliers, 1917–18; 3rd Bn Royal Defence Corps (3rd Home Service Garrison Bn Kings Liverpool Regiment), Pembroke Dock

Newhaven Garrison: No. 1 Depot RGA, Newhaven, until 1914; Sussex RGA (TF) (HQ, Brighton, then Newhaven in 1914); Sussex Fortress RE (TF), HQ, Seaford; 3rd (Reserve) Bn Royal Sussex Regiment

Plymouth Garrison: No. 3 Depot RGA, Plymouth Citadel; Nos 36, 38, 41, and 45 Companies RGA, Plymouth; Devonshire RGA (TF) (HQ Devonport); No. 20 Company Fortress RE, Devonport; No. 30 Company Fortress RE, Plymouth; Devonshire Fortress RE (TF), Mutley Barracks, Plymouth; 3rd (Reserve) Bn Devonshire Regiment; 5th and 6th (Reserve) Bns Worcestershire Regiment, 1914–17; 3rd (Reserve) Bn East Lancashire Regiment, until mid-1917; 3rd (Reserve), 4th and 5th (Extra Reserve) Bns Royal Munster Fusiliers, Devonport

Portland Garrison: Nos 16, 28, and 30 Companies RGA, Weymouth; Dorsetshire RGA (TF), HQ, Weymouth; No. 6 Company Fortress RE, Weymouth; Dorsetshire Fortress RE (TF), HQ, Sidney Hall, Weymouth; Wiltshire Fortress RE (TF), HQ Church Road, Swindon (South Coast defences); 3rd (Reserve) Bns Dorsetshire Regiment, Wyke Regis; Wiltshire Regiment, Weymouth, 1914–17; 1st (Home Service) Garrison Bn Dorsetshire Regiment, Weymouth, 1916–17

Portsmouth Garrison: III Reserve Brigade RFA, Hilsea Barracks; No. 2 Depot RGA, Fort Rowner, Gosport; Nos 29, 37, 42, and 67 Companies RGA, Portsmouth; Nos 11 and 33 Companies RGA, Golden Hill, IoW; Nos 32 and 34 Companies RGA, Sandown, IoW; Hampshire (Wessex) RGA (TF), HQ, Southampton; Nos 4 and 42 Companies Fortress RE, Gosport; No. 22 Company Fortress RE, Yarmouth, IoW; Hampshire Fortress RE (TF), HQ, Hampshire Terrace, Portsmouth; 3rd (Reserve), 4th and 5th (Extra Reserve) Bns Prince of Wales's Leinster Regiment; 3rd (Reserve) Bn Hampshire Regiment at Gosport Barracks; 2nd (Garrison) Bn Munster Fusiliers; 1st (Home Service) Garrison Bn Berkshire Regiment; 1st (Reserve) Garrison Bn Worcestershire Regiment, 1916–18; 3rd (Reserve) Bn Duke of Cornwall's Light Infantry, Freshwater, IoW; 3rd (Reserve) Bn Oxfordshire & Buckinghamshire Light Infantry until late 1917; 2nd (Home Service) Garrison Bn Royal Munster Fusiliers, Cosham from 1917; 14th Bn

Royal Defence Corps (1st Home Service Garrison Bn Royal Berkshire Regiment), Portsmouth

Scapa Flow: Orkney RGA (TF), HQ Kirkwall; Royal Marine Artillery Southern and Western Fire Commands

Severn Garrison: Detachment of No. 35 Company Fortress RE, Cardiff; Glamorgan Fortress RE (TF), HQ, Park Street, Cardiff; 4th (Extra Reserve) Bn Lancashire Fusiliers, Barry

Sunderland part of Tyne Garrison: 3rd (Reserve) Bn York and Lancaster Regiment; 3rd (Reserve) and 4th (Extra Reserve) Bns Sherwood Foresters; 9th Bn Royal Defence Corps (1st Home Service Garrison Bn Leicestershire Regiment), Easington

Tay Defences: North Scottish RGA (TF), HQ Broughty Ferry, covered Tay and Aberdeen; Detachment of No. 49 Company Fortress RE, Broughty Ferry; City of Dundee Fortress RE (TF), HQ, Taylors Lane, Dundee; 2/4th Bn Black Watch, Broughty Ferry, then to Norfolk, 1916; 4th (Extra Reserve) Bn Highland Light Infantry, Arbroath

Tees Garrison: Durham RGA (TF), HQ West Hartlepool; Detachment of No. 16 Company Fortress RE, Middlesbrough; North Riding of Yorkshire Fortress RE (TF), HQ, Bright Street, Middlesbrough; 4th (Extra Reserve) Bn Prince of Wales's Own West Yorkshire Regiment, Redcar and West Hartlepool; 3/5th–3/9th Bns Durham Light Infantry, Redcar, 1916; 3rd (Reserve) Bns Princess of Wales's Own Yorkshire Regiment, West Hartlepool; Cheshire Regiment, West Hartlepool, 1917–18; East Lancashire Regiment, Saltburn and Marske from mid-1917; Welsh Regiment, Redcar; 1/7th (Cyclist) Bn Welsh Regiment, Middlesbrough; 10th Bn Royal Defence Corps (2nd Home Service Garrison Bn Princess of Wales's Own Yorkshire Regiment) Hartlepool

Thames and Medway Garrison: No. 14 Company RGA, Shoeburyness; Nos 2, 18, 19, and 22 Companies RGA, Sheerness; No. 39 Company Fortress RE, Sheerness and Gravesend; Kent Fortress REs (TF), HQ, Submarine Mining School, Gillingham; 1st (Reserve) Garrison Bn Suffolk Regiment, Tilbury, Gravesend & Isle of Grain; 3rd (Reserve) Bns Gloucestershire Regiment, Sittingbourne-Maidstone; Royal West Kent Regiment, Leysdown, Sheppey; Northamptonshire Regiment, Gillingham; Wiltshire Regiment, Sittingbourne from autumn 1917; 5th and 6th (Reserve) Bns Middlesex Regiment, Chatham and Gillingham; Kings Royal Rifle Corps, Queenborough and Sheerness; Rifle Brigade, Minster and Eastchurch; 13th Bn Royal Defence Corps (2nd Home Service Garrison Bn Northamptonshire Regiment), Sheerness; 15th and 16th Bns Royal Defence Corps (1st Home Service Garrison Bns) Royal West Kent Regiment, Rochester & Middlesex Regiment, Chattenden

Tyne Garrison (*see* Sunderland): Nos 12 and 47 Companies RGA, Tynemouth; Tynemouth RGA (TF) HQ, North Shields; Detachment of No. 16 Company Fortress RE; Durham Fortress RE (TF), HQ, Western Road, Jarrow-on-Tyne; 5th Cyclist Bn East Riding Regiment, Newbiggin; 3/5th and 3/6th Bns Warwickshire Regiment, Blyth; 3/4th, 3/5th, and 3/6th Bns Gloucestershire Regiment, Seaton Delaval; 3/7th and 3/8th Bns Worcestershire Regiment, Blyth; 3rd (Reserve) Bns Duke of Wellington's West Riding Regiment, North Shields; South Staffordshire Regiment, Forest Hall, Newcastle; Northumberland Fusiliers; Prince of Wales's West Yorkshire Regiment; North Staffordshire Regiment, Wallsend; 3/4th and 3/1st (Bucks) Bns Oxfordshire & Buckinghamshire Light Infantry, Seaton Delaval; 3/4th Bn Royal Berkshire Regiment, Cambois, Blyth; 3rd (Reserve) and 4th (Extra Reserve) Bns Durham LI, South Shields and Seaham 1/1st Northern Cyclist Battalion, Morpeth then Alnwick; 7th Bn Royal Defence Corps (2nd

Home Service Garrison Bn Prince of Wales's West Yorkshire Regiment) Whitley Bay

Home Defence Divisions

(These were initially numbered in the order in which they were posted overseas)

The 42nd–44th and 46th–56th Divisions were pre-war First Line TF formations; the 45th, and the 57th–69th Divisions were Second Line TF formations raised in 1914; the 71st–73rd Divisions were raised exclusively for Home Service in 1916
42nd Division posted to Egypt and the Suez Canal, 1914
43rd Division posted to India, 1914
44th Division posted to India, 1914
45th Division posted to India, 1914
46th Division assembled in the Luton area, and posted to the Western Front, 1915
47th Division assembled in St Albans area, and posted to the Western Front, 1915
48th Division assembled around Chelmsford and posted to the Western Front, 1915
49th Division assembled in the Yorkshire/Lincolnshire area and posted to the Western Front, 1915
50th Division manned Tyne defences in 1914, and posted to the Western Front, 1915
51st Division assembled in the Bedford area, and posted to the Western Front, 1915
52nd Division manned Scottish coast defences until posted to the Western Front in May, 1915
53rd Division assembled on the Welsh border before moving to Northampton, and then to Bedford prior to sailing for the Dardanelles in July, 1915
54th Division assembled at Brentwood and was deployed across East Anglia at Norwich, Bury St Edmunds and Chelmsford, prior to sailing for the Dardanelles in July, 1915
55th Division posted piecemeal to the Western Front, 1914–15, and reformed in France in 1916
56th Division posted piecemeal to the Western Front, 1914–15, and reformed in France in 1916
57th Division assembled in Kent absorbing remnants of 55th Division. Following re-equipping moved to Aldershot area and was posted to Western Front, 1917
58th Division absorbed remnants of 56th Division and manned East Coast defences throughout 1916, then posted to the Western Front, 1917
59th Division assembled in early 1915 in the Luton area, then to St Albans and Dublin in 1916; relieved by the 65th Division, and posted to the Western Front in 1917
60th Division assembled at White City then moved to Surrey and Salisbury Plain prior to being posted to Salonika in 1916
61st Division assembled in the Northampton area in early 1915, then to Salisbury Plain prior to a move to the Western Front in May, 1916
62nd Division (185, 186, and 187 Brigades) assembled at Matlock Bath, Derby and surrounding towns, then to Newcastle, via Retford, and into East Anglia. After a final move to Bedford, Northampton and Wellingborough, the division was sent to France, in January 1917

63rd Division (188, 189, and 190 Brigades) at Newcastle (Swalwell Camp) manning the Tyne defences, until July 1916, when it was broken up and the RN Division (posted to Western Front in 1914), was transferred to the army as a new 63rd Division

64th Division (191, 192, and 193 Brigades) assembled at Perth, Blair Atholl, Scone, Falkirk and Blairgowrie, manning the Firth of Tay defences, then to Norfolk in March 1916 with HQ in Norwich, and brigades in Kelling, Taverham, and North Walsham

65th Division (194, 195, and 196 Brigades) concentrated on Bridge of Allan and towns around Dunfermline manning the Firth of Forth defences. In March 1916 moved to Essex with HQ at Chelmsford with brigades at Billericay, Danbury and Chelmsford, then posted to Dublin in January 1917, releasing 59th Division for service in France, with HQ at the Curragh and units scattered across Ireland, broken up March 1918

66th Division (197, 198, and 199 Brigades) from 1916 stationed in Suffolk manning east coast defences, then sent to France in February 1917

67th Division (200, 201, and 202 Brigades) assembled around Windsor with brigades at Staines, Sunninghill and Ascot, and then to Second Army, Central Force at Sevenoaks, Reigate, and Tonbridge. In 1917, it moved to Ipswich and Colchester

68th Division (203, 204, and 205 Brigades) at Bedford, Northampton, and Newmarket; then into Suffolk and Norfolk at Yarmouth, Benacre Park, Herringfleet, Henham Park, and Lowestoft

69th Division (206, 207, and 208 Brigades) assembled in Peterborough, Stamford, Thetford; then to Doncaster, and to the Nottinghamshire camps of Clipstone, Thoresby, and Welbeck, with HQ at Retford; then to Barnard Castle and Guisborough

There was no 70th Division.

71st Division (212, 213, and 214 Brigades) formed November 1916 at Fleet, Aldershot and Guildford, before moving to Colchester

72nd Division (215, 216, and 217 Brigades) formed November 1916 at York, moving south to Bedford, Ipswich, and Bury-St-Edmunds, before being broken up in March 1918

73rd Division (218, 219, and 220 Brigades) formed 1916 in Blackpool, then to Essex: at Danbury, Southend, and Chelmsford before being broken up in March 1918

Camps used as bases for Reserve and Training Brigades

Aldershot Area: Blackdown, Bordon and Tidworth.

Salisbury Plain and the South West: Blandford, Bournemouth, Chisledon, Fovant, Hursley Park, Larkhill, Ludgershall, Rollestone, Stockton, Sutton Mandeville, Sutton Veny, Torquay, Wareham, Winchester and Wool.

Home Counties: Crowborough, Dover, Halton Park, Purfleet, Romsey, St Albans, St Leonards, Seaford, Shoreham, Shorncliffe, Tunbridge Wells, Wimbledon and Witley.

East Anglia: Bungay, Colchester, Harwich, Hunstanton and Ipswich.

East Midlands: Clipstone, Thoresby Park, Welbeck, Belton Park, Saltfleet and Louth.

West Midlands: Cannock Chase (Rugeley and Brocton), Oswestry and Prees Heath.

North East: Blyth, Catterick, Bridlington, Harrogate, Hornsea, Newcastle, Ripon, Scarborough, Seaton Delaval and Whitley Bay.

North West: Altcar and Southport.

Ireland: Aghada, Ballinvonea, Belfast, Buncrana, Buttevant, Cahir, Clandeboye, the Curragh and Randalstown.
Scotland: Bridge of Alan, Dundee, Dunfermline, Glencorse, Inverkeithing, Kinghorn, Kirkcaldy, Montrose and Wormit.
Wales: Kinmel Park (Rhyl), Morfa (Conwy) and Pembroke Dock.

Concentration Areas for Anti-Invasion Reinforcements

Eastern Command: Bishops Stortford, Newmarket, Orpington, Romford and Thetford.
Northern Command: Darlington, Durham, Gainsborough, Selby and York.
Scottish Command: Alloa, Falkirk and Stirling.

APPENDIX IV

The RFC and RNAS in Defence of the Skies: Stations and Aerodromes

RNAS Home Defence Airfields

ALDEBURGH (Suffolk)
ATWICK RACECOURSE, Hull (Yorkshire)
BACTON (Norfolk)
BARLOW, Selby (Yorkshire)
CHELMSFORD (Essex)
CHINGFORD (Greater London)
COVEHITHE (Suffolk)
DETLING (Kent) to RFC 1917
EASTCHURCH (Kent)
EAST FORTUNE (Lothian)
GOSPORT Fort Grange (Hampshire)
GRAIN (Kent)
HENDON (Greater London) to RFC 1916
HOLT (Norfolk)
LOWTHORPE (Yorkshire)
MANSTON (Kent)
NARBOROUGH (Norfolk) to RFC 1916
OWTHORNE (Yorkshire)
REDCAR (Yorkshire)
ROCHFORD, Southend (Essex) to RFC 1916
SEDGEFORD (Norfolk) to RFC 1917
WALMER (Kent) satellite of Dover 1917
WEST AYTON (Yorkshire)
WESTGATE (Kent)

RFC Home Defence Aerodromes

ASHINGTON (Northumberland)
BEKESBOURNE (Kent)
BERWICK-upon-TWEED, Horndean (Northumberland)

BEVERLEY (Yorkshire)
BRANCROFT (Yorkshire)
BUCKMINSTER (Lincolnshire)
CATTERICK (Yorkshire)
CHIDDINGSTONE CAUSEWAY (Kent)
COPMANTHORPE, York (Yorkshire)
CRAMLINGTON (Northumberland)
CROYDON (Surrey)
DETLING (Kent)
ELSHAM (Lincolnshire)
GOLDHANGER (Essex)
HAINAULT FARM, Fairlop (Essex)
HARLING ROAD (Norfolk)
HELPERBY (Yorkshire)
HINGHAM (Norfolk)
KIRTON-in-LINDSEY (Lincolnshire)
LEADENHAM (Lincolnshire)
LONDON COLNEY (Greater London)
MATTISHALL (Norfolk)
MONTROSE (Tayside)
NORTHOLT (Greater London)
NORTH WEALD BASSETT (Essex)
NORWICH, Mousehold Heath (Norfolk)
RIPON (Yorkshire)
SEATON CAREW (County Durham)
SCAMPTON, Brattleby (Lincolnshire)
STAMFORD (Lincolnshire)
STIRLING (Central)
STOW MARIES (Essex)
SUTTONS FARM, Hornchurch (Essex)
TADCASTER (Yorkshire)
TELSCOMBE CLIFFS (Sussex)
THIRSK RACECOURSE (Yorkshire)
THROWLEY (Kent)
TURNHOUSE (Lothian)
USWORTH, Hylton (County Durham)

RNAS Seaplane Stations

AULDBAR (Angus)
BANGOR, Abergwyngregin (Gwynedd)
BARROW-IN-FURNESS (Cumbria)
BEMBRIDGE (Isle of Wight)
BRIDPORT (Dorset)
BURGH CASTLE (Norfolk)
CALSHOT (Hampshire)
CATFIRTH (Shetland)
CHICKERELL, Weymouth (Dorset)
CROMARTY FIRTH (Highland)
DUBLIN

DUNDEE (Tayside)
FALMOUTH BAY, Bonython (Cornwall)
FELIXSTOWE (Suffolk)
FISHGUARD (Goodwick)
GREAT YARMOUTH, South Denes (Norfolk)
HICKLING BROAD, sub-station (Norfolk)
HORNSEA (Yorkshire)
HOUTON BAY (Orkney)
KILLINGHOLME (Lincolnshire) to USN 1918
LEE-on-SOLENT (Hampshire)
NEW GRIMSBY, Tresco (Scillies) removed from Porthmellon
NEWHAVEN (Sussex)
NEWLYN (Cornwall) RNAS Land's End, to RAF 1918
PETERHEAD (Aberdeen)
PIEROWALL BAY (Westray)
PLYMOUTH, Cattewater later Mount Batten
PORTLAND (Dorset) to RAF, 1918; closed 1919.
PORTHMELLON, St Mary's (Scillies) moved to New Grimsby
ROSYTH (Fife)
SCAPA BAY (Orkney)
SCARBOROUGH, Scalby Mills (Yorkshire) seaplane sub-station
SEATON CAREW (County Durham)
SMOOGRO (Orkney)
SOUTH SHIELDS (Northumberland)
STENNESS (Orkney)
STRATHBEG (Aberdeen)
TORQUAY (Devon)
WESTGATE (Kent)
WHIDDY ISLAND, Bantry Bay (County Cork) used by USN in 1918

RNAS Kite Balloon Stations

BEREHAVEN (County Cork) US Navy balloon base; offered to Air Ministry 1919
BUNCRANA, Rathmullen Fort, Lough Swilly (County Donegal), to Air Ministry 1919
CALDALE (Orkney), initially an airship station
DEVONPORT (Devon) HMS *Valiant* served as a kite balloon vessel
HOUTON BAY (Orkney)
IMMINGHAM (Lincolnshire)
LERWICK, Grimista (Shetland) to RAF, 1918
LOWESTOFT (Suffolk)
MILFORD HAVEN, Castle Hill (Pembrokeshire)
NORTH QUEENSFERRY (Fife)
SCAPA FLOW, HMS *Canning*, Kite Balloon Depot Ship from 1915
SHEERNESS (Kent)
SHOTLEY (Suffolk) offered to Air Ministry 1919
TIPNER, Portsmouth (Hampshire)
TOR POINT, Wilcove, Merifield (Cornwall)
TORQUAY, detachment from Merifield (Devon)
WESTGATE (Kent)

RNAS Airship Stations

CALDALE (Orkney)
CAPEL (Kent)
CAREW (Pembroke)
CRANWELL (Lincolnshire)
DOVER, Guston Road and Marine Parade (Kent)
EAST FORTUNE (Lothian)
HOWDEN (Yorkshire)
INCHINNAN, Glasgow
KINGSNORTH (Kent)
LLANGEFNI (Anglesey)
LONGSIDE (Aberdeen)
LUCE BAY (Wigton)
MILTON (Pembroke)
MULLION (Cornwall) transferred to RAF, 1918
POLEGATE (Sussex)
PULHAM (Norfolk) Admiralty experimental station.

RNAS Airship Sub-Stations and Mooring-Out Sites

AULDBAR (Angus)
BALLYLIFFAN (Donegal)
BARROW-in-FURNESS (Lancashire)
BENTRA, Belfast Lough, for Northern Channel patrols from Luce Bay
BRIDPORT (Dorset)
BUDE (Cornwall)
CHATHILL, Holy Island (Northumberland)
GODMERSHAM PARK, near Canterbury (Kent)
JOHNSTOWN CASTLE (County Wexford) used by USN
KILLEAGH (County Cork)
KIRKLEATHAM (Yorkshire) for Howden
LAIRA Plymouth (Devon)
LARNE (Antrim)
LOWTHORPE, Bridlington (Yorkshire) for Howden
MALAHIDE (County Dublin)
RAMSEY (Isle of Man)
SLINDON (Sussex)
TOLLER, Dorchester (Dorset)
TORQUAY (Devon
UPTON, Poole (Dorset)
WEST MERSTHAM (Kent)

Bibliography

Appleby, C., Cocroft, W., and Schofield, J., (eds) *The Home Front in Britain 1914-18: An Archaeological Handbook* (York: CBA, 2015)

Barclay, G., *The Built Heritage of the First World War in Scotland* (Edinburgh: Historic Scotland and RCAHMS, 2013)

Beatty, J., *The Lost History of 1914: How the Great War was not Inevitable* (London: Bloomsbury, 2012)

Beckett, I., and Simpson, K., (eds) *A Nation in Arms* (Barnsley: Pen & Sword, 1985 and 2014)

Bernhardi, F. von, *Germany and the Next War* (London: Longmans, Green, 1914)

Binder, J., *Life in a Northamptonshire Market Town during the Great War 1914-18: The Diary of John Coleman Binder* (Oundle: Oundle Museum Trust, 2013)

Bird, C., *Silent Sentinels: Norfolk's 20th Century Defences* (Dereham: Larks Press, 1999)

Bird, C., *Norfolk's First and Second World War Anti-Invasion Defences in the Weybourne Area* (Weybourne: The Muckleburgh Collection, 2014)

Brown, M., Pattison, P., and Williams, A., *Coastal Artillery Fortifications on the Isle of Grain, Kent* (Cambridge: RCHME, 1998)

Burridge, D., *Defending the Gateway: The Fixed Defences of Dover in the 20th Century* (Dover: published by author, 2001)

Carradice, P., *First World War in the Air* (Stroud: Amberley, 2012)

Clark, N., 'Twentieth Century Coastal Defences of the Firth of Forth' in *FORT* 14 (Liverpool: FSG, 1986)

Clements, W., *Defending the North: The Fortifications of Ulster 1796-1956* (Newtownards: Colourpoint, 2003)

Cooksley, P., *The Home Front: Civilian Life in World War One* (Stroud: Tempus, 2006)

De Courcey, A., *Margot at War* (London: Weidenfeld & Nicolson, 2014)

Dobinson, C., *Twentieth Century Fortifications in England* (York: CBA, 1996/2000); *Volume 1.1 Anti-Aircraft Artillery 1914-46* (York: CBA, 1996); *Volume 1.2 Anti-Aircraft Artillery 1914-46* (York: CBA, 1996); *Volume VI.1 Coast Artillery, 1900-56* (York: CBA, 2000); *Volume VI.2 Coast Artillery, 1900-56* (York: CBA, 2000)

Dorman, J., *Guardians of the Humber: The Humber Defences 1856-1956* (Hull: Humberside Leisure Services, 1990)

Dorman, J., *Orkney Coast Batteries 1914-56* (Kirkwall: author, 1996)

Dorman, J., and Guy, J., *The Coast Artillery Defences of the Firth of Clyde* (Deal: authors, 2009)

Downing, T., *Secret Warriors* (London: Little Brown, 2014)

Emden, R., and Humphries, S., *All Quiet on the Home Front* (London: Headline, 2003)

Faulkner, N., and Durrani, N., *In Search of the Zeppelin War* (Stroud: Tempus, 2008)

Fitch, T., and Poirier, M., *Into the Danger Zone: Sea Crossings of the First World War* (Stroud: The History Press, 2014)

Foster, J., *The Guns of the North-East: Coastal Defences from the Tyne to the Humber* (Barnsley: Pen and Sword, 2004)

Francis, P., Bellamy, P., and Crisp G., *20th Century Air-Raid Precaution Railway Control Centres* (Ware: ARG, 2014) in CD form.

Francis, P., www.airfieldinformationexchange.org/community/showthread.php?6805-FIRST-WORLD-WAR-Home-Defence-(Ground-Forces)

Freeman, R., *The Great Edwardian Naval Feud* (Barnsley: Pen & Sword, 2009)

Gilbert, M., *A History of the Twentieth Century Volume 1 1900-33* (London: Harper Collins, 1997)

Gooch, J. (ed.), 'The Bolt from the Blue', in *The Prospect of War: Studies in British Defence Policy 1847-1942* (London: Frank Cass, 1981)

Gulvin, K., and Hughes, Q., 'The Twydall Profile' in *FORT 5* (Liverpool: FSG, 1978, reprinted and revised, 1995)

Guy, J., *The 15-pdr Breech Loading Converted Field Gun used in Coast Defence Service during World War I* (Mold: FSG *Casemate* 98, 2013)

Hamilton-Paterson, J., *Marked for Death: The First War in the Air* (London: Head of Zeus, 2015)

Hall, M., *From Balloon to Boxkite* (Stroud: Amberley, 2010)

Hanna, M., *On Patrol: The Story of TB1 & the 7th Flotilla 1914-15* (n/d, unpublished)

Hastings, M., *Catastrophe, Europe goes to War 1914* (London: Collins, 2013)

Hawes, J., *Englanders and Huns: The Culture Clash which led to the First World War* (London: Simon & Schuster, 2014)

Hiley, N., introduction to Le Queux, W., *Spies of the Kaiser* (London: Tower Publishing, 1909) new edition (London: Frank Cass, 1996)

Hogg, R., 'The Tyne Turrets: Coastal Defence in the First World War' in *FORT* 12 (Liverpool: FSG, 1984)

James, Brig. E., *British Regiments 1914-1918* (Heathfield: Naval & Military, 1978)

Kent, P., *Fortifications of East Anglia* (Lavenham: Terence Dalton, 1988)

King-Hall, S., *A North Sea Diary* (www.vlib.us/wwi/resources/northseadiary.html)

Knight, E., *The Harwich Naval Forces 1914-18* (www.leonaur.com Oakpast reprint of *c.* 1920 text, 2011)

Lewis-Stempel, J., *The War Behind the Wire* (London: Phoenix, 2014)

Linzey, R., *Fortress Falmouth, Vol II History and Gazetteer* (Swindon: EH, 2000)

Macmillan, M., *The War That Ended Peace* (London: Profile, 2013)

Mallinson, A., *1914: Fight the good Fight* (London: Bantam, 2013)

Maurice-Jones, Col. K., *The History of Coast Artillery in the British Army* (Woolwich: Royal Artillery Institution, 1959)

Mitchison, K., *Defending Albion: Britain's Home Army 1908-1919* (Basingstoke: Palgrave Macmillan, 2005)

Moon, H., *The Invasion of the UK: Public Controversy & Official Planning 1888-1918* (London, King's College: unpublished Ph.D. thesis, 1968)
Morris, R., *The Man Who Ran London During the Great War* (Barnsley: Pen and Sword, 2009)
Nicolson, J., *The Perfect Summer* (London: John Murray, 2006)
Oldham, P., *Pillboxes on the Western Front* (London: Leo Cooper, 1995)
Osborne, M., *Defending Britain* (Stroud: Tempus, 2004)
Osborne, M., *Always Ready: The Drill Halls of Britain's Volunteer Forces* (Leigh-on-Sea: Caliver Books, 2006)
Osborne, M., *First World War Searchlight Position, Lincoln* (Lincoln: Lincolnshire History & Archaeology 41, 2006)
Osborne, M., *Pillboxes in Britain and Ireland* (Stroud: Tempus, 2008)
Patrick, C., & Baister, S., *William Le Queux: Master of Mystery* (Purley: authors, 2008)
Pye, A., and Woodward, F., *The Historic Defences of Plymouth* (Truro: Cornwall County Council and FSG South-west, 1996)
Rawlinson, Cdr A., *The Defence of London* (London: Melrose, 1923)
Rawson, A., *British Army Handbook 1914-1918* (Stroud: Sutton, 2006)
Reynolds, B., and C., *The London Gunners Come to Town: Life and Death in Hemel Hempstead in the Great War* (Tring: CODIL, 1995)
Richmond, Admiral Sir H., *The Invasion of Britain* (London: Methuen, 1941)
Saunders, A., *Channel Defences* (London: Batsford, 1997)
Severo, R., *A Footnote: Kaiser's Plan to Invade US* (New York: New York Times, 24/4/1971)
Seymour, M., *Noble Endeavours: The Life of Two Countries, England and Germany* (London: Simon & Schuster, 2013)
Smith, V., *Chatham's Defences in the Nineteenth Century* (Canterbury: Kent Defence Research Group, Kent Archaeological Society, *c.*1975)
Smith, V., *Defending London's River* (Rochester: North Kent Books, 1985)
Smith, V., *Front-Line Kent* (Maidstone: Kent County Council, 2002)
Smith, V., Anstee, A., and Mason, S., *Britain's First World War Defences* (Bourne: *After the Battle* 165, 2014)
Sockett, E., *Stockton-on-Tees 'Y' Station* in *Fortress* 8, (Liphook: Beaufort, 1991)
Stell, G., *Orkney at War: Defending Scapa Flow* (Kirkwall: The Orcadian, 2010)
Summers, A., *Militarism in Britain before the Great War* in *History Workshop* No. 2, (Oxford: OUP, Autumn 1976)
Thomson, B., *Odd People: Hunting Spies in the First World War* (London: Biteback, 2014, reprint of *Queer People*, 1922)
Tooze, A., *The Deluge* (London: Penguin/Allen Lane, 2014)
Warlow, Lt Cdr B., *Shore Establishments of the Royal Navy* (Liskeard: Maritime Books, 1992 and 2000)
Warner, G., *World War One Aircraft Carrier Pioneer* (Barnsley: Pen & Sword, 2011)
White, J., *Zeppelin Nights: London in the First World War* (London: Bodley Head, 2014)

Index